Facing the Truth

FACING THE TRUTH

South African faith communities and the Truth & Reconciliation Commission

edited by
James Cochrane, John de Gruchy and Stephen Martin

David Philip Publishers
Cape Town

Ohio University Press
Athens

First published 1999

in Southern Africa by David Philip Publishers (Pty) Ltd.,
208 Werdmuller Centre, Newry Street, Claremont 7708, South Africa

and in North America by Ohio University Press, Scott Quadrangle,
Athens, Ohio 45701

ISBN 0-86486-399-3 (David Philip Publishers)
ISBN 0-8214-1307-4 (Ohio University Press)

CIP data are available.

Printed in South Africa by The Natal Witness (Pty) Ltd

Contents

Contributors

Roger A. Arendse is a doctoral student at the University of Cape Town. He has also lectured at the Faculty of Theology and Religion, University of the Western Cape.

H. Russel Botman is Associate Professor of Theology in the Faculty of Theology and Religion, University of the Western Cape.

David Chidester is Professor of Comparative Religion and Director of the Institute for Comparative Religion in Southern Africa in the Department of Religious Studies, University of Cape Town.

Jame Cochrane is Professor and Director of the Church and Public Policy Programme, Department of Religious Studies, University of Cape Town.

John de Gruchy is Robert Selby Taylor Chair of Christian Studies at the University of Cape Town, and Director of the Religion and Social Change Unit, University of Cape Town.

William Johnson Everett is Herbert Gezork Professor of Christain Social Ethics at the Andover Newton Theological School in the Newton Centre, Massachusetts.

Heidi Grunebaum-Ralph is a doctoral candidate in the Department of English at the University of the Western Cape.

Charity Majiza is General Secretary of the South African Council of Churches.

Tinyiko Sam Maluleke is Professor of Theology at the University of Natal, Pietermaritzburg.

Stephen Martin is a doctoral candidate in the Department of Religious Studies, University of Cape Town. He is also Research Coordinator of the Research Institute on Christianity in South Africa.

Carl Niehaus is South African Ambassador to the Netherlands.

Robin M. Petersen is a lecturer in Theology in the Faculty of Theology and Religion, University of the Western Cape.

Oren Baruch Stier is Assistant Professor of Judaic Studies in the Department of Religious Studies at Florida International University. He was formerly Joint Senior Lecturer in Jewish Religion and Culture at the University of Cape Town.

Foreword

The Most Rev. Njongonkulu Ndungane
Archbishop of Cape Town

The work of the TRC was never going to be easy or comfortable. Events have proved this to be so. And those of us in South Africa's faith communities may be proud that Archbishop Tutu came from our ranks to bring to bear a Christian witness of justice and love to the TRC process.

Neither was the Commission's onerous responsibility going to be exercised with ease. It stumbled across many vested interests as it sought to uncover the truth in the limited time available to it. It will be to its lasting credit that the TRC never allowed any stumbling blocks to cripple its work. It is a recognition of a long and painful process that it was able to report, albeit with some arguing strenuously that its findings are faulty.

South Africans should not be surprised by this. The truth is never easy to find; it is even more difficult to reveal. Indeed, when Pilate, nearly two thousand years ago, agonised over 'What is truth?', he could not see Truth, in the form of the Living Christ, standing before him.

The TRC's problem has similarly been one of interpretation. This does not negate its invaluable contribution to the emergence of truth and the beginnings of the process of reconciliation. Indeed, its work will be the benchmark, for generations to come, for people in post-conflict situations in many parts of the world who seek to emerge with some degree of stability and on a road that points to progress.

Many believed that the Commission would concentrate solely on the perpetrators of apartheid, and the heinous deeds they did. Their requests for amnesty, it was believed, would perhaps be more closely scrutinised than those of others. In the event, an even-handedness prevailed; this had to be the case given the Commission's mandate – a mandate approved by all those who advocated a process of amnesty.

Indeed, one can fully understand the point of view of those who were part of a noble struggle against the heretical policy and actions of apartheid, and yet who find themselves lumped together in the Report of the Commission with the very perpetrators of this terrible era. Sacrifices were made in the struggle, in the cause of liberation, and we salute those who did so. Mistakes, inevitably, were also made. Thus South Africans should understand that there will always be two planes on which the evil deeds of the past are measured.

Given the fact that the Commission laboured under the disadvantage of not being a judicial commission, the work it has done has been remarkable, to say the least. Truth has been exposed in all its nakedness. This has been most uncomfortable for many. It is good that this is so.

On the positive side, many people have discovered what happened to the whereabouts of their loved ones, and have been able to come to terms with the terrible and ghastly events of our immediate past history. For that alone, the TRC deserve commendation.

The fact that some have sought to exonerate themselves from the findings of the Commission does not diminish the manner in which, without fear or favour, it has delivered its Report. It will not be popular among some for indicating that it was not going to do political favours for selected interests.

But now is the time to move on. A cut-off point has been reached. As a country we must find mechanisms whereby we can close the book on the past. One way of doing this, without forgetting the many lives that were inextricably damaged, some snuffed out, is to create a living memorial in their honour. It would be fitting if we could create an Annual Award, named for our great heroes, and which would be applied to benefit the poor, the dispossessed, those discriminated against and marginalised in society. I will be undertaking extensive consultations and investigations to ascertain the feasibility of such an award, as I believe our past should be memorialised.

Much truth has been exposed. As a nation, our challenge is now to move forward and complete the process of reconciliation and reconstruction that has started. Let reconciliation do its work. Let us understand the work in this respect has just begun. Future generations must take the baton and move to full reconciliation.

Abbreviations

AIC	African Initiated Churches
AFM	Apostolic Faith Mission
ANC	African National Congress
ATR	African traditional religion
BCSA	Baptist Convention of South Africa
BK	Belydende Kring
BOSS	Bureau for State Security
BUSA	Baptist Union of Southern Africa
CAIC	Council of African Initiated Churches
CCG	Conservative Christian Group
CESA	Church of England in South Africa
CI	Christian Institute
CLSA	Christian League of Southern Africa
CODESA	Convention for a Democratic South Africa
COI	Call of Islam
CPSA	Church of the Province of Southern Africa
DRC	Dutch Reformed Church/ Nederduitse Gereformeerde Kerk
DRMC	Dutch Reformed Mission Church/ Sendingkerk
ELCSA	Evangelical Lutheran Church of Southern Africa
FF	Frontline Fellowship
GDL	Gospel Defence League
GK	Gereformeerde Kerk
ICT	Institute for Contextual Theology
IDASA	Institute for Democracy in South Africa

IFCC	International Fellowship of Christian Churches
JMC	Joint Management Centre
JUT	Jamiatul Ulama Transvaal
LIC	Low Intensity Conflict Strategy
LMS	London Missionary Society
MCSA	Methodist Church of Southern Africa
MJC	Muslim Judicial Council
MK	Umkhonto weSizwe
MYMSA	Muslim Youth Movement of South Africa
NIR	National Initiative for Reconciliation
NMS	National Management System
NSMS	National Security Management System
PAC	Pan Africanist Congress
PCR	(World Council of Churches) Programme to Combat Racism
PCSA	Presbyterian Church of Southern Africa
RICSA	Research Institute on Christianity in South Africa
RWCG	Right-wing Christian Group
RPC	Reformed Presbyterian Church of South Africa
SACBC	Southern African Catholic Bishops' Conference
SACC	South African Council of Churches
SADF	South African Defence Force
SAHMS	South African Hindu Maha Sabha
SCA	Student Christian Association
SCM	Student Christian Movement
SDA	Seventh Day Adventist Church
SPROCAS	Study Project on Christianity in Apartheid Society
SPROCAS II	Special Programme for Christian Action in Society
SSC	State Security Council
SWAPO	South West African People's Organisation
TEASA	The Evangelical Alliance of South Africa
TRC	Truth and Reconciliation Commission
UCCSA	United Congregational Church of Southern Africa
UDF	United Democratic Front
UMCSA	United Methodist Church of South Africa
URCSA	Uniting Reformed Church in Southern Africa
WCC	World Council of Churches
WCRP	World Conference on Religion and Peace
ZCC	Zion Christian Church

Facing the Truth

Introduction

Faith, Struggle and Reconciliation

John de Gruchy, James Cochrane and Stephen Martin

After years of struggle, South Africa's transition to democracy eventually came about through a process of tough negotiation. During the course of that process it was widely recognised that the fostering of national reconciliation was a prerequisite for a peaceful transition, ongoing stability and economic growth. Thus the final clause of the 1993 Interim Constitution, entitled 'On National Unity and Reconciliation', contained these words:

> This Constitution provides a historic bridge between the past of a deeply divided society characterised by strife, conflict, untold suffering and injustice, and a future founded on the recognition of human rights, democracy and peaceful co-existence and development opportunities for all South Africans irrespective of colour, race, class, belief or sex.
>
> The pursuit of national unity, the well-being of all South African citizens and peace require reconciliation between the people of South Africa and the reconstruction of society.
>
> The adoption of this Constitution lays the secure foundation for the people of South Africa to transcend the divisions and strife of the past, which generated gross violations of human rights, the transgression of humanitarian principles in violent conflicts and a legacy of hatred, fear, guilt and revenge.
>
> These can now be addressed on the basis that there is a need for understanding but not revenge, a need for reparation but not for retaliation, a need for *ubuntu* but not for victimisation.

The clause ended with a paragraph on the need for amnesty for those who had been engaged in certain political crimes as a necessary precondition for reconciliation and reconstruction. Although the mechanisms for achieving these goals were not specifically addressed, they provided the basis for the eventual establishment of the Truth and Reconciliation Commission (TRC).

While the establishment of the TRC arose out of the negotiation process, its sources predate the beginning of that process. No one person or organisation deserves all the credit, but clearly an important role was played by the working group established by Dr Alex Boraine, Executive Director of the Institute for Democracy in South Africa (IDASA), which explored the possibilities for such a commission. This involved several major workshops and conferences, and wide-ranging international and local consultation, over several years. Gradually the shape of the TRC began to emerge, and eventually, by the time the new parliament convened in 1994, much of the groundwork had been prepared for the Bill on National Unity and Reconciliation.

Indicative of the urgency of initiating the process of reconciliation is the fact that the establishment of the TRC was approved during the first session of the new South African parliament, on Friday 21 October 1994, and on 15 December 1995 it passed the Promotion of National Unity and Reconciliation Act. Its mandate was to provide a record of gross human rights violations committed by both the upholders of apartheid and the liberation movements between 1 March 1960, when the liberation movements were banned, and 6 December 1993, after which, it was agreed, armed conflict and political violence could no longer be justified or tolerated. It was further mandated to identify the victims and investigate their fate, to recommend possible measures of reparation, to process applications for amnesty and indemnity, and to make recommendations with regard to measures necessary to prevent future gross human rights violations.

Although the TRC was established and funded by the state, it was free to act without interference from the state or political parties and organisations. This was important in establishing the capacity of the Commission to achieve its goals and its integrity and credibility in doing so. The seventeen commissioners, led by Desmond Tutu, the emeritus Anglican Archbishop of Cape Town, were appointed by President Mandela only after a long process of hearings, and were reasonably representative of the broad political, ethnic and cultural spectrum in South Africa.

The TRC began its work in February 1996. Unlike the Nuremberg Trials which followed the Second World War, it was established not by foreign powers for the sake of punishing war criminals, but as an instrument constituted by South Africans for the sake of dealing with the past in a way which would bring healing and reconciliation. The South African Council of Churches (SACC) (1995: 24) captured its motivation in these words:

> The Commission for Truth and Reconciliation is not another Nuremberg. It turns its back on any desire for revenge. It represents an extraordinary act of generosity by a people who only insist that the truth, the whole truth and nothing but the truth be told. The space is thereby created where the deeper processes of forgiveness, confession, repentance, reparation and reconciliation can take place.

This statement, one of several emanating from churches and other faith communities on the TRC, is indicative of the important link between some sections within these constituencies and the formation of the commission, as well as its eventual operations.

The need for faith communities to play an important role in the process of nation-building and reconciliation had already been stated by President Mandela in an important keynote address in Potchefstroom in December 1992. Addressing the Free Ethiopian Church of Southern Africa, he acknowledged the role which some churches had played in the struggle against apartheid, and went on to challenge the church 'to join other agents of change and transformation in the difficult task of acting as a midwife to the birth of our democracy and acting as one of the institutions that will nurture and entrench it in our society'. While the position of faith communities in the conflicts of the past, their role in the transition to democracy and their commitment to being instruments of transformation remain contested – not least in the report that begins this volume – there can be little doubt that their influence constitutes an important dimension of the work of the TRC.

The notion of reconciliation has been central to theological debate in South Africa for many years. In Christian churches, this dates at least to the publication by the SACC and the Christian Institute of *The Message to the People of South Africa* in 1968 and finds its most critical expression in the *Kairos Document* almost twenty years later. In the early 1970s, the Special Programme for Christian Action in Society (SPRO-CAS II), which was one of the outcomes of the *Message*, was an important programme for relating reconciliation to the realities of South Africa. After the publication of the *Kairos Document* in 1985, prophetic voices within the churches called on the churches to confess their guilt for apartheid on behalf of the nation, and to work for reconciliation on the basis of justice. Archbishop Tutu and Dr Beyers Naudé were key figures in this regard, but they were not alone. There were also a number of major conferences and documents that focused on reconciliation and the need for repentance and reparation. The *Kairos Document* also made an impact in other faith communities, and some Muslim voices in the Western Cape, where interfaith cooperation was especially strong, expressed disappointment at not being asked to sign it.

Even though they differed in emphasis, the *Kairos Document* (1985), the National Initiative for Reconciliation (1985), the SACC's Soweto Conference on 'Confessing Guilt' (1989), the Rustenburg Conference (1990), and the Cape Town Consultation of the World Council of Churches (WCC) member churches in South Africa (1991) carried forth this call for repentance. The SACC and its member churches regularly made similar appeals, even though the churches themselves were not particularly good at putting their resolutions into practice. Mention should also be made of other faith communities and of the interfaith movement, of which the World Conference on Religion and Peace (WCRP) and its *Declaration of Religious Rights and Responsibilities* played an especially important role. It is notable that Archbishop Tutu, who would eventually become Chairperson of the TRC, also held leadership posts in the SACC and WCRP. In short, faith communities and their members helped shape the consciousness within which the idea of the TRC was nurtured. But faith communities also played other roles in South Africa's past.

It was only as the TRC entered its final phase of hearings that it was decided that special hearings should be held for certain major players during the apartheid era other than the various instruments of the apartheid regime or its victims. Thus organised business, the media, the legal profession and other sectors were invited to make submissions both in writing and at hearings specially convened for them. The faith communities, comprising all religious traditions represented in South Africa, were invited to do the same.

In many ways, the faith community hearings were symbolic of the endpoint of the involvement of religious communities in giving support either to apartheid or the struggle against it. Not since 1903–5, when the South African Native Affairs Commission (the Lagden Commission) instituted hearings to investigate the role of Christian missions, and especially African initiated churches (then referred to as Ethiopian churches), in fostering social unrest and even rebellion, have religious communities in South Africa been called upon by the government of the day to give an account of their social and political roles. Of course, during the apartheid era there were several state commissions (the Schlebusch Commission, for example) which investigated the activities of church organisations such as the Christian Institute.

But the TRC faith community hearings were somewhat different, for they included all faith communities, irrespective of their tradition, who were willing to participate. It was not that a government-sponsored commission was sitting in judgement on the faith communities, but that they freely accepted the need to take responsibility for their past and to indicate their commitment for the present and future. The extent to which they have acknowledged their past can be judged from what is contained in these pages. The extent to which they will honour their commitments is something that only future generations will be able to judge.

FACING THE TRUTH: A STRUGGLE NOT OVER

In 1997, the Research Institute on Christianity in South Africa (RICSA) in the University of Cape Town's Department of Religious Studies was approached by the TRC to advise on the setting up of the faith community hearings. Supplied with a set of submissions from faith communities, and with a very clear understanding that it was to adopt a wholly non-confessional, professional position, RICSA produced a document which sketched the historical background of the communities, providing also a summary of the submissions, a recommended structure for the hearings and suggested questions. On this basis the commissioners then asked RICSA to produce a report on the faith hearings, which two members attended, for use in drafting the appropriate section of the Commission's final report. This report was prepared using the original RICSA document as well as transcripts of the hearings, and was supplemented with secondary materials.[1] It also drew on extensive subsequent comment sought from a variety of people representing various faith communities.

Given the scope of the TRC's mandate, the faith community hearings were but a small dab on a much larger canvas. Even so, the RICSA Report had to distil over a thousand pages of written submissions and oral testimony into sixty pages. The final report of the TRC includes only a substantially abridged version. The unabridged document, as produced by RICSA, is made available in this book in order to allow for further analysis of the role of faith communities and to prompt a deeper and wider discussion.

The RICSA Report describes and analyses 'in a nutshell' (see Caputo 1997) how faith communities understood themselves in relation to apartheid, and what they hope to do in the future to contribute to truth and reconciliation. Yet it is significant for our purposes that there are many gaps not filled, stories not told, confessions not made and actions for the future not spelled out – both by those who made submissions and those who did not. If there is one prime purpose for this book, it is to insist that the gaps are still there to be addressed, the stories must still be told, the confessions must be given space and actions must be made practically real. The nutshell offered here is meant to be cracked open; the book aims to interrupt any premature closure of the debate, which still challenges faith communities. It calls faith communities and their members to acknowledge that the TRC is in every respect a beginning – and only a beginning. As the SACC statement alluded to previously implicitly recognises, the setting up of the TRC was a first step: 'The space is thereby created where the deeper processes of forgiveness, confession, repentance, reparation and reconciliation can take place.'

We take it that the entire life of the TRC has been about beginning to create that space, to make an opening through which others may go. Too many people, not least those for whom membership in a faith community means a great deal, have viewed the TRC as something more than an instrument for opening up space. Too many have expected it to uncover the whole truth, to be the instrument of reconciliation, only to find themselves disillusioned. Because it cannot meet their wishes, others still have questioned the extent to which the TRC work has received public coverage. Some (whites in the main) even claim to have become bored by the whole thing. Perhaps Tinyiko Maluleke is correct in suggesting, in his contribution to this volume, that the Commission itself may have been guilty of promoting unrealistic expectations.

Participation in the TRC process on the part of faith communities *per se* has been far from strong, despite the ecumenical input at its point of origins and the presence on the Commission of several people with prominent religious affiliations. A particularly unfortunate reality is that while most white South Africans remain strongly committed to one or another faith tradition, they have made their presence felt at the TRC hearings largely by their absence.

To be sure, there are important debates about the 'religious' character of the TRC itself, both about its language, widely felt to be dominated by Christian discourse, and the make-up of its commissioners. But this should not detract from the responsibility of religious communities for taking up the original intentions of the TRC in whatever form is appropriate, and in as many forums as possible. The space opened up at the faith hearings remains to be claimed and contested by South Africa's faith communities.

South Africa remains a deeply divided society. In this context the TRC was limited by its mandate to deal with 'gross human rights violations' and it could never be expected to deal with the deeper material bases of injustice and their threat to a healed and whole society. Second- and third- generation rights, in particular economic rights, have remained beyond its scope. It is vital that they are addressed, however, and that faith communities work out their responsibilities in this regard.[2]

The TRC, vital to the reconciliation process as it is, was but a beginning, a line that was drawn and crossed. And as the essays in this book show, there are many critical questions to be asked about the TRC and the goals it set itself. Whatever its limits and problems, however, the TRC has introduced an important agenda into the public sphere. It is the public as a whole, in all of its dimensions and through all of its diverse, contested and fragmented institutional and organisational forms, that must continue the task.

Part of the legacy of the TRC is the important questions it leaves to be debated in the coming years. They include, first, the difficult question of determining what 'truth' is, especially as linked to the notion of painting as complete a picture of the past as possible. This is not straightforward. Not only is truth contested and often particular to specific communities and perspectives, but much of what we might know through records has been obscured, erased or destroyed. Much of what we do know cannot be fully verified or falsified. Truth-telling in the forensic, juridical mode therefore fails to provide a 'complete' picture, if it even aspires to that.

However, an understanding of the context of the past (which was also part of the mandate of the TRC and, indeed, of the institutional hearings which included faith communities) means that at least a 'frame' has been provided for its portrayal. And what has emerged in forensic terms provides a preliminary sketch for a fuller picture. It also enables the public to begin to question what may be trusted in others, how trust may be established and sustained.

Perhaps the TRC drives us towards an acknowledgement that truth is above all a dialogical process to which we must commit ourselves, a process involving a multifaceted, always incomplete work of (re)construction. Truth is something, ironically, that we will have to build on the back of lies, of untruth and deceit. A theological as much as it is a forensic or philosophical challenge, this forces us to think of ways to enter into sustained discourse with one another. Such discourse involves a willingness to give a clear account of ourselves and to hold the other accountable in a similar way, to act with integrity and to learn to judge its lack. This notion of 'integrity', in turn, requires not only that we attest ('give testimony') to who we are, but that we offer the promise that we can be trusted and believed, and demonstrate in our behaviour that this promise can be redeemed.

The problematic question of determining the meaning and scope of reconciliation is also raised by the TRC. Reconciliation, if there is such a thing, cannot be established on the basis of juridical or pseudo-juridical processes, or even through confession and forgiveness as mere linguistic acts. Reparation must come into the picture, and this has not been adequately defined. In this context, the Christian practice of the Eucharist, with its explicit reference to Matthew 5:23–4 that one should not share the bread and the wine until one has made restitution to those whom one has harmed, is an awesome social challenge.

Other questions emerge – questions which already are sparking important debates within South Africa. Does amnesty serve justice? What is the price exacted for the pain of victims in the TRC and related processes? What of the beneficiaries of the system that hurt so many people? This question in particular has not been adequately addressed – if at all. It raises the probing question of what makes for a perpetrator, and the related question of how far the line of responsibility for gross human rights violations goes. In the light of this, the question of the meaning and extent of – and responsibility for – reparation is deepened. But perhaps the most pertinent question of all concerns how we will ensure that all of the above questions are addressed in practical actions aimed at healing what can be healed, transforming what must be transformed and building what is desired and desirable.

All of these questions, we believe, are fundamental to faith communities. They are questions of vision, of fundamental orientation in the world. They go to the heart of religion. They have both personal implications for believers and public implications for their believing communities.

The editors offer this book as a stimulus to members of faith communities, their institutions and organisations. If the faith community hearings presented the church struggle in a nutshell – a kind of 'church and apartheid for beginners' – there were also gaps emerging within and between the discourses of the various faith communities, and between themselves and the Commission as well. Opening up these gaps deconstructs the discourse, including the idea among Christian communities, for example, that there was such a thing as a 'church struggle' into which everyone fitted unambiguously. In the end, neat identities ('we were this', 'we were that') fall away. For this reason we have placed Carl Niehaus's provocative and sobering essay after the RICSA Report. Niehaus opens the gap further between the often triumphalistic profession of religious communities and their actual participation in the reconciliation process – something which sets the tone for the rest of the book. Indeed, in this book we are pushing the gaps (and calling for those who read the book to do so) with our foot in the door, leaning in. But we also wish to reinvigorate our religious discourses about truth and reconciliation, suggesting new ways of understanding, new configurations, new paths to constructing our present and future institutional life. Several of the essays produced here explore such possibilities.

The RICSA Report makes a number of recommendations for investigation into various areas. One is the crucial role of right-wing Christian groups in supporting the state and being a pipeline for its propaganda, not only in conservative churches but also in so-called 'mainline' churches. The failure of the faith hearings to address this was a serious oversight. Roger Arendse fills in some of the history and supplies a number of important leads for other researchers to pursue. Perhaps more importantly, Arendse suggests ways that local churches and ministers can address the context within which right-wing Christianity arises. This is a challenge, for many ministers do not attend to the social basis of theological ideas.

Tinyiko Maluleke takes a slightly different tack in critiquing the TRC from the point of view of black theology. For Maluleke, the silence of black critical comment on the Commission is directly related to its functioning as a silencing discourse. The TRC represents the triumph of a certain understanding of reconciliation which fails to honour black perspectives on reconciliation forged during the struggle years. This triumph is a triumphalism that drowns out dissent and positions the TRC, against its own professions, at the centre of the reconciliation debate – something which marginalises the black majority.

A different kind of critique of the TRC, and indeed of the faith community hearings, is found in Robin Petersen's account of the African Initiated Churches (AICs) and the TRC. Indeed, Petersen here suggests a reading which allows the voice of the AICs, who represent the largest faith grouping in South Africa, to speak in criticism of the TRC and its understanding of social action. For Petersen, a prophetic critique was implicit in the very way that the AICs engaged the Commission during the hearings. This mode of engagement points to new understandings of 'being prophetic', which also challenge the categories that faith communities used to describe their activity under apartheid, and that RICSA also used in its report.

But what of the role of so-called 'mainstream' Christianity, particularly that represented in the Dutch Reformed Church (DRC), in providing succour for the perpetrators of apartheid? This is the theme that Russel Botman takes up. Following on Arendse's approach to the religious context of socialisation, Botman investigates the role of the DRC in establishing what he terms 'the value orientation' that became a foundation stone of South African racism. His is a challenge to churches, and in particular the DRC, to reconceive its role in the past and future in terms of an ethic of responsibility, a call that is perhaps similar to David Chidester's conception of faith communities as seeing their future in terms of a servant role – something to which Niehaus also alludes.

It may indeed seem ironic to many that the DRC at the faith hearings claimed its calling in the past, and specified its commitment to the future, as 'prophetic'. Certainly this term emerged within the discourse of the faith communities as highly contested. David Chidester wonders whether the term provides an adequate basis not only for understanding the past but for moving ahead into the future. The idea of 'prophetic' (as an orientation around which to centre accounts of the past) speaks of a coherent narrative, in which agents of struggle and agents of oppression were well defined. Chidester reconceives the past, however, not in terms of prophetic agents of struggle but of sites of struggle. Flashbulb memories replace coherent narratives, as they displace triumphalist nationalisms. And yet the question of constructing national unity, for healing the divisions of the past, remains.

The zeal for wholeness interfaces with the crucial question of healing and memory. Drawing on representations of the Holocaust and construction of Holocaust memorials, Oren Stier and Heidi Grunebaum-Ralph equate the zeal for a whole picture of the past with the positing of hermetically sealed spaces of remembrance. Individual memory is collapsed into the founding moment of a collective, leaving the pain of the 'singular' unfelt and silenced, bringing about a premature closure. Sharing Chidester's (and Maluleke's) suspicion of nationally enshrined meta-narratives, they urge the right to 'deferred closure' rather than the formal institutionalisation of remembrance.

The work of mourning points to the challenge for the future. For while mourning must go on, and sites of memory honoured, at the same time a new society must be built. What is the challenge for the future? Finishing the reflective essays on a theological note, William Johnson Everett links the ongoing work of the TRC to the remaking of civil society and the reconstruction of 'the religious and deep cultural anchors of people's lives'. He does this by attending to the history of modern constitutional democracy and applying two key ideas: respect for a higher law than that of the constitution and public life, linking them to theological ideas of covenant and publicity.

Although the point of this volume is to open up discussion, and therefore not to give the 'last word' either on the faith hearings or on the role of faith communities under apartheid, a brief 'afterword', which includes reflections from Charity Majiza, General Secretary of the SACC, and from the editors, draws the volume to a close. 'After words', the rest is in the hands of South Africa's faith communities. An appendix contains selections and extracts from the submissions. These are not intended to be in any way comprehensive, but rather to represent some of the different flavours on display at the TRC faith hearings. A list of written submissions and a list of testimonies given to the hearings are also included.

The opinions expressed within each essay are heartfelt and passionate, and there has been little conceptual 'ironing'. Some contradictions emerge over interpretations of the role of faith communities in South Africa's transition. The careful reader will notice that crucial concepts such as 'church' are not used in the same way by the different authors, and (in this case) talk of 'the church' may refer to the collection of institutions, to denominations, to local faith communities or to individual Christians. Perhaps this serves to demonstrate the ongoing way that such concepts remain contested, and to further debate. It is also important to note that the activities of faith communities in addressing their past – where such actions are taking place – are ongoing. As this volume was completed there were important developments within, for example, the Reformed and Presbyterian families of churches. We therefore urge that this volume be read with an awareness of the dynamic processes within and between faith communities.

Thanks are due to all contributors who worked under tremendous pressure. In particular, his co-editors wish to acknowledge the excellent work that Steve Martin has done in producing the original RICSA Report, largely the result of his careful sifting and research, and largely written by him. The editors also express deep gratitude to Charles Villa-Vicencio and Wendy Arendse at the TRC and to Piet Meiring, coordinator of the faith hearings, who made documentation available. All references to the testimonies at the hearings will be to the official transcripts produced by the TRC and available on the Commission's web site (www.truth.org.za/hrvtrans/faith/index.htm). The full written submissions are also available on RICSA's web site (www.ricsa.org.za/trc), as is an interactive version of the RICSA Report, with links to other key primary and secondary materials.

Faith Communities and Apartheid

A Report prepared for the Truth and Reconciliation Commission by the Research Institute on Christianity in South Africa

Faith Communities and Apartheid
The RICSA Report

1. WHY FAITH COMMUNITY HEARINGS?

To an outsider the Truth and Reconciliation Commission (TRC) is a very strange body. Set up with constitutional warrant and parliamentary decree, the Commission is also led by two former church leaders, one in the splendour of an Archbishop's attire. Religious language permeates the process, with terms like 'reconciliation' and 'confession' strongly in evidence. Hearings are punctuated with moments of silent prayer and reflection.

• Religion has played an important public role in the past with which South Africans are struggling to come to terms. Particularly (though not only) 'Christian doctrine, language and sentiment are . . . interwoven in the social and cultural history of South Africa.'[1]

• Christian churches gave their blessing to the universally condemned system of apartheid. The politicians that invented apartheid came from churches. Some of the apartheid laws, for instance the Mixed Marriages Act, were motivated by churches (especially the DRC), and churches actively implemented apartheid policies.

• Out of churches, mosques, temples and synagogues also came many of apartheid's strongest foes, including many of South Africa's present political leadership. Churches, mosques, temples and synagogues gave theological legitimisation to resistance to apartheid. For some leaders in the resistance movement, theology was an important site of struggle precisely because of its position in legitimising apartheid; and it was necessary to turn the theological weapons of the oppressor against the very oppressor.

• Churches, mosques, temples and synagogues also bade their members to eschew the political in the quest for the eternal. In so doing they did not extricate themselves from involvement, however. Some churches pressing for a solution beyond politics were covertly involved as agents of the state. Others have come to admit that not to have opposed oppression, even in the name of protecting the identity of the church as church, was to have failed in their vocation and to have lent tacit support to the regime.

• Churches, synagogues, mosques and temples also suffered under apartheid. Their land was appropriated by being declared 'white' under the notorious Group Areas Act. Their schools were closed. Removals affected numerous congregations, forcing many to shut down. On the other side the St James Church within the Church of England in South Africa (which confessed to tacitly supporting the state) was attacked in the name of resistance to apartheid.

• Many faith communities have important international links which were mobilised both to defend and to oppose apartheid. The changing names of church denominational structures from 'South' to 'Southern' Africa reflect their growing regional identities. This also means that such communities are in a position to assess the regional effects of apartheid oppression, as their members in neighbouring states were also affected.

• Finally, like business, faith communities (especially churches) benefited from apartheid. They were beneficiaries of removals as victims left empty buildings and manses. Their support of the state gave them legitimacy in the eyes of the powerful, and many of the powerful were counted as loyal members. Even those churches that espoused neutrality or a 'Christian alternative' to ideological conflict received concessions from the state because they were not seen as its opponents – something that was more than apparent to members of non-Christian communities.[2]

In the light of all this, it should not have come as a surprise that the question of a special hearing on the role of faith communities during the apartheid years should have been raised early in the life of the Commission. Add to this the fact that churches, synagogues, temples and mosques claim an enormous committed constituency, with lines cutting across many of the racial, class and ethnic barriers that a post-apartheid South Africa is trying to transcend, and one can see the importance of bringing them more fully into the reconciliation process. Moreover, such communities are themselves places where real reconciliation needs to take place and where the values and processes of democratic citizenry need to be entrenched.[3] Indeed, people on both sides of the apartheid struggle were often members of the same faith community both nationally and locally, and many people who did not see themselves as on any 'side' found the struggle confusing, not the province of religion, or secondary to other questions felt to be more central to their religious worldviews. The wide spectrum of positions, convictions and worldviews which one finds in religious communities, even within one tradition of faith, is a caution against strong dualist views on the apartheid struggle and a challenge to learn for the future how to come to terms with the search for a common language of accountability in building a 'conciled and reconciled society'. Reconciliation and the enhancement of human dignity in such communities could be a leaven for the whole society.

At its hearings in East London, the Commission was greatly encouraged by the willingness of faith community leaders to apologise for their role in giving support to – or their failure to sufficiently oppose – apartheid oppression. This was in marked contrast to the business hearings the week before, most of which consisted of claims of hardship under apartheid and dubiously founded celebrations of opposition to it – flying in the face of the fact that the precursors of apartheid were the various legislative Acts ensuring cheap and accessible labour for industry and mining. On the other hand, sadly, it must be observed that faith communities seem to have gone the way of the business sector in claiming that 'now that society has changed' they can go on building up their own institutions. Another reason for having faith communities as part of the TRC process, therefore, is to remind them that, like the business sector, they have a moral obligation to be involved in the transformation of a society they so profoundly affected.

2. FAITH COMMUNITIES IN SOUTH AFRICA

2.1 Problems of definition

As long as the Commission merely wanted a 'churches' hearing (as originally intended)[4] there was no definitional problem. South Africa as a Western-style state had its 'religious' and its 'secular' components structured within 'church' and 'state' sectors. Muslim, Hindu, and Jewish communities were able to survive in South Africa largely by conforming to the political context and taking the same place institutionally as churches did. When the Commission recognised that other faith communities had to be included, the problem arose as to how this should be done.[5] It was decided to have a 'faith communities' hearing rather than simply a churches hearing.

What is a 'faith community'? What are its boundaries? How much can it be identified with the actions and interests of its constituents? For while it is true that many faith communities represent in principle a loyalty that cuts across ethnic, racial, gender and class divisions, this is not always so in practice. The Dutch Reformed Church from an early period could not maintain itself as a single community and had to develop an identity as a racially segregated *volkskerk*, splitting off its non-white members into 'mission churches'. African Initiated Churches (AICS) can be accounted for in many different ways – on the basis of a class analysis, as a part of a 'cultural struggle', or as a response to racism – as well as in terms of the attempt to create an indigenous ecclesial identity.[6] Likewise, theological divisions amongst Muslims also reflect cultural and class distinctions between the Malay and Indian origins of that community, exacerbated by apartheid's division of 'Indians' and 'coloureds'.[7]

It is not the place of this report to conduct a theoretical analysis of the relations between class, race, gender and ethnic factors on the one side and 'faith' on the other. For the purpose of this report, we take it for granted that faith communities exist – that is, communities defined by loyalty to a particular faith tradition – but within a context of many other competing loyalties.

The term 'faith community' is also problematic because it seems to indicate a degree of homogeneity amongst organisations as diverse as the South African Council of Churches, the Ramakrishna Institute, the Baptist Union, the Call of Islam and the Uniting Reformed Church congregation of Messina – all of which made submissions as faith communities to the TRC, and which confessed their own failures.[8] Remembering that the original intention of the hearings was for Christian churches to assess their conduct under apartheid, the term 'faith communities' may still contain this intention, only in different terms. It certainly seemed generally (though not always) appropriate to churches, but less so to other faiths. Do practitioners of African traditional religion, for example, constitute a faith community in the same way as, for instance, members of the Church of the Province of South Africa (CPSA)? Arguably the boundaries existing between African traditional religion (ATR) and, say, Christianity are of a different nature from those between Christianity and Judaism. This was made evident in the fact that many 'spokespersons' for the African religious community are also practising Christians, and are not recognised as members (let alone representatives) of the African religious community by other practitioners of ATR. Indeed the invocation of the Genesis creation story by the representative of ATR at the hearings to substantiate his claims about the philosophy of *ubuntu* (human feeling, humanity) would have been seen as a syncretistic betrayal of the African religious community he claimed to represent.[9]

The groups that made submissions to the TRC under the name 'faith communities' obviously differ according to tradition (Christian, Islamic, Jewish, Hindu and Traditional). But they also represented different kinds of organisations – some highly organised, with a defined and centralised leadership structure; others more loosely associated, with emphasis on the local community; still others with close ties to ethnic or tribal boundaries. With its links to the *amakhosi* (chiefs) in KwaZulu-Natal, the Ibandla lamaNazaretha Church resembles African traditional communities more than it does many Christian churches, while the Baptist Union's decentralised and voluntarist nature makes it institutionally more similar to South African Hinduism than to the strong hierarchical character of the Roman Catholic Church. There are also important theological and ideological similarities and differences amongst and between faith communities represented. The ideological perspective of the Institute for Contextual Theology (ICT) was much closer to the Call of Islam (as articulated by Faried Esack) than it was to the Church of England in South Africa (CESA).

All this is to recognise that we are not dealing with homogeneous phenomena when looking at faith communities. This has implications both for the question of representation and for issues of accountability – which we must return to below.

2.2 A note on our position

Given the heterogeneous nature of faith communities in South Africa, it is difficult to locate a single norm that all would share and that could function as an evaluative yardstick for their behaviour within society during the period with which the Commission is concerned. Perhaps the term 'gross human rights abuses' points to one such norm. Unfortunately the meaning of this term was not clearly defined by the Commission. The fact that faith communities came (for the most part) with confessions of complicity and wrongdoing implies, however, that they certainly operated according to a norm or set of standards they felt they had violated, whether derived from their tradition (as the Seventh Day Adventist Church and Salvation Army) or from a general societal or constitutional understanding of human rights (which characterised much of the discourse of the English-speaking churches).

It is fair to say that one term that is shared amongst almost all faith communities is the term 'prophetic'. The exception to this would be the African religious community, although it is arguable that a figure like the nineteenth-century Xhosa leader Nxele was as prophetic a figure as Christianity or any other religion in South Africa has produced. This prophetic strand exists, not purely within a faith community, but in tension with its social-legitimising function. This social-legitimising function is usually ambiguous – it can be a boost for nation-building (as can be seen by the recognition of the role of faith communities by President Mandela) or it can plunge into idolatry (as we saw under apartheid).

This report holds that given the nature of the apartheid regime, faith communities, functioning according to their deepest traditions, ought to have been prophetic and vocal and denouncing rather than blindly legitimising social structures. This perspective is broadly shared by all who made submissions, and it will form our point of departure in section 3.

Put another way, this report holds that the faith communities hearings constituted a summing up of the church struggle in South Africa (though expanded to include other faiths), and that all communities present there either explicitly or strongly implied that that struggle was a just one and that they should have contributed more to it. This report shall take this point of view, and argues that South Africa is still a site of struggle – especially socio-economically. Therefore it is appropriate to use the same terms of analysis (victim, perpetrator and agent of social change) in looking back, because these same categories present themselves as possibilities as we look ahead to the future.

2.3 Faith communities in South Africa: a brief picture

The Commission exacerbated the problem of defining faith communities by inviting submissions simply of those institutions it deemed to be 'players' in the former years.[10] Fortunately as word got out, other institutions and individuals made submissions, promising a larger and more accurate picture.

The submissions that were received by the Commission can be organised broadly into those that came from groups connected to the Christian, Muslim, Jewish, Hindu, Buddhist and Baha'i faith traditions.[11] There were also submissions claiming to represent 'the African traditional religious community', as well as a representation from women in religion.[12] Within these traditions there are different categories of submissions: those from individuals (of which there were three), local faith communities (e.g. Hatfield Christian Church), denominational representatives, ecumenical and interfaith groups, which were not faith communities in the strict sense but organisations made up of persons and groups representing various denominations or communities, and special groups which worked within specific traditions (e.g. the Belydende Kring, which worked within the Dutch Reformed family of churches). There were submissions from theological bodies, including the ICT and the Muslim Jamiatul Ulama – neither of which represented all Christians or Muslims respectively but saw themselves as resources for their communities. There was also a submission from the WCRP, a coalition of adherents of various faith traditions which formed its South African chapter in 1984.

It must be recognised that no presentation of faith in South Africa (or anywhere else for that matter) is beyond contestation. The complex picture presented by faith communities in South Africa – with or without reference to their position under apartheid – is in large part due to the ways religion has contextualised itself under South African conditions (see section 2.1). There are a number of possible ways to present South

Africa's faith communities and their submissions to the TRC. One is to look at how each saw itself in relation to apartheid and to the liberation movements. In their submissions, faith communities located themselves in terms of being 'supportive' of the old regime (notably the DRC), as 'neutral' with reference to the old regime (usually invoking a 'nature of the church' vs 'nature of the state' argument), or as 'opposed' to the old regime (usually, though not necessarily always, in solidarity with the liberation movements).[13] We will expand on this in examining and analysing the submissions. But first we must introduce the various players who will feature in this more specific discussion.

This is not intended as a comprehensive account of South Africa's faith communities.[14] No doubt it will be argued that some of the players mentioned represent minority groups, such as the Baha'i faith, while scant mention is made of groups with relatively large followings.[15] Many such groups declined to represent themselves before the Commission and so will only feature here to provide background for those that did appear. Space constraints mean that only a few sentences can be given to each grouping, often without relation to their size or importance.

2.3.1 General comments on the history of South African religion

Apartheid mythology taught that the first settlers entered a religious vacuum when they landed at the Cape and encountered its indigenous inhabitants. This is manifestly untrue. Far from being an 'empty container' into which religion could be emptied, Khoisan culture was already religiously rich. While the early settlers included a small number of Catholics and Jews, only the Reformed faith was officially recognised. In 1804 the De Mist Order set the stage not only for a proliferation of Christian denominations at the Cape, but also for other religions. Both Judaism and Islam were well established by the middle of the nineteenth century. Christianity remained strongly favoured, however, with some churches subsidised by the Cape government. The passing of the Voluntary Act in 1875, while recognising the importance of religion in the Colony, effectively reconstituted faith communities alike as voluntary societies.

The Union of South Africa made little pretension of being a 'Christian' state, and the relation between its early leaders, Jan Smuts and Louis Botha (and even Barry Hertzog), and Christianity was not politically significant. The rise of African nationalism, however, was closely connected with Christianity – especially that which carried with it the liberal values of the original missionaries. Ironically, as the century wore on, many missionaries championed segregation policies, often in the teeth of opposition from their converts. While many, if not most, of the policies identified with apartheid and its violation of human rights were anticipated in the decades before, an ideological change came in 1948 with the coming to power of D.F. Malan's new National Party. The National Party espoused an ideology called 'Christian nationalism' – a synthesis of neo-Calvinism, reformed pietism and Fichtean romanticist nationalism which would soon transform the country.[16]

For many years, the Dutch Reformed Church (DRC) acted as an organ of legitimisation for Christian nationalism and apartheid and was *de facto*, if not *de jure*, the established church.[17] Gradually, however, the state took upon itself the role of 'guardian of the faith' – something which gave the DRC space to distance itself from its previous function of legitimising of apartheid. This new role for the state was evident most strongly in the Preamble to the 1983 Constitution. Ironically, it was this now blatantly 'Christian' constitution that attempted to co-opt Muslims and Hindus (who constituted an important part of the coloured and Indian communities) into the tricameral system. And it was this constitution that was strongly opposed by a coalition of Christian, Muslim and other religious groups, in solidarity with liberation movements, many of whom already had origins in or strong connections with religious communities.

2.3.2 African traditional religion

Often classified as 'primal religion', African traditional religion may simply refer to the religion of Africans practised from antiquity to the first contact with European settlers.[18] As practised today, however, 'the religion of Africans' is contested amongst those who espouse a 'purified' form (purified especially from all Christian or missionary influences) and those who have adapted the religion or mobilised its resources within the Christian tradition.[19] African religion has provided 'an open set of resources' for negotiating human existence, and the 'traditional' in ATR is not only something 'handed down' but something 'taken up'.[20] What this means for the Commission's investigations is simply that the contextual element is always present, whether positively or negatively; that is, the fact that contact with other religions changed the shape of ATR does not in itself constitute an abuse. On the contrary, ATR as a religion was able to transform itself into a map for the negotiation of life in a colonial and postcolonial context. The abuse comes when such expressions are suppressed in the name of another religion, such as 'Christianity'. But it should also be noted that ideas of 'traditional' were also useful to oppressive regimes that wanted to lock Africans into a particular way of life.

2.3.3 Protestant Christianity

2.3.3.1 Ecumenical churches. While not representing the largest number of adherents amongst the faith communities, by far the majority of the submissions, as well as the most extensive and detailed, came from

Protestant churches. The amount of space given them is not an indicator of their special importance, but rather to aid in understanding some of the nuances in their submissions.

Protestant Christianity in South Africa has two originating strands: mission and settler. Mission Christianity existed for the purpose of propagating Christianity amongst indigenous peoples. In the process, the missions established schools and hospitals, helped in the development of vernacular languages, published newspapers, and engaged in many other activities which had widespread cultural and social significance. Settler Christianity was brought along with the Europeans who emigrated to South Africa and functioned in part to give them a sense of continuity with institutions of the mother country. By the middle of the twentieth century mission and settler Christianity had consolidated into many different denominations.

Mission Christianity recognised the need for African Christians to develop their own structures, which led to the formation of denominations such as the Bantu Congregational Church (now part of the United Congregational Church), the Tsonga Presbyterian Church (now the Evangelical Presbyterian Church), and the Bantu Presbyterian Church, which would later be renamed the Reformed Presbyterian Church (RPC). While the Reformed Presbyterian Church counted officials of the former homelands among its members, it is different in kind from a church such as the United Methodist Church, which was set up in the Transkei specifically as an alternative to the anti-Bantustan Methodist Church of Southern Africa.

One of the oldest Protestant movements in South Africa is the Moravian Church. Indeed, the first missionary in South Africa was Moravian. With a strong ecumenical tradition, the Moravian Church was a founder member of the SACC and its predecessor, the Christian Council. Moravian missions had two foci: the Eastern Cape (mainly amongst Xhosa-speakers) and the Western Cape (mainly amongst the coloured population). In the 1990s the two sections united in one church.

Some mission and settler churches of the same tradition combined to form one multiracial denomination, though not usually integrated at local levels, and these have generally been known as 'the English-speaking churches', notably the Methodist, Presbyterian and United Congregational Church of Southern Africa (UCCSA). The CPSA represents the dominant stream of Anglicanism and is grouped together with these other churches (although it has in its history attempted to build formal ties with the DRC).[21] The smaller CESA, though also tracing its roots to the arrival of the first English settlers at the beginning of the nineteenth century, is conservative-evangelical in theology and is not normally grouped with the mainline English-speaking churches.

Although the black constituencies of the multiracial Protestant churches soon became the largest part of their membership, their leadership has until recently tended to come from their white minority. Also they have a history of supporting middle-class black aspirations but shying away from more radical social and economic demands.[22] This helps account for their ambivalence in supporting liberation movements, while voicing opposition to apartheid policies. The ethos of these churches could be described as 'ecumenical' and indeed they have been seeking union for several decades. They are also institutions that have undergone much change – particularly with reference to the racial make-up of their leadership.

Most of the churches mentioned above are members of the SACC, an inter-church organisation which was originally formed in 1936 as the Christian Council of South Africa, which in turn was anticipated by a series of regular General Missionary Conferences. The SACC was constituted in 1968 and soon saw its relations with its white-dominated English-speaking member churches become strained over the WCC's Programme to Combat Racism (PCR), which diverted funds to support liberation groups. In the early seventies it had reached a turning point, being declared by the government a 'black organisation'. Significant within this phase of ecumenical Christianity was the activity of the Christian Institute (CI), which openly identified itself with the black consciousness movement.[23] The CI was banned in 1977. In the 1980s, the ICT helped to radicalise the Council's theological agenda.[24] Many of its member churches at an institutional or denominational level, however, remained cautious. For these reasons, its activities and those of its member churches cannot be simplistically identified.

While, as we stated, Protestant Christianity in South Africa is broadly ecumenical, not all Protestant churches are members of the SACC. The Salvation Army withdrew in the early 1970s over its alliance with the PCR and support of the End Conscription Campaign, as did the mostly white Baptist Union of Southern Africa (BUSA). The mostly black Baptist Convention of South Africa (BCSA), which split from the Union in 1987, is a member of the Council.[25] The Salvation Army rejoined the SACC in 1994. CESA, with its conservative theological and political ethos, has never been a member – a fact which it strongly asserted during the apartheid struggle to indicate its patriotism.

2.3.3.2 Evangelical churches and groups. 'Evangelical' is difficult to define as it can be used as a synonym for 'Protestant'. This is indicated in the official title of the Lutheran churches, viz. Evangelical Lutheran Church of Southern Africa. Many individual Christians within the ecumenical churches consider themselves 'evangelical' and here the term is used theologically as distinct from liberal or some other kind of theology. While we have distinguished this group from the 'ecumenical' group above, it must be recognised that not all evangelicals are anti-ecumenical (indeed, they are 'ecumenical' with reference to other evangelicals).

As used here, the term refers to groups including denominations which have a conservative-evangelical theological ethos (e.g. BUSA and CESA – see the previous section), independent or semi-independent groups which exist within 'mainline' Protestant churches, including para-church agencies such as the Scripture Union (an organisation devoted to the evangelism of children and youth), and some independent congregations of evangelical orientation such as the Rosebank Union Church in Johannesburg.[26] Generally speaking, evangelical Christianity has been politically conservative and sometimes reactionary. [27] As a result more progressive evangelicals formed organisations such as Concerned Evangelicals in the late 1980s, and produced documents expressing strong public opposition to apartheid.[28] Some 'migrated' to more ecumenical churches while others engaged in debates that led to denominational splits. The legacy of all these groups is represented in the submission of The Evangelical Alliance of South Africa (TEASA), a new coalition of evangelical bodies founded in November 1995 which has a membership of 31 denominations representing about 2 million people.

The first missionaries of the Seventh Day Adventist (SDA) Church arrived in South Africa in 1887, and the church was organised in 1892 as the South African Conference of Seventh Day Adventists. It was an integral part of the world body, becoming a Union comprising the Cape and Natal–Transvaal conferences, along with Cape (coloured) and black missions in 1901. An Indian mission was organised in 1956 in Natal–Transvaal. In 1960, the church was reorganised into two distinct groups, one for black ('Bantu') members and the other for the rest. These merged in 1991. The SDA Church in South Africa numbers fewer than 100,000 baptised adult members.

The BUSA came into being in South Africa in 1877 and was predominantly British. By the end of the century, British immigration swelled the number of South African Baptists. Though from a nonconformist heritage, Baptist congregations were also typical 'settler' churches, serving to reinforce loyalty to the Empire. The Baptist Missionary Society was formed in 1892 and the movement soon spread beyond the white, English-speaking community. Known for prizing local congregational autonomy, nevertheless there were institutions which allowed Baptists to engage the public sphere, such as the Christian Citizenship Committees. It was only in 1976 that the Union advocated integrated congregations, and the long-standing tension between progressive (mostly black) and conservative members grew until 1987 when the BCSA was constituted as a separate body.[29]

2.3.3.3 Dutch Reformed Churches. The DRC is the largest of the four white Afrikaans-speaking churches within the Dutch Reformed tradition, but it is the only one to have made a submission to the TRC.[30] The other three churches are the Hervormde Kerk, the Gereformeerde Kerk and the Afrikaanse Protestante Kerk,[31] the last-mentioned a result of a schism within the DRC when the DRC began to move away from supporting apartheid policies.[32]

Although it had ecumenical strands, with the Cape and Transvaal Synods participating in the Christian Council until 1940, the DRC distanced itself from the ecumenical movement after the Cottesloe Consultation in 1960, and functioned in many ways like an official, established church throughout the apartheid years. Along with the National Party and the Afrikaner Broederbond, the DRC was closely identified with Afrikaner nationalism and its 1.3 million members at present account for 60 per cent of Afrikaners. After the transition to democracy in 1994, the DRC became an observer member of the SACC.

Like some of the English-speaking missionary churches the DRC formed its own 'mission churches' – the NG Sendingkerk (coloured, 1881, but stemming from a synod decision of 1857), the NG Kerk in Afrika (African, originally 'the NGK Bantu Church of South Africa', 1951) and the Reformed Church (Indian). While its origins predate the advent of apartheid, this 'family' of churches came to exemplify the expression of the apartheid ideal in the church. Ecumenical efforts within the 'family' were tied to opposing this ideal. In 1978 a unification of the former DRC family churches was proposed and, in 1994, the NG Kerk in Afrika and the Sendingkerk united under the name of the Uniting Reformed Church in Southern Africa (URCSA). The vision of the URCSA is to bring all the former segregated churches together in one denomination – something which has yet to be fulfilled as negotiations with the DRC and Indian Reformed Church are ongoing.

Within the DRC, 'family' groups arose specifically opposing the theological justification of apartheid. Most notable (and unfortunately absent from the Commission) was the CI, led by a former Moderator of the Southern Transvaal synod, Beyers Naudé. Established in 1963 after the DRC had rejected the Cottesloe Consultation's Statement, the CI was ecumenical in orientation and became increasingly identified with the liberation movements. It was banned in 1977. The Belydende Kring or 'Confessing Circle' (formerly called the 'Broederkring') was formed in 1974 and was made up of dissident ministers within the African, Indian and coloured NG churches who were engaged in the struggle against apartheid.

2.3.4 Historically African churches

By 'historically African churches', we mean churches that were started by Africans as a response to colonialism or missionary suppression of African aspirations or culture. Often referred to as African 'Independent', 'Instituted', 'Indigenous' or 'Initiated' Churches, these have been referred to as a unique, 'fourth type' of Christianity in the world, taking their place alongside Protestantism, Catholicism and Orthodoxy.[33] In 1991, AICs accounted for more than one third of the Christian population in South Africa.[34]

AICs are sometimes dubbed 'syncretistic' in their attempt to combine African traditional elements with mission Christianity. It is more helpful to understand them as 'contextual innovations' – as indeed all faith communities in South Africa must be understood.[35] The first AICs were not so much a synthesis of African traditional religion and Protestant Christianity as an attempt by a rising African middle class to construct a Christianity that was like its Protestant forebears but under the control of Africans. This 'type' was termed by Bengt Sundkler as 'Ethiopian' and was not represented at the Commission.[36]

While the Ethiopian churches 'were African replicas of Christian denominations and were an explicit response to racial inequality', Zionist Christianity arose from the economic conditions of an urban proletariat.[37] Within 'mainstream' Zionism, by far the largest group is the Zion Christian Church (ZCC), which in the 1980s grew from 2.7 to 7.4 per cent of all Christians in South Africa.[38] The ZCC combines worship with sponsorship of successful business and other enterprises, and is perhaps best known for its openness to political leaders, who are invited to its annual gathering at Moria.[39]

Also belonging within the family of African Initiated Churches is the amaNazaretha, popularly known as 'the Shembe Church'. This is the second largest AIC in southern Africa, numbering about half a million members, the majority of whom are Zulu. Mobilising specifically 'Zulu' cultural resources, the church hierarchy mirrors Zulu social structure, something that makes it distinct amongst AICs.[40]

The ethos of the AICs varies and it is even more difficult to generalise in their case than in that of the other faith communities. Opinions vary on the extent to which members of these churches were involved in the political struggle against apartheid, and as yet much research needs to be done on the subject.[41] Clearly those within the Ethiopian tradition, which had long identified with African nationalism, were committed to the liberation movement along with their black compatriots in the mission and settler churches. The ethos of Zionist churches has been less overtly political, and some churches such as the ZCC have insisted on their political neutrality. Indeed, the ZCC appears to have been aligned with more conservative political forces, even though it now rejects such a claim.[42] But it would be misleading to generalise about these churches. Comprised largely of the marginalised poor, it is inconceivable that all their members refrained from the struggle against apartheid. While the Council of African Initiated Churches (CAIC) is a member of the SACC, some other AICs (including especially the ZCC) have displayed reluctance to be involved in ecumenical activity, whether with other AICs or with bodies such as the SACC.[43] The ZCC, however, now has an ecumenical office in Johannesburg.

2.3.5 The Roman Catholic Church

Much of what can be said of English-speaking Protestant Christianity in terms of social and ecumenical ethos could be written of the Roman Catholic Church. Like the Protestant English-speaking churches, the Roman Catholic Church has a long history of involvement in education, health work and other forms of social engagement. Unlike the Protestant churches, however, it refused to accede to government demands to close its schools following the Bantu Education Act of 1953, financing them with funds raised locally and overseas.[44]

Roman Catholicism was regarded with suspicion by the Afrikaner nationalist government, with the *Roomse gevaar* following close on *swart gevaar* and *rooi gevaar*. This made it marginal within the South African Christian scene.[45] In some ways this made the Roman Catholic Church more cautious at times in its opposition to apartheid, though its record in opposing apartheid is at least equal to that of any of the other English-speaking churches. The hierarchy of the Catholic Church in South Africa is similar to that of other churches, with the Southern African Catholic Bishops' Conference (SACBC) taking an important leadership role – especially in the 1980s. Since the 1960s, the Roman Catholic Church has been ecumenically engaged, and after some years as an observer of the SACC it became a full member in 1995. Eleven per cent of South Africa's Christians in 1991 declared themselves Roman Catholics.

2.3.6 Pentecostal and charismatic Christianity

After Roman Catholics, Pentecostal and charismatic Christians account for the largest group of Christians in the world. In South Africa, Pentecostal churches, including those in AICs, account for one quarter of the population.[46] South African Pentecostalism is represented both in some of the 'spirit-type' AICs and in those churches which have long been white-controlled, notably the Apostolic Faith Mission (AFM), Assemblies of God and Full Gospel Church of God. While the Assemblies of God did not make an official submission, included in the TEASA team at the hearings was the Rev. Colin LaVoy, a national leader. Also included was Dr

Derek Morphew of Vineyard Ministries, a prominent charismatic group of churches. This illustrates the close ties between Pentecostal, charismatic and evangelical Christians in South Africa.

Much of what was said about the DRC could be repeated of the AFM, which over the years has provided a space for many ex-DRC members who wanted a more emotionally orientated expression of Christian faith and worship. While it developed out of the early racially inchoate Pentecostal movement, it soon grew to reflect the racially segregated structure of the DRC. The power and constitution of the church was controlled by white members and before 1991 only whites could be 'legal' members.[47] In 1990, the three non-white sections formed a 'composite' church – from 1993 under the leadership of Frank Chikane. In 1996 the various sections united. The AFM's support of apartheid was explicit, something which may help account for some African Pentecostals' unwillingness to criticise the policy while separating themselves from their white colleagues institutionally.[48]

Many newly established independent charismatic churches now exist throughout South Africa, especially in white suburbs. The Hatfield Christian Church in Pretoria (five thousand members) and Rhema Church of Johannesburg (some ten thousand members) are prominent examples – especially of so-called 'mega-churches'. In ethos, these churches strove (at least outwardly) in the eighties to eschew political involvement – particularly by dissuading their members from becoming involved in the anti-apartheid movements.[49] But since the Rustenberg Conference in 1990, where Ray McCauley emerged as a leading figure, they have had a higher public profile. The International Fellowship of Christian Churches (IFCC), which links most of these churches together, has grown remarkably since its founding in 1984 and now has over 400 member churches. From 1992 the IFCC has held observer status at the SACC.

2.3.7 Islam[50]

While Islam may have been in South Africa since the fifteenth century its origins within South Africa are usually traced to the late seventeenth and early eighteenth centuries.[51] During this period, the Dutch East India Company brought slaves from the Indonesian archipelago to the refreshment station at the Cape of Good Hope. They also used the Cape as a banishment outpost for anti-colonial leaders. Many of these slaves and exiles were Muslims. If Islam at the Cape has a 'founder', it would be Sheikh Yusuf of Macassar, who arrived as a political prisoner in 1694 and, despite restrictions placed on him, was able to communicate tenets of Islam to slaves and free blacks. While only three of his party would remain after his death in 1699, by the 1830s his tomb was a popular site.

Islam developed a strong base among Malay slaves during the late eighteenth and early nineteenth centuries – facilitated in part by the relaxing of the law which punished its practice by death.[52]

Many of the indentured Indian labourers and free traders that came to the Transvaal and Natal in the late nineteenth and early twentieth centuries were Muslims, and they planted religious roots wherever they settled. Islam has been marginalised by the state for most of its existence in South Africa. This reflects imported European–Christendom constructions of 'otherness', with Islam existing at the boundaries of Europe. Over the years, however, many Christians and Muslims in South Africa have made common cause around social and moral issues, particularly against apartheid oppression. According to the official 1991 census, Muslims numbered approximately 1.1 per cent of the population, although this number is probably too low.

The Muslim Judicial Council (MJC) was formed in 1945 in the Cape. It was set up to promote unity amongst Muslims but also to promote unity amongst all oppressed non-Europeans. Generally taking an apolitical stance the movement was radicalised only some years after the death in detention of Imam Abdullah Haron.[53] Haron's death also created a leadership vacuum amongst Muslim youth, one that was filled by the Muslim Youth Movement of South Africa (MYMSA), which was established in 1970 – one year after his death.[54]

A split within the MYMSA led to the formation of the Call of Islam (COI) in 1984, a group whose understanding of Islam was in broad agreement with the principles of the United Democratic Front (UDF).[55] The COI clergy leadership emerged as prominent spokespersons, leading to the radicalisation of the MJC – at least at a public level. A more radical group, Qibla, had already been formed in 1980 and supported the Pan Africanist Congress (PAC) agenda.[56] The MYMSA, Qibla and COI were united in opposition to the tricameral constitution – and opposed to the more conservative Jamiatul Ulama in the Transvaal (JUT, formed originally in 1922), which supported tricameral politics.[57] The conservative Ulama movements generally also opposed the ecumenical cooperation between Muslim groups and what they termed 'infidels' (Christians, Jews, Hindus and secularists).[58]

2.3.8 Judaism[59]

The Jewish community in South Africa is relatively small, numbering less than 0.3 per cent of the South African population.[60] Like Muslims, Jews came to South Africa in two main waves: the first, of mainly British and German origin, immigrated in the early nineteenth century; the second of persecuted Jews of Eastern European origin, arrived toward the end of the nineteenth century. While English-speaking Jews were considered 'safe', others were subject to harassment both by other whites and by the state.[61] Indeed, it has been said that 'the Jewish community has been subjected to more discriminatory legislation than any other white group' – especially laws controlling immigration.[62]

In 1841, the Tikvat Israel Synagogue in Cape Town was built, providing a focus for Cape Town Jewry. More followed, with Oudtshoorn providing an example of a vibrant community. The two main representative bodies for Jews are the South African Jewish Board of Deputies (formed in 1912) and the South African Zionist Federation (1898). Originally South African Jews looked to the Chief Rabbi of Britain for spiritual leadership. Eventually, synagogues in the Transvaal federated under a chief rabbi in 1933; an amalgamation of Cape and Transvaal groupings (which had remained fairly independent centres) took place in 1986. South African Judaism, as in other places, is divided into orthodox and reformed groups. The Chief Rabbi of South Africa represents Orthodox Judaism. Reform Judaism, which started in South Africa in 1933, is known for its relative conservatism in practice and comprises 17 per cent of South African Jews.[63]

The ethos of Judaism generally in South Africa is a kind of non-observant orthodoxy which reveres certain traditions (such as synagogue attendance on important occasions and feast days) but which also is less strict with reference to other traditions (such as refraining from driving on the Sabbath and keeping kosher outside the home).[64] While Jews made their greatest contributions to South African society as individuals, there have also been organisations which have played roles. During the last years of apartheid, Jews for Justice and Jews for Social Justice were important voices of protest. The Gesher Movement, formed in Johannesburg in 1996, aims 'to serve as a Jewish lobby speaking with one independent voice, "to enlighten" the Jewish community in the new South Africa, and to combat Jewish racism.'[65]

2.3.9 Hinduism[66]

The Hindu community makes up 70 per cent of the one million South African Indians. The first Indians came to South Africa in 1860 to work as indentured labour, mainly on sugar plantations in Natal. After the term of their indenture ended, many stayed on as farmers – despite government attempts to repatriate them in the 1920s. The so-called 'free' or 'passenger' Indians arrived towards the end of the nineteenth century, and set up trade and merchant businesses. Indians in South Africa are a very diverse group, including four major language groups with distinctive (though sometimes overlapping) worship practices, religious rites, customs and dress.

From the turn of the century, the need arose for the various Hindu communities and religious institutions to come together under the banner of a national body. The Hindu Maha Sabha was formed in 1912, to provide a coordinated means to discuss the religious, cultural, educational, social and economic welfare of the Hindu community. It embraces the four main language groups, temple societies and neo-religious organisations which subscribe to the views of Hinduism.

2.3.10 Buddhism

While some Buddhists came to South Africa from India, and other Indians have converted to the religion since its arrival late in the nineteenth century, most South African Buddhists are white converts. Buddhism in South Africa does not have centralised structures but is present in small organisations and centres. The first Buddhist society was formed in 1917 in Natal. Buddhism grew amongst whites through the work of Molly and Louis van Loon and others, who travelled and learned its practices abroad. The Dharma Centre, rooted in the Zen tradition, was set up at Somerset West in 1984 by Heila and Rodney Downey.[67]

2.3.11 The Baha'i faith

While present in South Africa since 1911, the Baha'i faith only began to grow in the 1950s. While committed to inclusivity, the South African Baha'i community worked to promote its black leadership. This was, as it says, 'a result of [its] great emphasis on spiritual, moral, and ethical aspects of community life.'[68] The Baha'i faith places great stress on offering itself as model for reconciliation, both racial and religious.

3. AN ACCOUNT OF THE SUBMISSIONS

3.1 Three caveats

In addition to the problems with defining 'faith community', there are also problems inherent in assessing the submissions themselves. Some were extensive and detailed, chronicling with a high degree of introspection the highs and the lows of the respective community's life during the apartheid years. Others were sketchy and vague, making generalisations (especially about being 'opposed to apartheid') without supplying specific instances. The impression created by this is that, judged in terms of quantity, those communities that went into more detail about the past were more 'involved' – whether for or against apartheid. While imprecise, perhaps such impressions cannot be helped in a report of this nature. On the other hand, those communities which supplied the most detail seem to be the most ready to own up to the past and to move ahead into the future, although doubts remain about the various documents supplied by the DRC[69] – despite their relative length.[70]

Much of the evidence that we have to draw upon comes from the submissions themselves. This creates another problem: that communities may have a selective memory or even suppress the truth. This occurred during the hearings when the mostly white Baptist Union testified to opposing human rights abuses under apartheid, of taking their protests to the government of the day and so forth. Following this, the mostly black Baptist Convention's presentation strongly relativised the Union's claims to have opposed the old regime, accusing it of active complicity. Whether this was an instance of 'white' vs 'black' perceptions or a deliberate attempt on the part of the Union to mislead the Commission, it shows that we are dealing with perceptions and perspectives that are highly particularistic and relative to a number of 'hidden' factors, including the ongoing construction of identities within and between faith communities.[71]

Perhaps then we should regard the submissions not so much as what faith communities did, but rather what they said they did during the years under consideration.[72] This means that our report will have to go beyond the accounts in the submissions to examine other sources relating what various faith communities did during that time. It will mean attending to the unsaid as well as the said. Not only will this help fill in the picture of those years, but it will also allow us to begin to evaluate the preparedness of faith communities to deal with their past and move into the future.

The third caveat will come up again, so we only mention it briefly here. When for instance the CPSA submission is examined, of whom and for whom does it speak, confess and ask forgiveness? Its individual members? All its individual members? Its leaders? Its parishes? What does it mean when a church apologises to its spiritual leader (in the CPSA's case, Archbishop Tutu, for failing to support his call for economic sanctions in the 1980s)? At the hearings, the Moderator of the DRC said that he spoke on behalf of 'the greater portion of the church' when it came to commitment to reconciliation with the other sectors of the DRC family, but the church still had to consult locally with its individual members before a formal statement could be made.

The answer to the question of who speaks for whom is never clear or unambiguous. In this way, however, faith communities are no different from other kinds of bodies and sectors that have testified before the Commission, including business and the media. It is worth mentioning that the different ways that faith communities are organised also shape the issue of representation. A hierarchical church such as the CPSA finds it far easier to send a representative (or to make representation) at hearings than a community which stresses the autonomy of the local congregation, such as the UCCSA, or of its individual members. This also has strong implications for how different faith communities can be held accountable, not only for the past, but for following through on the promises they made.

What follows is a synoptic report on the submissions to the TRC by faith communities and the statements made at the hearings. A distillation of some 500 pages of written submissions and three full days of transcripts from the hearings, it is far from comprehensive, aiming rather at representing the diverse nature and activity of faith communities during the period under consideration. It focuses on what the communities actually said or wrote to the Commission, although, as stated already, it will supply other details to help fill in the picture.

3.2 Reflecting on gross human rights violations of the past

The original letter to the faith communities sent by the Commission posed these questions:

> Given the prominence of references to morality and religion in the submissions of various political parties and amnesty applications, in which way, if any, did the theology and activities of your denomination contribute to the formation of the motives and perspectives of those individuals, organisations and institutions responsible for gross human rights violations, either in upholding the previous system or in opposing it?
>
> The conflicts of the past have been described as a 'holy war'. With the benefit of hindsight, what was the contribution of your [community or organisation][73] in creating a climate or a justification for gross human rights violations to be committed?
>
> In which ways, through acts of commission and acts of omission, did your [community or organisation][74] contribute to the conflict of the past?
>
> In which ways did you fail to live up to those principles of your faith which oppose human rights violations?
>
> In which ways did your [community or organisation][75] actively oppose (gross) human rights violations?'[76]

Some general observations about the responses of faith communities to these questions may be in order, before turning to the details of the submissions in the next sections of this report.

• With some notable exceptions, faith communities in their responses were virtually unanimous in apologising for playing a role, whether through omission or commission, in the abuses of the past.[77] Again with notable exceptions, faith communities – even the most conservative – recognised that strategies of disengagement contributed to the maintenance of a 'climate' which allowed human rights abuses to continue. One of the striking admissions came from the CESA, which recognised how a theology of disengagement could be 'manipulated' into support for the state. Certainly, as the submission of the International Federation of Christian Churches confessed, such theology gave 'tacit support' to state structures. The Seventh Day Adventist Church noted that attempting to stay out of party politics was effectively a vote for the status quo. Along with those who admitted passive complicity, many if not most apologised for not 'doing enough' to oppose apartheid.

• No group apologised for active complicity in human rights abuses, whether on the part of the state or of the liberation movements.[78] However, some of churches admitted they supplied chaplains to both sides of the struggle, contributing to interpretations of that conflict as 'holy war'.[79] Communities admitted that some of their members may have been responsible for human rights abuses on the side of the state during the apartheid years, though how and where their theologies or organisational activities contributed to the actions of those guilty of human rights abuses was not generally spelt out.

• No group confessed to having actively supported or being complicit in the policies of apartheid as they were actually implemented by the state.[80]

We can broadly speak of two ways in which faith communities acted as agents of oppression: by deliberate acts, if not of outright support of apartheid, of tacit support and implication in state structures; and by failing to act in accordance with their own traditions by allowing oppression to continue. Some of the groups which apologised for 'failures' to better oppose apartheid mentioned poor communication with members and being reactive rather than proactive.[81] While providing important lessons for future community and ecumenical action, and underlining the third caveat above, these do not constitute support for oppression and will not be dealt with here.

While we shall make use of the terms, it is clear that there are different ways of understanding 'complicity', and probably also 'solidarity' with the victims, as well as 'responsibility'. The hearings and submissions both demonstrated that there is a wide divergence in understandings, with some communities considering themselves 'engaged' by their own standards – even 'prophetic' – but decidedly not when compared to others.[82]

In some analyses of faith communities, the term 'apolitical' may apply (with the implication that to be apolitical was to be in tacit support of the former regime)[83] while other ways of seeing might define engagement (or indeed 'politics') differently.[84]

It is possible to summarise the identities of faith communities in their submissions as assuming three roles in relation to the climate of the period under question (sometimes one, sometimes two, sometimes all three at the same time – see our third caveat above): agents of oppression, victims of oppression, and opponents of oppression.

3.2.1 Faith communities as agents of oppression

In the first section we noted the importance of faith communities as alternative centres of loyalty. In most cases faith communities claim to cut across divisions of race, class and ethnicity. As such it would seem that faith communities would present a key point of opposition, by their very existence, to the policies of the apartheid state. But also, the norms and values proclaimed by faith communities would or should have challenged directly the policies of the state.

That this was not the case lies behind many of the communities' apologies to the South African people. Indeed, contrary to their own deepest traditions, many faith communities mirrored apartheid society.[85] They thus not only failed in terms of South African society, but they failed their own faith tradition.

The following section concerns 'acts' of commission and omission. It is worth mentioning that some submissions spoke also of an ethos where racism was tolerated – including between whites.[86] At the same time, churches played an important role in reinforcing the idea that South Africa was a relatively normal society with a few racial problems.

3.2.1.1 Acts of commission and legitimisation

• Direct support of apartheid

The submissions noted how individual members of churches – even of churches outspoken against government policies – co-operated with the regime or with the Security Branch.[87] Nico Smith, a former *dominee* who was himself outspoken against apartheid, admitted that 'many of these willing executioners ... were members of our congregations'.[88] Even amongst Catholic clergy, *Roomse gevaar* notwithstanding, there was 'an unhealthy alliance of altar and throne'.[89] All this created a climate where any challenge to the consciences of whites was rarely, if ever, issued.

This went beyond tacit support of apartheid's foot soldiers. As is apparent from previous hearings, many state operatives claimed to have found positive support in the teaching of the Afrikaans-speaking churches, most notoriously the DRC, which 'blessed their weapons of terror'.[90] In its response, the DRC confessed to having 'misled' its members on 'apartheid as a biblical instruction'.[91] The DRC from the outset provided theological and biblical sanction for apartheid, even though as its submission claimed some of its theologians questioned this justification.[92] It was only in 1986 that such sanction was officially questioned.[93] Even in their documents submitted to the TRC, the DRC continued to make a distinction between 'good' and 'bad' apartheid, arguing that they supported apartheid when applied with justice. In other words, apartheid was not evil or unjust in essence, but only became bad when it took on the character of an ideology.[94] This was in marked contrast to those communities, such as the UCCSA, that called apartheid evil 'in principle'.[95]

The complicity of the DRC with the policy of apartheid went beyond simple approval and legitimisation, however. The church actively promoted the policy – not least because it served the Afrikaner interests with which it identified itself. The DRC confessed that it 'often tended to put the interests of its people above the interests of other people'.[96] There were no examples given of when it did not put the interests of the Afrikaner community above those of others.

While only the DRC gave official sanction to apartheid laws in principle, other faith communities confessed to actions which amounted to acquiescing with apartheid laws, wronging those who bore the brunt of apartheid.[97] The Presbyterian Church of Southern Africa (PCSA) confessed to giving 'qualified support' to government during the early sixties, which included defending the Bantustan policies in 1965 and the right of the state to suppress 'unlawful subversion'.[98] Other examples of faith communities 'falling into line' could be offered. But perhaps the strongest way they gave it legitimacy was in the shape of the churches themselves and the way they conformed to the norms promoted by apartheid – something to which we shall return.

• Complicity and participation in state structures

Apartheid South Africa understood itself as a 'Christian society'. This meant that the Christian churches were expected to lend succour to the agents of the state in battle (through the South African Defence Force) or in infiltrating the camps of its enemies (through the South African Police or its various security bodies). This was done overtly by sponsoring chaplains and in more subtle ways by 'praying' for soldiers or officers.[99]

Again the leader in this was the DRC. As Ds. Neels du Plooy, a former South African Defence Force (SADF) chaplain, testified earlier to the Commission, objectors to service in the SADF were termed 'unbelievers' while all who served were given a New Testament with a special message from P.W. Botha inside, telling them that the Bible was their 'most important weapon'. In his testimony before the Commission on 23 July 1997, Du Plooy spoke of how 'the appointment of chaplains and the involvement of the church in the military were governed by an official agreement between the state and the church. This agreement was approved at a national synod level as well as at parliamentary level.'[100] Many of the perpetrators of human rights abuses were never challenged on these issues by the DRC but were tacitly or otherwise encouraged in their activities.[101]

This was a failure amongst the Afrikaner churches (and other Afrikaner institutions) in general which, in the words of Ponti Venter of the Gereformeerde Kerk at the hearings, 'acted as no more than limbs ... of the volk and the state'.

From the first years of its existence under the control of white missionaries, the former Sendingkerk and NG Kerk in Afrika were shaped by 'tacit' apartheid, which accounts for why their decisions 'were often ambiguous', with 'both clergy and lay members participating in the structures of apartheid'.[102] Eventually, however, with the emergence of its own leadership these churches would become important critics of the state.

But it was not only the DRC which was complicit in state structures.[103] The Apostolic Faith Movement church, dominated by white Afrikaners, also admitted to having numerous members who were 'employed in the structures of the former government', with many holding 'top positions in the former government organisations'.[104] Of course, holding a position, even a top position, does not entail direct implication in specific violations. It does, however, mean participating in the machinery that created the conditions under which such violations took place.

The Baptist Union, according to the BCSA submission, in the 1980s elected an SADF Brigadier as president, with the elections taking place at a national assembly held in the military barracks in Kimberley.[105] Other churches confessed that their members participated in state machinery, with the Reformed Presbyterian Church admitting that some of its members took part in homeland structures. But they were by no means alone in this regard, as members of most faith communities were involved. The difference was more a matter of whether or not the faith communities as such gave their support. Special mention should be made of the accusation against Indians (including some Hindus) that they participated in tricameral politics. The perception of Indian and Hindu complicity, according to the South African Hindu Maha Sabha, was largely created by state propaganda.[106]

• Active suppression of dissidents within their ranks

While some faith communities confessed that they did not give sufficient support to activists in their communities (see below under acts of omission), others suppressed, censured and condemned dissidents, even branding them as 'heretics'. Notable here is the case of the Rev. Frank Chikane, General Secretary of the SACC, who was tortured under the supervision of an elder in the white section of his church; the latter went off to a church service afterwards.[107] The BCSA noted incidents where black Baptist ministers were tortured by deacons of white Baptist churches.[108] Along with this active suppression should be placed confessions of failing to support dissidents and activists within church ranks. This will be dealt with in the next section.

Even the most seemingly benign activity could be construed as subversive. Venter spoke of the National Initiative for Reconciliation's (NIR) Potchefstroom supporters endeavouring to supply study space for black matriculants during the 1980s. Local churches, under the watchful eye of the security forces, termed the plan 'communist-inspired' and no church in town would grant it support.[109]

• Religious apartheid (church structures)[110]

The term 'religious apartheid' can be used of the privileged position of the Christian faith in a so-called Christian society alongside non-Christian religions – the latter being tolerated strictly on the terms of the former. We shall deal with this in the section on faith communities as victims. But religious apartheid is evident within as well as between faith communities, and can also be seen especially within the Christian church.

Despite the fact that they held to different loyalties that reached beyond the boundaries of the state, South African churches, whether implicitly or as matters of policy, allowed themselves to be structured along racial lines. The most obvious example of this in the Dutch Reformed 'family' of churches has already been mentioned.

Like the DRC, the Apostolic Faith Mission was divided formally into four sections (African, white, Indian and coloured). Strikingly, while previously the president of the AFM had attributed this sectionalisation to 'spontaneous segregation', which indicated an implicit understanding of South African racial dynamics on the part of its Afrikaner founders,[111] in his submission on behalf of the church he identified 'the winds of ideological issues' as the cause of the structural divisions in his church.[112] Lutherans were also racially divided, with whites consistently refusing to join in the unity movement which would become the Evangelical Lutheran Church. The Student Christian Association split into separate white (SCA) and black (SCM) organisations.[113]

But the other churches which on the surface appeared non-racial – including those who spoke against the government policy of apartheid – were not guiltless. Some, such as the Salvation Army, confessed a tacit support of racism. And while the Roman Catholic Church officially disavowed racial divisions, 'effectively there was a black church and a white church',[114] something which reinforced the separate symbolic universes in which South Africans lived. Even in those communities where black clergy were recognised in principle, it was often done so with paternalism. In practice these clergy were not sufficiently empowered as leaders within church structures. The PCSA submission stated that even in 1997 it was rare to see a black minister serving a white congregation.[115] At any rate, it went on, stipends were drastically different for black and white clergy, reinforcing racial stereotypes of lifestyle differences.[116] Only in 1995 did the PCSA hold a General Assembly meeting in a black township.[117] The MCSA confessed to similar problems at the hearings.[118] The BCSA accused the BUSA at the hearings of unilaterally creating a scale of benefits based on race, with some black ministers earning as little as R50 per month despite thirty years of service to the Union.[119] While the SDA was unified at its highest level, many of its structures became segregated as the church began to 'pattern itself after the thinking of the politicians'.[120]

This discrimination was not unknown in faith communities outside of Christianity. Hence whether legislated or not, and even in the face of their own resolutions to condemn racist government policies, many South African faith communities nevertheless confessed to having mirrored the racial divisions of their society.

• Propagating 'state theology'

The term 'state theology' is derived from the *Kairos Document*, which used it to refer to the theology that gave legitimacy to the apartheid state. Within the discourse of 'state theology' the God of the Bible was identified with the ultimate principle of the apartheid state. The effects of state theology were to 'bless injustice, canonise the will of the powerful and reduce the poor to passivity, obedience and apathy'.[121]

The most obvious example of a community propagating state theology was the DRC, although it has never (even in its submission to the Commission) confessed to actually 'bowing down' to the monster apartheid disclosed itself to be. Right-wing Christian groups[122] were also schools of state theology, acting as arms of the state infiltrating evangelical and Pentecostal denominations.[123] This has become especially evident in investigations into the Information Scandal of the late seventies, where it was disclosed that government was funding groups such as the Christian League – forerunner of the Gospel Defence League.[124]

Evangelical churches were used by government agencies in order to 'neutralise dissent'.[125] The AFM confessed that it lent support to this idea in its claiming to hold forth a message of charity and love while saying that opposition to apartheid was 'communist-inspired and aimed at the downfall of Christianity'.[126] Other churches acted as if it was in the interest of 'Christian civilisation' to support the state's 'total onslaught' strategy, and therefore to propagate state theology indirectly. Claiming to speak for 'eleven million evangelical Pentecostals', Assemblies of God leaders travelled around the world denouncing the activities of anti-apartheid Christians.[127]

• Bias toward the rich and powerful

While the constituency of the Christian churches was largely poor and black, one of the ironies of the churches' life has been their bias toward the privileged and powerful. We have already mentioned the DRC's bias toward Afrikaner whites. The so-called English-speaking churches have displayed similar ties with business elites.[128] In so far as apartheid was as much about protecting the material interests of whites, this 'bias' toward the wealthy is also a kind of legitimisation.

Churches have also displayed an undue respect for the institution of government – which perhaps is related to their bias toward the rich and powerful (and also connects with churches favouring the practice of opposition by resolution-making, rather than supporting practices of opposition which challenge the machinery of society and economy). Readings of the Bible were often used to buttress this idea.[129] While other faith communities may have been guilty as well, given their social location it was usually much less the case.

3.2.1.2 Acts of omission

• Avoiding responsibility

The idea of 'responsibility' differs amongst groups, with some communities (mostly, though not only, English-speaking churches) seeing themselves as consciences of the nation.[130]

Communities expressed a strong sense of moral responsibility to speak against injustice. Hence their silence in the face of injustice was especially regrettable. Offering a variety of reasons, including complicity with white business interests, poor or inadequate theology or other reason, faith communities and their leadership confessed silence in the face of apartheid wrongs. In their submission, the Roman Catholic Church thought this perhaps its greatest sin. The Salvation Army also, despite its heritage of 'standing up and being counted', noted its lack of courage here. Even the Uniting Reformed Church, which in the 1980s was an important player in opposing the theological justification of apartheid, confessed taking too long to make a stand. This meant 'silent approval' of state actions.[131]

In his submission, Faried Esack accused the Muslim leadership of failing to speak out strongly against apartheid, and especially of remaining silent after the death in detention of Imam Abdullah Haron in 1969 – despite the injuries on his body.[132] Hindu 'leaders' failed their communities by not protesting against apartheid and created the impression that Hindus were part of the system, the Hindu Maha Sabha noted. These 'irresponsible' leaders should have been removed, and the community failed in not doing so.[133]

• Lacking courage

Those communities that did speak out against injustices confessed a certain timidity, that they could have been more aggressive in campaigning for reform[134] and in attacking the evil that 'wrecked both bodies and souls'.[135] Reasons given for this varied. For the Jewish community the memories of Nazi atrocities were fresh and so they feared to give the impression that they were against the state. The mostly German ELCSA also spoke of its minority cultural status.[136] Sometimes it was to protect the interests of its wealthy constituents. Sometimes it was simple failure of nerve,[137] or refusal to place privilege at risk.[138] The Catholic Church made a similar observation about itself, citing its tenuous position as *die Roomse kerk*.[139] But Nico Smith and the other pastors, representing many different denominations, who signed his open letter also admitted their fear led them to be unfaithful to the Christian gospel.[140]

The DRC in its *Journey* document spoke of how it used its privileged position in relation to government to oppose abuses behind closed doors, but did not speak out strongly enough. This confession is notable in that it is not nearly as strongly worded as the confessions of other churches who opposed apartheid.

• Failure to translate resolutions into action

Along with a confession of the failure to speak, confession of failure to act was common in the submissions. Many communities which were opposed to apartheid in principle found it difficult to translate strong resolutions into practical action, and in the nature of institutional politics resolutions were watered down by the time they were actually passed.[141] Such failures, as the URCSA admitted, 'represent a blatant omission and silent approval of the conditions and main cause of human rights violations.'[142]

• Failure to support members involved in anti-apartheid activities

As already stated, many activists were members of faith communities, though faith communities (even ones that they led) did not necessarily support their activities. ELCSA confessed to not encouraging its clergy to speak against atrocities and failing to support those that did. The CPSA apologised to Archbishop Tutu for failing to support his call for economic sanctions against the former regime. In doing so, the CPSA 'allowed others to precede [it] and take the flak'.[143] The Baptist Union had a number of activists, including some detained on Robben Island, but refused to acknowledge them.[144] It was in fact the Baptist Convention that reminded the Union of this.

This same confession could have been extended to institutions that were engaged in anti-apartheid activities and were, at least in words, supported by faith communities. When the Christian Institute was declared 'affected' by the Schlebusch Commission in 1975, preventing it from receiving external funds, little or no material support came from those churches that had verbally supported it in synods and assemblies. Similarly, when it was banned two years later, along with its executive leadership, little action was taken or support given to many of those affected within South Africa.

Muslim leaders were accused of denying space and legitimacy to Muslims engaged in anti-apartheid activities.[145]

• Wrongly understanding their own heritage or faith tradition

Some communities confessed that they misunderstood or even repressed dimensions of their own tradition. Here particular traditions are in view, such as (within Christianity) the Salvation Army's tradition of supporting the poor and the Reformed tradition's doctrine on church–state relations, which teaches that Christians not only are permitted, but have an obligation to resist an unjust state.[146] The apolitical stance taken by the Salvation Army 'enabled us to minister more freely' but was an 'affront to God and humankind'.[147] The Seventh Day Adventist Church, despite its emphasis on the holiness of the Sabbath, failed to understand the prophetic meaning of the Sabbath and Jubilee year in the biblical traditions. It confessed that 'true Sabbath keeping and keeping silence in the face of oppression are mutually exclusive'.[148]

In effect, what communities were confessing here was equivalent to medical doctors confessing to violating their Hippocratic Oath. That is, membership in these communities carries certain obligations rooted in rich traditions of prophetic protest. Not only did such communities confess that they failed to live up to generally accepted norms of justice and goodness, but they betrayed their own tradition. Their actions gave the lie to tenets of their fundamental beliefs.[149] The fact that some communities recognised this is important to note, as it is also an implicit affirmation of the liberative and reconstructive potential of their particular tradition in a new dispensation.

3.2.2 Faith communities as victims of oppression

Apartheid viewed the strategy of its enemies as a total onslaught, and countered it with a total strategy which viewed society and its institutions – including faith communities – as battlefields, and their members as 'hearts and minds' which must be won over or sidelined. Under apartheid no institutions (especially those that counted different racial groups as members) could remain unaffected. Communities of faith *qua* communities were affected in the same way as other communities. Members of churches, temples and mosques were removed under the Group Areas Act and those institutions suffered as a result, with many being forced to close down.[150] Members of faith communities also suffered under 'immorality' and other petty legislation.[151]

The effects were also more direct, and faith communities were attacked as faith communities, as alternative centres of loyalty or (in the eyes of the state) disloyalty.[152] Media campaigns and other forms of demonisation promoted the idea that churches opposing the state had abandoned their loyalty to Christ, taking another, anti-Christian cause. Ministers who did not toe the state line were prohibited from participating in religious programmes on television.[153] Anti-apartheid activists in turn defined their churches as 'sites of struggle'.[154] The church was from the point of view of the state an important area of low intensity conflict.[155]

The battle for symbols is an important dimension of all religion, and no faith community existed during the apartheid years (or has since) apart from engaging in it. The question of who constitutes 'the true believer' was raised by all sides in various communities (and within as well as between communities) during the years of apartheid. But this battle went beyond symbols to the support by right-wing Christian groups of direct attacks on faith communities, which included raiding offices, bombing and attempts on the lives of leaders.

3.2.2.1 Direct attacks by the state on members and organisations. Perhaps the most famous cases of churches being attacked directly by the state are the banning of the Christian Institute in 1977 and the bombing of Khotso House, the headquarters of the South African Council of Churches, in 1988. This latter action of the state should be seen in the context of an ongoing battle with the SACC, waged on symbolic (media disinformation) and legal (Eloff Commission) fronts as well. Indeed the SACC in its submission noted that it was often a target of security raids and in 1985, on the day the State of Emergency was to be announced, Khotso House was surrounded by SADF personnel. Many SACC staff members and associated personnel were detained and some tortured. Others died under mysterious circumstances.[156] In 1989 state operatives injected poison into the clothing of the SACC General Secretary, Frank Chikane, almost killing him.[157]

Six weeks after the bombing of Khotso House, the headquarters of the Southern African Catholic Bishops' Conference was destroyed by arsonists who, it is now known, were agents of the state.[158] Fr. Smangaliso Mkhatshwa, the Secretary General of the SACBC, was detained and tortured by the state many times. Other faith communities testified to their leaders, members and offices being targeted. Post was intercepted and phones tapped. The state used its machinery to hinder free movement of church officials and representatives.[159] Passports were denied. Ministers were detained without trial.

The CPSA singled out Fr Michael Lapsley, who lost both arms and an eye in a savage parcel bomb attack in April 1990, as 'living icon of redemptive suffering within [the CPSA]'. It is significant to note that this attack happened after the unbanning of the liberation movements with which he identified himself.

Leaders of other faith communities were also detained, tortured and killed. Notable in the submissions of the MJC, the Call of Islam and the MYM was the name of Imam Abdullah Haron, of the Al-Jamia Mosque in Claremont, Cape Town. Haron was detained for four months in 1969 under the Terrorism Act and tortured to death.

3.2.2.2 Closure of buildings, schools and institutions. We have already noted that, inevitably, faith communities were influenced by Group Areas legislation, congregations were forced to relocate and historical buildings lost.[160] Among those mentioned in the submissions were the LMS church at Graaff-Reinet, built in 1802, and the stone church at Majeng in the Northern Cape, built in 1874 and bulldozed in 1975. Their congregations were declared 'trespassers in their own homes'.[161] The Moravian Church spoke of suffering the loss of a number of churches, especially in Port Elizabeth and Cape Town.[162] They were forced to sell properties to state-run community boards at low prices – something which seriously hindered efforts to re-establish congregations after removal.[163]

Bantu Education forced the closure of mission stations and schools which had provided education for Africans for many years. In the process land was expropriated. Several churches, such as the Methodist Church of Southern Africa (MCSA), the United Congregational Church of Southern Africa (UCCSA) and the Church of the Province of Southern Africa (CPSA), with a long tradition in mission education, lost large numbers of primary schools and many secondary schools as well. A number of names synonymous with mission education were affected. The MCSA spoke of losing Kilnerton and Healdtown and the UCCSA Adams College and Tiger Kloof. The Reformed Presbyterian Church (RPC) spoke of the loss of Lovedale and Blythswood to the governments of Ciskei and Transkei.[164] Indeed many properties belonging to the RPC were in so-called 'white' areas and they were forced by law (which prohibited ownership of such properties) to sell them.[165] Hospitals and other institutions were also affected by Group Areas legislation, with the Seventh Day Adventist Church, to give one example, forced to close its hospital in Alexandra.[166]

Several submissions make reference to the closing of the Federal Theological Seminary (Fedsem) in Alice and the taking of its land.[167] This institution, established in 1961, symbolised the churches' autonomy from the state-imposed norms of Bantu theological education. It was significant for its ecumenical character and its being a centre for emerging black theology in the 1970s. According to the UCCSA, the order to close Fedsem 'was one of the most vicious acts of the regime directed specifically at the churches and their policy of developing articulate black leadership'.[168]

While many communities suffered loss, however, others benefited from that loss. The Volkskerk, a coloured split-off from the DRC, worshipped in a building in the centre of Stellenbosch which they had built themselves, but lost it in the early sixties under the Group Areas Act. The building was taken over by a white Christian congregation. The URCSA congregation in Messina made a similar allegation against its neighbouring DRC congregation.[169] According to the Hindu Maha Sabha presentation at the hearings, Hindu religious sites were readily bought up by Christian churches after removals. The fact that faith communities – sometimes within the same tradition – both suffered and benefited from the same series of removals highlights the need for reconciliation between communities, and of some kind of reparations. (See section 4.2 below.)

3.2.2.3 Repression and abuse of religious values and laws. Ignoring the many different religious allegiances of its subjects, the apartheid state saw itself as the guardian of Christian civilisation in southern Africa. As already noted in the introduction, other faith communities were barely tolerated from the time of the arrival of colonists in the seventeenth century. The apartheid state perpetuated this, and again education was an important site. Christian National Education was imposed on non-Christian faith communities – something that was mentioned especially within Muslim and Hindu submissions.[170] This repressed the expression of certain religious values in education and imposed other, alien values. This was even true, though, in the case of a Christian community such as the Shembe Church, where taboos concerning shaving were not honoured in schools and children were forced to remove their hair, causing ritual defilement.[171]

Related to the repression of religious values in education was the repression of religiously orientated law, especially in the case of Islam and Hinduism. Muslim marriages, noted the JUT, were not legally valid, making their children illegitimate.[172] But the state was also able to use religious laws to suit its own ends, as pointed out by the Muslim Youth Movement. In its submission, it recalled how the Ulamas were co-opted onto a South African Law Commission committee on the recognition of Muslim marriage in 1986 – a cynical attempt on the part of the state to gain the approval of the Islamic community.[173]

While this is a contested point in other faiths, according to its submission the religious values of the Baha'i faith preclude opposing governments. While its racially mixed worship practices and its black leadership resulted in state surveillance, so-called 'Black Baha'is' were traitors in the eyes of some other blacks. Its statement at the hearings noted the tragic execution of four of its adherents at its places of worship in Umtata and Mdantsane as a consequence.[174]

3.2.2.4 Manipulation by state propaganda. The apartheid state attacked faith communities in other ways. Evangelical groups such as the Church of England saw themselves as being subjected to state propaganda, especially about the struggle against communism, which in part played on white fears and (mis)used the same Bible which the church saw as authoritative. This created the conditions under which it confessed its failure to understand its own tradition, as it allowed itself 'to be misled into accepting a social, economic and political system that was cruel and oppressive'. Declaring itself 'apolitical', CESA thus 'failed to adequately understand the suffering of our many black members who were victims of apartheid'.[175]

It might be an overstatement to term this kind of manipulation 'victimisation' alongside the more direct and violent attacks by the state on anti-apartheid leaders. However, the fears of white church members made them vulnerable to propaganda, leading them into sins of omission. Even the English-speaking churches whose leadership was at least in word opposed to apartheid were 'vulnerable to the right'.[176]

3.2.2.5 Victimisation by other faith communities. As Faried Esack observed at the hearings, the 'past' was only partly about apartheid, security laws and so forth. 'It was also about Christian triumphalism.'[177] In a sense, all non-Christian faith communities were victimised by an aggressively 'Christian' state, and Esack pointed out that '*die Islamse gevaar*' took its place alongside the other enemies of the state. There were other kinds of victimisation of faith communities by other faith communities – even within Christian churches. The submissions indicate that this took a number of forms, from denominational splits to the appropriation of buildings declared off limits to blacks under Group Areas legislation.[178] Theology was a battleground, with 'heresy' being a term used not only of those who disagreed about classical dogma and its interpretation, but also of the meaning of such dogma in practice.[179] Indeed accusations of heresy often went beyond the boundaries of doctrinal dispute.

A number of denominational splits took place around questions of commitment to the struggle, with conservative 'splinters' proliferating.[180] While these institutions often claimed 'theological' reasons for their existence as alternatives to mainline groups, the state was active amongst them as well. Indeed many served the state as 'shadow' institutions and denominations set up to oppose those working against apartheid policies.[181]

The demonisation of other faith communities characterised conservative Christian groups. In 1986, at the same synod where its policy of uncritical support for apartheid was beginning to be challenged, the DRC proclaimed Islam a 'false religion'.[182] The victimisation of African traditional religion by Christians was brought out in Nokuzola Mndende's submission, which spoke of how Africans were forced to become Christians, as a baptismal certificate was a common form of identification.[183]

3.2.3 Faith communities as opponents of oppression

In their submissions, faith communities described themselves as opposing apartheid in many different ways. No community claimed it did 'enough', but all claimed at least some degree of opposition, if not to apartheid, then to state abuses. They issued statements and formulated confessional documents linking opposition to apartheid with their theological traditions; they withdrew from state structures, engaged in civil disobedience, and circulated petitions. Some engaged the state by openly identifying with liberation movements while others met with officials in private.

But when we realise that many who perpetrated human rights abuses were members of churches – including churches voicing opposition – we are again confronted with the problem of precisely who was being represented when opposition was being voiced. While many resolutions were adopted at a variety of levels (see below), faith communities had difficulty communicating them to their constituents.[184] And the actions of local communities may or may not have been in agreement with those resolutions.[185] Indeed, the resolutions themselves were frequently not effected once made – a kind of passive abstention from acting on decisions made. This was even more pronounced in the way ecumenical statements and actions were treated by churches. 'The SACC was supported in its statements by its member churches. It was supported in its actions by individual members and small groups among those churches . . . who were willing to act accordingly.'[186]

While many perpetrators of human rights abuses were members of faith communities, whose leadership may or may not have owned responsibility for their actions, many individuals who fought against such abuses were also members of faith communities.[187] Two examples will suffice: Frank Chikane of the Apostolic Faith Mission and Beyers Naudé of the DRC, neither of whom were supported by their church bodies. Faith communities at a local level also took certain stands which may or may not have reflected stands taken at denominational or translocal levels.

Faith communities at a translocal level also took stands. Inevitably these actions were taken by leadership on behalf of grassroots members and may or may not have reflected the views of their constituency in general. But we can, for example, talk about how the Presbyterian Church of Southern Africa 'acted' against apartheid.

The nature of 'active opposition' is difficult to judge. For some groups, for instance the Presbyterian Church of Southern Africa, active opposition took the form of resolutions condemning apartheid, civil disobedience and declarations of support and solidarity with the liberation movements. For others, such as the Zion Christian Church, opposition to apartheid took place in terms of 'self-esteem' and support of education. Indeed one way of reading Zionist practice is in terms of a 'hidden transcript' and covert opposition.[188] Other groups might not see this as opposition at all, or at best passive opposition. Indeed, what is understood at one point as resistance may later be termed anachronistic or out of touch.[189]

In understanding the role of faith communities (especially Christian churches) in opposing apartheid, it is helpful to map out a 'continuum of opposition'.[190] This is founded on the idea that the broader struggle against apartheid went through various stages, and that while early resistance came out of the heritage of mission Christianity, churches more often than not lagged behind the societal movements, rather than leading them. Initially, resistance (and here we speak of resistance not specifically to apartheid but to the broad policies of segregation and land expropriation within which the apartheid policies took shape) took place in the form of separation, as Africans constructed alternative religious institutions to those dominated by whites. The second form of opposition, characterising white missionary response to the Hertzog Bills, and also to growing labour militancy, pleaded with the consciences of government not only to take responsibility for black development, but also to forestall instability. Ecumenical institutions developed, and began to make formal representations to government. With the coming to power of the National Party in 1948, the English-speaking churches 'lost the ear' of the state and turned to formal protest and then passive resistance. But by this time (the mid-fifties) a tradition of resistance politics had already been entrenched in the broader social movements and the late rallying of the churches only around the question of segregated worship demonstrated that their own institutional interests remained their primary concern.

From the 1960s onward there was a gradual shift in the churches. More and more sought to break the colour barriers, speaking of identification and reconciliation. By this time the major black political organs had been banned, however, creating a vacuum which churches only in the late 1980s would begin to try to fill. While they were willing to identify with non-racial aspirations, they were unwilling to identify with the now underground institutions which blacks entrusted to bring about those aspirations.

With every shift, more and more churches were left behind. Indeed the more conservative churches, such as the Baptist Union and CESA, only came around to formal representations in the mid-1980s – and even then their representations (like those of the ecumenical churches fifty years earlier) were as much a plea for social stability as for an end to injustice. Some African Initiated Churches (like the ZCC) maintained their separatist stance – even against ecumenical protest. More progressive evangelicals, embracing a Third Way, turned to passive resistance, moderate defiance and the rhetoric of reconciliation, but stopped short of declaring support for the liberation movements. Some went as far as to challenge the legality of government policies, without challenging the legitimacy of the state itself. Indeed by this time (the late 1970s) the National Security state was in place and the rule of law virtually suspended.

Meanwhile some Christians declared that the time for white leadership in opposition to apartheid was over, and that the ball had passed to black liberation movements. While the Programme to Combat Racism had begun to give support to liberation movements as early as 1970, it was only in the next decade that the so-called mainline churches followed suit. Once again the South African churches lagged behind – this time behind their overseas ecumenical partners. But institutions like the Christian Institute, the SACC and the ICT came to identify openly with resistance movements, eventually filling an important role in the late 1980s.

This 'continuum of opposition' is reflected broadly in what follows.

3.2.3.1 Official statements and resolutions. Most faith communities place great value on collective statements, whether doctrinal or ethical. Numerous statements on apartheid were issued during the period under examination and were mentioned in the submissions. We can only highlight those that indicate the variety of ways faith communities presented their opposition.[191]

We start with ecumenical statements. While the history of the relation of the former mission and settler churches, which would form the Christian Council in 1936 (the forerunner of the SACC), to policies of segregation is ambiguous, by the time of the period covered by this Report the churches which would become members of the SACC would reject all discrimination based on colour, sex or race.[192]

Amongst the Protestant churches, the UCCSA and the PCSA made special mention of the Cottesloe Statement, as did the SACC.[193] This conference was sponsored by the WCC in the wake of the Sharpeville tragedy and produced a statement 'that opposed apartheid in worship, in prohibition of mixed marriages, migrant labour, low wages, job reservation and permanent exclusion of "non-white people" from government'.[194]

The fact that this statement went beyond strictly 'church' matters in the eyes of the state is significant.[195] Cottesloe also featured in the DRC's *Journey* document as 'an important stop'.[196] Not only did it result in the marginalisation of some of its representatives (including Beyers Naudé) but it caused 'a deep rift between the Dutch Reformed Churches and many other recognised Protestant churches in the country'.[197] More than this, it set a precedent for state interference not simply in the affairs of the DRC (with which it was already in a special relation) but in those of the ecumenical churches.

The Message to the People of South Africa (1968) directly attacked the theological foundations of nationalism, positing that a Christian's 'first loyalty' must be given to Christ, rather than to 'a subsection of mankind'.[198] Christian groups began to engage in intensive social analysis in the early 1970s. The Study Project on Christianity in Apartheid Society (SPRO-CAS) was launched after the *Message*. SPRO-CAS set up six commissions, covering education, legal, economic, social and religious areas, and later the Special Programme of Christian Action in Society (SPRO-CAS II) was organised to carry out the report's recommendations.

Throughout the 1970s, the SACC published materials expressing opposition to apartheid and envisioning a post-apartheid society. In its submission, it highlighted the Resolution on Conscientious Objection (1974), which also questioned the appointment of military chaplains to the SADF, and the Resolution on Non-Cooperation, which urged Christians to withdraw from state structures. Of its statements in the turbulent eighties, notable is the Call for Prayer to End Unjust Rule, which mobilised Christian symbolic resources against the 'Christian' state, and the Lusaka Statement of 1987, which urged the churches to support the efforts of liberation movements – and occasioned 'fierce opposition' from SACC members.[199]

Another watershed statement was produced by the Institute for Contextual Theology in 1985: the *Kairos Document*. It was contentious, with some churches rejecting its analysis and theology outright as a sell-out to ideology, while others (notably the UCCSA) set up special study groups in local churches.[200] While the document was blamed for polarising the debate over the relationship between churches and liberation movements, arguably it merely gave expression to polarisations that had emerged already. Not all anti-apartheid Christian leaders signed it. The *Kairos Document* had an impact beyond the Christian churches and was also mentioned by the Muslim Youth Movement's submission.[201]

While the DRC's protests were limited to private meetings with state officials, it is notable that scholars from the smaller Afrikaans-speaking Gereformeerde Kerk produced a statement opposing apartheid and its Christian justification in 1977 entitled *Koinonia Verklaring* [*Koinonia*

Declaration]. While the GK declined to make a submission to the TRC, two members made a private submission and drew upon the legacy of this statement.[202]

In the meantime, publications attacking the theology behind apartheid were being produced, perhaps the most devastating by Douglas Bax of the Presbyterian Church.[203] At a denominational level, discrimination in general and the policy of apartheid in particular were rejected as 'intrinsically evil' by the Roman Catholic Church in 1960, and as heresy in 1982 by the UCCSA.[204] In 1986, the PCSA and the UCCSA passed resolutions making rejection of apartheid a matter of *status confessionis*, essentially arguing the claim that the church in South Africa stood in relation to apartheid in the same way as the German church did to Nazism during the 1930s.[205] The Uniting Reformed Church, which noted in its submission a heritage of not pronouncing strongly on apartheid, produced in 1982 the Belhar Confession, the first church confession to be produced on South African soil.[206]

Notable was the international dimension to such confessions, with overseas links also holding conferences and producing statements (see below under sanctions). However, not all overseas structures were heeded by their South African counterparts, with the Salvation Army in South Africa remaining silent about apartheid crimes even though apartheid had been condemned by its then General, Eva Burrows, in London in 1986.[207] The Seventh Day Adventist Church also confessed that their position on apartheid was 'out of step' with its overseas body.[208]

Shortly after the Cottesloe Statement was launched, the Call of Islam Declaration was issued in Cape Town by the MJC along with the Cape Town Muslim Youth Movement, Claremont Muslim Youth Association, Cape Vigilance Association, Young Men's Muslim Association, and a number of individuals and leaders. This was a declaration of apartheid being contrary to Islam, and condemned group areas, pass and job reservation legislation.[209] A 1964 national conference called by the MJC protested concerning the impact that the Group Areas Act was having on mosque life, passing a series of resolutions urging that under no circumstances should mosques be abandoned. Muslim leaders also participated in the UDF's 'Don't Vote' campaign, arguing that a vote for the tricameral parliament was *haraam* – unclean. In this way, they used the specific, particular language of Islam to communicate the wrongness of participating in apartheid structures.[210]

In addition to passing resolutions against the violent policies of the state, faith communities also expressed general concern in their statements during the 1980s over the violence sweeping the country.[211] Sometimes this meant recognising a certain tension between a community's solidarity with the liberation movements and its awareness of the violence with which apartheid was often opposed, as in the UCCSA submission.[212] Communities differed on the degree to which anti-apartheid violence was 'justifiable' (not simply 'understandable').[213] While it has been put forth that those responsible for the *Kairos Document* share guilt for supporting violent uprisings, it must be pointed out that (whatever their perspective on the armed struggle on the borders) they did not condone 'necklace' killings or 'kangaroo courts'.[214] Indeed, as the chairperson reminded the people at the hearings, many leaders accused of culpability in violence placed their lives on the line by intervening in necklacings. For those that claimed a 'third way' perspective, all violence was equally wrong and their statements condemned both sides of the struggle.[215] Where they leaned sympathetically towards the liberation movements, English-speaking churches drew upon the 'just war' tradition of the church – though it must be said that generally their submissions lack discussion of their declared positions *vis-à-vis* the armed struggle and popular uprisings.[216] This is perhaps symptomatic of their own internal divisions.[217]

3.2.3.2 Petitions, letters and private appeals. One way open to faith communities short of outright allegiance with liberation movements was petitioning government directly, either openly or behind closed doors. Many churches and faith communities petitioned the government on a wide range of issues, and this was also engaged in towards the end of the apartheid era by more conservative churches, such as CESA, which were less comfortable with direct opposition.[218] Positioning itself as 'politically neutral', the leadership of the Baha'i faith nevertheless also met with officials in private to present its philosophy of inclusivity.[219] But sometimes this was a strategy used by leaders of communities more public in their opposition. The MJC issued a letter in the seventies, protesting to government over human rights abuses during the 1976 riots.[220] SACC and other ecumenical Christian leaders adopted a stronger tone as well, warning leaders of the consequences of failure to change.[221]

The Dutch Reformed Church also met privately with state officials to 'express its doubts' about policies and their application. The church admitted, however, that such meetings rarely called the policies themselves into question, but only asked that they be 'applied with compassion and humanity'.[222] The DRC remained tied to state structures.

The Moravian Church spoke of pastoral letters it circulated to its members, informing them and helping them reach a better understanding of the issues in the country.

3.2.3.3 Withdrawing from state structures. Another way that faith communities – and here in this ostensibly 'Christian' land we must speak of churches – expressed opposition to apartheid was by withdrawing from state structures in which they were complicit, most significantly the military. This is not insignificant, as an important part of the legitimisation of state institutions was that they were protecting Christian civilisation.

The tricameral parliament was a problem for many faith communities, especially those which had coloured or Indian leadership (as mentioned in section 3.2.1.1 above).[223] Opposition from Muslim and Hindu communities was strong, with an 'overwhelming consensus' amongst Muslims declaring it 'contrary to the spirit of Islam'.[224] Hindu leaders who participated were ostracised. The UCCSA urged its members to distance themselves from the tricameral parliament and removed the Revs. Allan Hendrickse and Andrew Julies – two former chairs of the UCCSA who were members of the tricameral parliament – from their ministers' roll.[225]

Some Christian churches were opposed to combat as a tenet of faith. For Seventh Day Adventists and Quakers, to have served in the military (on either side) would have meant apostasy from their faith tradition.[226] Many leaders in the conscientious objection movement were Christians, and objected on the basis of Christian principles.[227] While not all their churches supported them, more and more became uncomfortable with their involvement in the chaplaincy. Individual Catholic priests refused to act as military chaplains or marriage officers, as did some clergy of the URCSA.[228] The Quakers and the SACC in 1974 issued resolutions supporting conscientious objectors. The UCCSA spoke of its 'constant support' for objectors, the principle of objection and the End Conscription Campaign. It also refused to be co-opted onto the SADF-sponsored Board for Religious Objection.[229] The PCSA, which had supported the rights of conscientious objectors from 1971, spoke of how in 1982 it initiated a process 'aimed at moving the denomination towards opposing service in the SADF'.[230] While it did not withdraw its chaplains until 1990,[231] in 1988 it met with delegations from the ANC and PAC to discuss the possibility of appointing chaplains to their liberation armies.[232] The UCCSA also supplied 'pastoral care' to the liberation movements, including the South West African People's Organisation (SWAPO),[233] while the CPSA only did so 'unofficially'.[234]

3.2.3.4 Civil disobedience. Another way that faith communities expressed opposition to the policies of apartheid was in deliberate disobedience to state laws. The PCSA, for example, embarked from 1981 on a campaign of defying laws concerning mixed marriages, group areas and quoting banned persons and publications.[235] This followed the work at a local level of the Rev. Rob Robertson, who in 1962 and 1975 started multi-racial and multi-class congregations in East London and Pageview, Johannesburg. Robertson's work, which represented 'the first move to take actual steps to reverse the segregating effects of apartheid on congregations and to set an example to the nation', came under fire from the state.[236]

Other local congregations deliberately flouted laws by promoting mixed worship. The Baha'i faith came under scrutiny for insisting that its members meet together across racial boundaries. The JUT also spoke of Muslims of different race groups worshipping and studying together.[237] Arguably these were not always deliberate acts of defiance,[238] but simply acts which conformed to the norms of the faith community's tradition – sharing a common faith across racial barriers. The fact that they flew in the face of the state only served to underline the wrongness of the state's policy.

Institutional resistance was expressed, for instance, in the Catholic Church's opening of its schools to all races in 1976 – something which engaged it in battle with the state until 1991.[239]

Civil disobedience was extended in support of mass defiance campaigns by some communities, as expressions of solidarity with liberation movements.

3.2.3.5 Solidarity with liberation movements. While some faith communities (mostly at a local level) participated from the outset with protests and defiance campaigns, with others (specifically the DRC) pledging loyalty to the state as a 'Christian' state, faith communities in general throughout the sixties and seventies sought various 'third way' approaches in-between lending full support to the liberation movements or to the state.

The aftermath of Soweto began to call forth more radical responses from faith communities. The RPC pointed out how in 1978 the Rev. D. M. Soga, its then Moderator, declared that a *kairos* had arrived for the churches in South Africa. In that community's first public stance against the government, Soga spoke of the 'daring' of the younger generation that was now rising up against oppression.[240] The United Democratic Front, started in 1983, had a strong representation from faith communities. The MJC affiliated with it, significantly, as it saw itself as an oppressed community in solidarity with other oppressed communities.[241]

As the eighties wore on and the climate intensified, several church denominations realised that the situation was such that their loyalty commanded them to take a stand either for the liberation movements or for the state. Mention has already been made of churches that supplied chaplains to the liberation movement. Contact between faith communities and liberation movements in exile took place throughout the eighties, with the UCCSA assembly meeting with ANC leaders in Gaborone in 1987.[242] While they were not represented in the submissions, a number of Afrikaner academics from the University of Stellenbosch in 1988 travelled north 'in search of Africa', and while they were not permitted to meet officially with the exiled ANC, there was contact at an informal level. This dispelled some of the state-sponsored propaganda about the ANC, and helped foster debate in one of the bastions of Afrikaner nationalism.[243] The WCRP also met with leaders in Zambia in 1988 to discuss religion in a post-apartheid South Africa.[244]

The Catholic Church mobilised its own structures (Young Christian Workers, Justice and Peace groups and so forth) and opened its parish halls to popular organisations for meetings and gave refuge to activists on church property or helped them leave the country.[245] The Catholic Church also participated in the Standing for the Truth campaign – an initiative that came from the SACC and was supported by its members and associates as well as other faith communities.[246]

3.2.3.6 Advocacy of sanctions. Some faith communities and organisations joined liberation organisations in appealing to their international partners to press for economic sanctions as the repression of the 1980s escalated.[247] Many, however, opposed sanctions, or at least were ambivalent on the question.[248] Some, such as the CPSA, which only came to its decision to support sanctions in 1989, confessed this as a failure during the hearings.[249] The Catholic Bishops, 'fearing a great increase of poverty and unemployment', supported sanctions with reservations.[250] The only one of the English-speaking churches to give unqualified support to sanctions from the outset was the UCCSA.[251]

Many people (mostly white) voiced opposition to sanctions, ostensibly because they would 'hurt blacks' as well as themselves. This was no less true of members of faith communities. However, communities were also striving to voice what the majority wanted and to bring them into the debates affecting them. In spite of surveys that were used by liberals to argue that a large number of blacks opposed sanctions, surveys also concluded that the majority recognised the leadership of people such as Desmond Tutu and Allan Boesak around the question.[252]

3.2.3.7 A voice for the voiceless. Faith communities have strong traditions calling on them to speak for the voiceless ones. But even though the majority of its constituents were black, the leadership of the English-speaking churches failed to express adequately their aspirations. Indeed, arguably the English-speaking churches 'spoke for' capital, while the DRC spoke for a now empowered Afrikaner elite.[253] It was left, said the SACC in its submission, to organisations such as the Council to be a 'legitimate voice' of South Africans. Indeed, the SACC became an internationally significant information centre, representing the oppressed before the world. It could do this because of its network of churches which reached every corner of society.[254]

South African faith communities have a rich tradition of expressing themselves in news publications, and this was an important way in which faith communities voiced the aspirations of blacks, as well as creating space for discussion and debate.[255] The Catholic Church started *The New Nation*, while the Muslim community started *The Muslim News* and *Al Qalam*. These publications went beyond sectarian interests to address the core issues of exploitation, and faced banning orders on numerous occasions.[256]

The policies of the apartheid state created turmoil in other countries, as well as domestically. This created a refugee problem. The UCCSA's regional identity allowed it to express special concern for refugees both in South Africa and in neighbouring states.[257]

3.2.3.8 Other ways of opposing oppression. Faith communities also protested by using fasting – a practice noted in the submissions of the Hindu community.[258] This drew upon the tradition of non-violent protest inaugurated by Mahatma Gandhi during his stay in South Africa.

3.2.4 Faith communities and South Africa's transition.

The picture of faith communities and their members involved in opposition to apartheid is not complete if it only ends with the unbanning of the liberation movements. As the 1980s drew to a close, some organisations were looking toward the future and preparing people for democracy. One example of many that could be given to illustrate the way the transition was anticipated is Diakonia, an ecumenical group in the Durban area, which published *The Good Society: Bible Studies on Christianity and Democracy* – anticipating voter education programmes in the run-up to the 1994 elections.[259]

Faith communities were engaged in a number of ways during South Africa's transition. A large number of Muslim organisations joined in a national conference as the negotiations between the De Klerk government and the previously banned movements got under way. Chief Rabbi Cyril Harris played a visible role, working together with other religious leaders. The WCRP held a conference in 1990, called 'Believers in the future', which issued a Declaration of Religious Rights and Responsibilities.[260] Amongst Christians the Rustenburg Conference and Statement in 1990 were of great significance and the confessions there anticipate those given at the TRC hearings.[261]

The National Peace Accord was launched in September 1991, with heavy involvement from the SACC, and was aimed at helping to create an ethos conducive to democratic transition. The SACBC and the SACC, together with a coalition of non-governmental organisations, launched 'Education for Democracy'. This project worked at local levels to create awareness of constitutional governance and key political concepts. It worked both amongst illiterate blacks and urban whites – the latter who had never experienced non-racial democracy and who still largely expected to retain their privileges in a new society. The Church Leaders Forum, representing a wide collection of denominations, met with government leaders and urged them on the path to a negotiated settlement. The group included traditional foes of the SACC, including the Rev. Ray McCauley of the Rhema Church and Prof. Johan Heynes of the DRC. After CODESA broke down, this forum worked to restart the negotiation process. More could be said about the role of church leaders in peace monitoring, election preparation and the resettlement of exiles.[262]

Does all this mean that the Christian church was engaged in South Africa's democratic transition? Sadly it is not possible to make a generalisation here, for, once again, Christians as individuals were engaged, along with ecumenical coalitions. The fact that the migration of such leaders and activists into government has created a huge leadership vacuum at an ecumenical level testifies to the close links between the ecumenical movement and progressive political activism. But at a denominational level, churches remained hesitant about entering the fray. The SACC in its submission spoke of how difficult it is to focus the churches' attention, as many now wish to enter into relations with the government on a denominational level.

One positive thing about the ecumenical activity of the early 1990s is the involvement of a wider spread of leaders, including evangelical and charismatic leaders who were not involved in progressive moments in the 1980s. Perhaps this ecumenical contact prepared them for their owning up to the guilt of their communities at the hearings. Certainly it was a bridge to their statements at the hearings where they committed themselves to active involvement in the transformation of the country beyond apartheid.

4. THE ROAD TO RECONCILIATION

4.1 A note on the use of the term 'reconciliation'

The idea of reconciliation was invoked in the English-speaking churches from the late 1960s, and was used in the 1980s by organisations such as the NIR to bring black and white, English- and Afrikaans-speaking churches together. What needed to be reconciled were 'groups', defined racially or ethnically. Apartheid was analysed as a racist ideology. Other

Christians, especially the authors of the *Kairos Document*, claimed that the South African problem was systemic economic inequality, rather than simple racial prejudice. Racial antagonism and racial policies were at the surface, rather than at the depths of the problem. Redressing injustice and bringing about social transformation was therefore the first step to real reconciliation.

This debate continues to the present, and was reflected in the TRC faith community hearings. Indeed, it is reflected in the debates around the Commission itself (see the critique in section 5). Many accuse the Commission of having a Christian-loaded understanding of reconciliation, but even Christians at the hearings had different understandings of the term. Some of the faith communities still thought that reconciliation equalled members of different groups 'getting together'. While certainly reconciliation cannot mean less than this (and for many white Christians, a first realisation of the deprivation of their fellow South Africans only came when they actually stepped into a township or shack settlement), it must mean more.[263] Other communities (especially the ICT) pressed their point that economic disparity was and remains the greatest legacy of apartheid, and that reconciliation must come with restorative justice. Reconciliation without restorative justice is a mere salve for the consciences of the privileged.

The Jewish Gesher movement supplied the Commission with a document outlining a Jewish perspective on reconciliation. It argued that reconciliation should be a celebration of South African diversity grounded in encounters between persons of different groups and identities, sharing a common ethical bond. The question of reparations is important (and indeed intrinsic to a Jewish understanding of reconciliation), but at the same time a single standard of justice for rich and poor must be held to. Reconciliation is a long and difficult process, involving the restoration of mutual responsibility. The temptation simply to take vengeance must be checked by commitment to a higher moral standard. The Ramakrishna Institute also was concerned that reconciliation in the eyes of some might simply mean 'turning the tables' – something that would further marginalise the Indian community.

The Islamic understanding of reconciliation, presented by Faried Esack and the MJC in their presentations at the hearings, is that of returning stolen property, resulting in an equalisation, a restoration of balance between victim and perpetrator. Interestingly, the understanding of the idea propounded by the ICT and some other Christian groups is closer to this than the understandings of more conservative Christian groups.

In its proposal for a Day of Reconciliation, the WCRP tried to harmonise the various faith communities around the idea of reconciliation. At the hearings, Dr Auerbach offered seven steps to reconciliation that all faith communities could agree upon:

> becoming aware of having done wrong; publicly acknowledging the wrongdoing; expressing remorse for the action or lack of action; making restitution for the harm caused; requesting forgiveness from the harmed person; making a sincere commitment not to repeat the wrongdoing; and accepting forgiveness where it is offered.[264]

These are points abstracted from the discourse of different faith communities, and whether they could be 'translated back' into that discourse, and how, remains an unresolved question.[265] Perhaps they can form a starting point for debate.

Much like the ideas 'race' and 'transformation', reconciliation is a term that is commonly used, assuming that its meaning is plain and unequivocal. A clarification of the meaning of the concept of reconciliation needs to take place within and between faith communities – but as a motivator, not as a substitute for action! The ambiguity of the term creates problems similar to those we noted in section 3.2 around the terms 'opposition' and 'legitimisation'. The fact is, however, that the faith communities used this term, and so for the remainder of this section we will continue to use it. In the last section we will suggest a more appropriate term, namely 'healing', for the faith communities for their own processes of renewal.

4.2 Faith communities as reconciled communities

Faith communities were unanimous in pledging themselves at the hearings to being agents of social transformation. But it was also acknowledged that communities needed to get their own houses in order before they could speak with integrity on a national level. One way to do this would be to replicate the national process at faith community levels. The idea of a 'TRC for the faith communities' was presented by several submissions.[266] Recalling that faith communities were sites of struggle as well as agents of struggle, it would seem to make sense that addressing the conflicts within faith communities would be a necessary precursor to retrieving their identity as agents of change. We think this a worthwhile recommendation, but it needs to address the cluster of issues highlighted elsewhere in the submissions, especially about the damage done within faith communities as a result of the conflicts of the past.

In order to address these conflicts, any such process or processes needs to take place within communities (internally), between communities (especially at an interfaith level) and also at the interface between faith community and public life.

4.2.1 Internal reconciliation

Sometimes within the same faith community, as mentioned above (see section 3.2.1.1), one member inflicted torture on another. Such wounds need addressing. At a structural level, the effects of 'religious apartheid' also need addressing. Several submissions and presentations noted the reunification talks going on between racially (and largely socio-economically) separate groups within the same denominational family (specifically the PCSA and RPC; the DRC and URCSA; the BUSA and BCSA).[267] Reunification would begin to address the inequalities in clergy stipends and the dependence of black congregations on white, of which, for instance, the PCSA spoke.[268] The Baptist Union and Convention, which split specifically over race issues, are presently engaged in negotiating a reunification of the churches. But this will only be a possibility if a common vision of the past can be agreed upon – something that seems beyond their grasp at present.[269]

The socio-economic dimension of such denominational splits needs to be revisited. What was not mentioned by the white-dominated (power-wise, not numerically) denominations was the strong resistance to reunification with black groups because that would mean sharing resources, land and personnel.[270] Similar tensions were noted in other churches where *de facto* if not *de jure* segregation took place – and continues to take place. Wealthy parishes continue to thrive while poorer parishes, often as a result of being caught in a debt trap incurred by costs of resettling after forced removals took place, continue to struggle.[271] This also needs to be addressed at appropriate levels.

4.2.2 Reconciliation with other faith communities

The SACC noted that the greatest pain it felt came not from the attacks of the state, but those from other Christian groups. On the Tuesday of the hearings, the chairperson of the Commission apologised to the non-Christian faith communities for 'Christian arrogance'. There was, unfortunately, little else in the way of recognition from the other communities of the inter-religious strife that corresponded to the apartheid state's general 'divide and conquer' ethos, nor a stated commitment to working across traditions to address the problems which all acknowledged as crucial to the future of the country.

The WCRP is committed to a linking of various faith communities, and could be a valuable facilitator of a process at an interfaith level.

4.2.3 Reconciliation with the nation

The way that faith communities confessed to failing in their role as witnesses within society points to several areas where a TRC process could begin to make them agents of transformation.

Christian churches are large owners of land, much of their occupation of it going back to the missionary period.[272] Several churches, including the Salvation Army, acknowledged that they needed to be called to account for how their land was acquired, and to participate in reparations.[273] The BCSA also called the BUSA to account here.[274] The MCSA at the hearings offered to investigate its land holdings in the former Transkei.

The MCSA at the hearings apologised to the nation for not fighting harder to retain its mission schools. In a country facing an education crisis, and with the legacy of Bantu Education still evident in poor matriculation results, the loss of mission schools generally seems an even greater tragedy. Commissioners at the hearings raised the possibility of the churches, particularly the CPSA and the MCSA, reopening their mission schools that were lost to the state under the Bantu Education Act. There was a positive response.

Apartheid profoundly affected South Africa's neighbouring states and its redress therefore has transnational dimensions, as the CPSA and the UCCSA both recognised at the hearings. A process of reconciliation needs to be extended to faith communities devastated by cross-border raids – especially in Botswana, Namibia, Mozambique and Zimbabwe.

4.3 Faith communities as reconciling communities

While not all communities owned up to the need for self-examination and self-critique, all had ideas on how they could help reconcile and rebuild the society. What follows is a brief résumé.

4.3.1 Aiding public processes of reconciliation

The TRC has provided dramatic models of confession, though under a national spotlight and in front of television cameras.[275] But for most people confession requires space – safe space. Faith communities generally offered their resources to aid the TRC process in this way. The CPSA, for example, offered itself as an agent for those who felt the need to confess, repent and seek forgiveness – especially those who were too late to be included in the TRC process. It also volunteered to act as an agent for those who wanted to make honest redress.[276] The PCSA made a similar offer, especially providing opportunity for personal confessions amongst members.[277] It also spoke of its 'be real' encounters, offering a space where stories are shared across cultural and racial boundaries.[278] The Salvation Army spoke of its distinctive 'testimony meeting' as also a space where stories can be shared publicly.[279] Scripture Union offered to work (as it has previously) on an interpersonal level, building relationships and bridges across races.[280]

4.3.2 Sharing or providing resources

Faith communities have a number of resources that they volunteered to mobilise in aiding the process of reconciliation. The URCSA noted that pastoral counselling of both victims and perpetrators would help facilitate confession and speed the reconciliation process, while special programmes could aid the rehabilitation of perpetrators.[281]

Of special concern was care for the victims of human rights abuses. What happens to them after the Commission is finished? The Catholic Church mentioned its Khulumani groups, and offered to consider enlarging the service.[282] The Salvation Army committed itself to nurturing the development of counselling skills amongst its membership.[283] Lutheran pastors have attended courses on the healing of memories, to assist members of congregations to listen – especially to those they have hurt.[284]

An important concern of the Gesher document was that people be empowered to move beyond a 'victim' identity – something which in itself is a great obstacle to reconciliation, as it understood the term.[285] TEASA committed itself to, among other things, breaking what it termed 'the victim syndrome' by running seminars on reconciliation.[286] Bishop Dandala of the MCSA noted at the hearings that churches can help people move from understanding their family members and friends who suffered under apartheid as 'victims', to celebrating them as 'heroes'. This is something that could be a tremendous hermeneutical and symbolic resource; but it also requires pastoral sensitivity, lest one particular framework of dealing with their past be imposed on people.

The contribution of facilities and services extends beyond counselling to outreach projects aimed at empowerment of the poor. One such project mentioned was the Jewish Tikkun, an initiative of Rabbi Harris and Bertie Lubner, an industrialist. Tikkun brings the considerable expertise of the Jewish community to bear in education, health, welfare, housing and other sectors.[287] The Seventh Day Adventist Church also noted its experience in welfare activities, especially the Adventist Relief Agency and Meals on Wheels, in addition to its medical and other health programmes. It committed itself to meeting the needs of 'the surrounding community'.[288]

The IFCC – which also contains a high number of businesspersons – also noted their co-operative projects with local authorities on housing, where an estate providing low-income housing is being constructed as a pilot project drawing on the volunteered expertise of its members.[289] They spoke of other projects, including a scheme in Mpumalanga to provide clean water to communities.

4.3.3 Symbolic and liturgical actions

The SACC spoke of Services of Reconciliation to provide symbols of a new covenant amongst South Africans.[290] The URCSA noted that reconciliation liturgies would transform acts of worship into acts of reconciliation, while a special faith communities' statement would be important to produce. They also put forward the idea of a memorial to martyrs and victims, as a reminder that such deeds should never happen again, as well as a week of reconciliation which would include a social audit, vicarious confession, and public commitments to upholding human rights.[291] We already noted the WCRP's proposal for a Day of Reconciliation on 16 December.

Important here is also the need to honour those who took the wrath of the state upon themselves. The Catholic Church suggested the building of a memorial for all who lost their lives in the struggle.[292] The idea of a memorial was echoed by other communities, and will be returned to in our recommendations below.

4.3.4 Moral reconstruction

Faith communities expressed concern for the moral reconstruction of South African society. They recognised that the struggles of the apartheid years and their legacy had left a moral vacuum – exemplified most strongly in crime statistics.[293] While it would be wrong to generalise, it is fairly plain that the more conservative churches were more likely to emphasise the importance of promoting values of 'decency' and 'hard work' than the ecumenical churches, which were concerned with promoting justice in the larger society. Especially the Shembe Church and the ZCC – two large AICs – expressed great concern for promoting personal transformation, with alcohol abuse featuring as a great evil.[294]

Amongst evangelicals there was an emphasis on building the new nation on divinely ordained 'values'.[295] Closely allied to this is the idea that reconciliation with God comes before reconciliation with others and also before social action on behalf of the poor, though as the CESA pointed out, it includes the call to love our neighbours.[296] The IFCC put it slightly differently: faith and works need to be fused to create a force for change.[297] A moral revolution – eradicating corruption, re-enforcing norms, and affirming human dignity – needed to follow South Africa's political revolution.[298]

4.3.5 New agendas

We noted the difficulty of working ecumenically today. There are many issues and many different positions, especially as more evangelical groups have joined the SACC, bringing new agendas. At the hearings, Hlope Bam noted that it was not possible for the Council to issue a strong policy statement on abortion because of internal differences around the issue. But the SACC spoke of one key issue which focuses all the faith communities, and one which most had a word to say for: poverty. This is perhaps the new agenda item for faith communities in their socio-economic and political role.

At the hearings there was much discussion of the wealth tax proposed by Prof. Sampie Terreblanche during the business hearings. This would involve a special tax on those persons and companies with assets over 2 million rands. Rabbi Cyril Harris said he had consulted Jewish business-people and they had generally expressed approval, though were concerned that such a tax could be a disincentive to needed investment. The IFCC supported the idea as well – though with the caveat that redistribution should accompany the tax. The ICT supported the idea but urged that the threshold be decreased from 2 million to 1 million rands in assets 'to increase the slice of the cake'.[299]

4.4 Faith communities and the TRC

While there was general support and enthusiasm for the work of the Commission, some groups, such as the ICT and the Catholic Church, expressed reservations about the TRC process. They claimed that it was fundamentally flawed as the result of an 'expedient' political settlement and morally problematic as it placed victims and perpetrators on the same footing.[300] 'Individual justice', said the Catholic submission, 'is being sacrificed for the truth.' There at least needs to be a mechanism, added the ICT, to make perpetrators take responsibility for their actions.[301] There was concern that the discourse of 'reconciliation' not exclude socio-economic transformation (see section 4.1) and that the final report make clear recommendations on redistribution of resources.

With regard to the TRC process, several people at the hearings expressed concern that the TRC was coming to an end and that the real challenge is in follow-up.[302] We have already shown how some communities volunteered resources to continue the process. The Catholic Church suggested that a national body could be set up to promote the common good with faith communities (churches) playing a key role.[303] They also recommended that an education programme be instituted around the forthcoming report of the TRC, to the end of developing a common history.

Another concern was the 'Christian' nature of the Commission itself – to which we shall turn in section 5.1.2.

5. REFLECTIONS AND RECOMMENDATIONS

5.1 Reflections on the process

Our account of what the faith communities thought of the process opens up space for critique and evaluation of the process of getting the faith communities together.

5.1.1 Omissions

A number of questions remain – gaps in the story which need to be filled in. A short résumé would include religious broadcasting and media and its role in state propaganda; theological training institutions and their role in helping produce an intelligentsia (many of whom are now serving in government), or alternatively in training ministers who would become agents or legitimators of apartheid at a congregational level.

The role of theology and its relation to ideology was given some space at the hearings, with the ICT invited to speak on the theology of liberation. TEASA spoke briefly of the way evangelical theology left itself open to legitimising state ideology. The DRC, CESA and IFCC spoke briefly of how liberation theology was understood in their churches. Much more analytical work, though, remains to be done.

The most serious omission, and we have referred to it previously, is that of what may be called 'right-wing groups' and their operations. There was at least one reference at the hearings (by Des Hoffmeister) to churches being used as fronts for such groups, but nothing was received from any such groups. Nor was anything received from the churches – such as the Congregational Church of South Africa – which actively supported right-wing groups.

Two groups in particular, the Gospel Defence League and Frontline Fellowship, were instrumental in seeking to undermine the credibility of churches, organisations and individuals who were well-known or leading opponents of apartheid.[304] These are widely believed to have received funding from the apartheid government's covert operations budget. Not only did they seek to discredit churches and their leadership in various ways, not least through the damaging of personal reputations, but their actions also led to state action against people and institutions. There was a widespread programme and concerted attempt by such groups to undermine the role of anti-apartheid churches in South Africa. It was indeed sadly ironic that this group was not addressed by the TRC, while those churches and individuals which were their victims (including persons such as Dr Beyers Naudé) confessed their failures.

Not only were right-wing groups active within the borders of South Africa, they were also active in the Frontline states – sometimes acting with overseas conservative Christian partners.[305] Similar groups were also active in other faiths, including Islam.[306] The picture of the role of faith communities in South Africa's past is simply not complete without an accounting of (and from) such groups.

The omission of other religious groups from the process is also serious. This may be partly due to the nature of some faith communities, such as Brethren churches, lacking centralised structures and being more local in character. Though we recognise that the Commission made some effort to get them on board, the fact that Lutherans were not represented at the hearings is a serious problem, given the history of Lutheranism in South Africa.[307] Also missing were other Pentecostal groups besides the AFM, such as the Assemblies of God. The way the Muslim community was dealt with will be noted in the next section.

5.1.2 Christian domination

The symbols of the TRC in general are often alienating to those who do not share Christian convictions, and sometimes strongly so. The fact that these particular hearings were held in a church with Christian symbols prominently displayed marginalised representatives of other faiths – as Faried Esack pointed out. Not only was the panel dominated by Christians, it was dominated by a particular brand of Christianity.[308] The hearings had an 'in-house' feel to them, with the chairperson being addressed by ecumenical leaders as a colleague and a friend. Indeed, Archbishop Ntongana said in his presentation that when he saw the panel, he thought he was in Khotso House (the headquarters of the SACC). Prof. Meiring was the only member on the dais who was not an SACC associate or former member of staff. This inevitably meant that the questions reflected a certain understanding of the role of religion (Christianity) in society. But the powerful presence of Archbishop Tutu, as Esack pointed out, also meant that the understanding of reconciliation with which the hearings worked was coloured by his own personality. The prioritising of reconciliation over truth and justice was evident in the panel's weak response to the Dutch Reformed Church representation, where it seemed as if the DRC's attendance at the hearings was sufficient to confirm them on the path to reconciliation.

As stated in the Introduction above, the Commission originally envisioned a 'churches' conference and only later moved to the idea of a 'faith communities hearing' idea. And it seemed that the inclusion of groups outside the Christian faith was an afterthought. The selection of representatives, particularly from the Muslim community, displayed a lack of insight about the diversity within faith communities outside of Christianity.[309] No one person or organisation can represent 'the Muslim community' because (like 'the Christian community') such an entity exists only as an abstraction and is easily open to manipulation by people who identify the 'true' community with their particular expression of it (see section 5.2.1). 'Muslims', like Christians, hold a variety of opinions which reflect economic, ethnic, class and other dynamics in their particular communities.

The result of all this was that, added to the overwhelmingly Christian ethos of the hearings, few Muslims will be able to 'own' the process.

5.2 Reflections on the submissions

5.2.1 Contested identities

The Truth and Reconciliation Commission has as its goal the reconstruction of 'what happened', an account of the past through the hearing of stories and confessions. This is a great challenge, given the different symbolic universes that South Africans live in, with their different legitimising structures. The upholding of these symbolic universes is largely the province of faith and faith communities.

Faith communities, as exhibited in the submissions and presentations, are (and always have been) agents in the ongoing contestation of social and cultural life. But these communities, their histories and their identities are themselves contested – particularly in a time of transition. The Jamiatul Ulama Transvaal claimed to have upheld the values of Islam against apartheid, while the Muslim Youth Movement in a separate submission protested against the JUT's speaking for Muslims. Faried Esack's submission claimed that not only the Ulamas, but the Muslim leadership in general failed to oppose apartheid adequately. Another Ulama, the Majlisul, claimed that Esack was 'a non-Muslim' and had no right to speak for the Muslim community.[310] Amongst Christians, and even within the same Christian tradition, communities struggled to come to a common understanding of the past. Denominations that split over apartheid issues, such as the Baptist Convention and Union, are unable to agree on 'what happened' and (at least the BCSA says this) cannot come near reunification (which both want). The same is true especially of the DRC family. We have already spoken of the DRC's inability to incorporate the pain of its former 'daughter' (now 'sister') churches into its narrative. Until it can do this, institutional reunification is impossible – as was evident from both the URCSA and BK submissions.

5.2.2 Shifting languages

In section 3.2 we noted briefly the ambiguity of language, especially around terms such as 'oppressor', 'victim' and 'engagement'. These can mean different things to different groups. But the very fact that different faith communities, representing a spectrum from conservative to radical, Christian to Muslim, could share a common language is notable. The terms of understanding the past were in the bipolar 'struggle' discourse of oppressed–oppressor, victim–perpetrator, guilt–innocence. Even groups which, during the apartheid years, would not have used this language had appropriated it.[311] There seemed to be a common roll of heroes, with references at the hearings, both celebratory and apologetic, to the chairperson. It seems that the ethos of the Commission (or is it that of the 'New South Africa'?) has had a profound effect upon at least the language within which faith communities understand themselves.

The exception to this rule was the ZCC and (to a lesser extent) the amaNazaretha. Here a different discourse, a different language, a different rhetoric was in place. This was the rhetoric of identity, of communal narrative, which was placed alongside the story of South Africa during the apartheid years.[312] And yet it would not be right to call it 'disengaged'. Indeed it is arguable that the appearance of Bishop Edward Lekganyane was aimed at changing or subverting the terms of engagement – at least for that part of the hearings.[313]

Could it be that faith communities are implicitly on their way to forging a new common history?[314] Such a common history would be good and yet problematic. It would be good in that a shared understanding of the past is an important prerequisite for reconciliation, and a shared language about the past is an important step along those lines. Indeed this is the goal of the Commission, though in tension perhaps with its giving space for particular voices to speak.

But such language needs also to be transcended by a new language of memory, both shared and individual. Shared memory is necessary because nation-building requires it. But shared memory in the service of nation-building can also do violence to the particular memories of suffering contained within communities and persons. A 'grand narrative' of struggle (which can easily erase or overlook ambiguities) in which the terms are easily and unambiguously defined (what were you – a victim or a perpetrator?) needs to be relativised by particular memories which are not reducible simply to either term, lest it becomes a new hegemony. This is as true of faith communities as it is of the larger society. Indeed one of the contributions faith communities can make is as sites where particular memories can be shared and stored.

Another problem contained within oppositional language is an either–or relation to the state: either a community was/is in a relation of 'legitimisation' to the state, or it was/is in a relation of 'opposition' to the state. While arguably the struggle is not over, and this language of either–or will continue to be appropriate as long as there are poor in the land, it needs to be supplemented by a new language appropriate to the new terms of engagement between faith communities and the state. Perhaps the term 'critical solidarity', used by the SACC, is helpful. But the meaning or meanings of that term need to be more fully spelt out.

5.2.3 Assessing the submissions

As already stated, some of the submissions give great detail about the particular faith community's involvement in past oppression. Interestingly, the groups with the largest black constituency and leadership, the AICs, took the occasion of addressing the Commission as an opportunity to present their distinctive faith, rather than account for their involvement in past abuses or opposition. The communities which went into the most detail about the past were the ecumenical Protestant churches, as well as the Catholic Church. In the case of the former it is not surprising, as Protestantism was the faith of most of the powerful in the shaping of South Africa.[315] But within Protestantism there are strong traditions of prophetic dissent, as well as state support. It is not surprising that Protestant Christianity understood itself as most active in opposing apartheid, as well as in giving tacit support to the state.

Protestant churches went into great detail about their written and spoken protests but (as evidenced in the way that our discussion 'thinned out' considerably as it moved from protest to declarations of solidarity with liberation movements) they struggled with translating protest into action. The particular style of protest amongst Protestant churches reflects their ambiguous status within South Africa. A characterisation written in 1988 is broadly applicable: 'Some individuals within the churches saw a vision beyond captivity, and Christian groups outside of the ecclesial structures rebelled against an ever-encroaching state tyranny. The institutional churches were left to protest without resistance.'[316]

Nevertheless, it must be stated that Protestant and Catholic Christianity at the hearings displayed self-criticism in confessing their complicity with the former regime, as well as admitting that their voice of protest was not loud or demanding enough.[317] While they did not go as far as to say that their manner of protest may have given a semblance of legitimacy to a regime widely regarded in the rest of the world as 'intolerant', they were generally forthright in owning up to the more obvious kinds of complicity, such as participation in state structures.[318] This was especially significant in the case of churches such as the UCCSA, whose overwhelmingly black membership meant that they were a church of victims, yet who readily admitted their failures and compromises.

An exception to the 'protest' involvement of Protestant churches is the Dutch Reformed Church, which, as was noted above, saw prophetic activity as only within the context of its privileged relation with the state.[319] To its credit, though, it was at least able to admit to that relation, although it is difficult to characterise as 'prophetic' a community that was one of the very pillars of apartheid (along with the National Party and the Afrikaner Broederbond). Indeed, in its *Journey* document it acknowledged that it had become part of the government's propaganda machine. The role of the DRC was more in keeping the wheels on the apartheid machine rather than in derailing it. Its steadfast refusal to condemn apartheid outright – standing alone within its ecumenical Reformed tradition and virtually alone amongst other Christian faith communities – makes many doubt whether it really has allowed itself to be confronted by the truth of its past. Certainly in its own eyes it is penitent, and its identity as a new Dutch Reformed Church is in line with the 'new South Africa' identity of institutions like the NP and the new Broederbond. But a community's self-understanding must allow itself to be confronted with the pain of those communities it oppressed – and this is the challenge of the TRC, not only for the DRC but for all faith communities. Is the DRC willing to integrate the pain of the former 'daughter churches' into its own narrative, its own 'journey'? At the hearings the DRC's insistence on being ready to 'move ahead into the future' contrasted sharply with the Uniting Reformed Church's claims that the DRC continued to block efforts at reunification of the churches separated by apartheid. Indeed, the URCSA's critique of the DRC points out a danger that all churches need to take account of: an enthusiastic embracing of a 'new' ecclesial identity, with a new language and a new legitimacy, may function as a shield against real transformation – in this case, against removing those barriers erected by 'church apartheid'. At any rate, the acid test for the DRC will be reunification and integration into a United Reformed Church.

We have already observed the interesting change of language on the part of the churches which formerly considered themselves 'apolitical'. The very recognition that 'the authority of the Bible' idea which they held so dearly was subject to ideological manipulation – as expressed in the CESA submission – is (hopefully) a sign of future vigilance and self-criticism. Also positive was the recognition that being 'apolitical' was impossible, and was in effect a vote for the status quo, which (wittingly or not) was to side with the 'oppressor' against the 'oppressed'. They recognised that they supported the former regime, even while at the time professing neutrality. And they recognised that, though chastened, they have a role to play in reconstruction. The question (especially for the more theologically conservative communities) is whether they understand the theological implications of the admissions and confessions they have made, whether they will be able to find a language for integrating these newly articulated convictions into their other identities and agendas. Their old theological wineskins may prove unable to hold the new wine of reconciliation and transformation. Here the help of other churches, especially the ecumenical churches, will be invaluable.

There is, however, a need for a self-critique of the theology of churches which described themselves as 'baffled, stunned and confused' at the revelations of the Commission about human rights abuses, some of which involved their members.[320] It is strange that persons in such communities were surprised at what is being exposed by the TRC, especially in the case of the AFM (one of whose prominent leaders, Frank Chikane, was a victim). Members of churches and other faith communities who were either involved in the anti-apartheid movement or were subject to state repression were not surprised at all. The question must be asked, Why? What was it that did not permit members of more conservative communities, which preached 'the dangers of ideology' and of 'reading scriptures politically', to see what to others was so plain? It is not enough to simply say 'we were duped' by propaganda, as certain conditions must exist before even the most subtle propaganda is believed. Again, the theological emphases of such communities need careful reconsideration, if the past is not to be repeated.

5.2.4 Reservations

When we speak of 'the churches' or particular 'faith communities' being ready or not ready to confront the past, we again encounter the problem of precisely who is doing the speaking and for whom and whose past is being confronted. When the leadership of denominations state a willingness to own the past and their role in it, this may or may not embrace all the clergy (or local leadership), let alone individual members. This was borne out in Nico Smith's letter of confession – a letter some might judge relatively mild in tone – in which pastors were given the opportunity of confessing complicity in lending succour to the agents of apartheid in congregations, and in failing to raise the awareness of their other members. However we judge the value of such a thing in scientifically appraising the mood of people, the fact that Smith sent out 12,000 copies and published it in newspapers across the country and, after six months, only 396 signatures were returned may indicate that confession and owning the past are not a priority at local levels. If we add the possibility that churches and communities at denominational levels may make confession for any number of reasons (not only out of a sense of guilt or remorse), we have little conclusive proof that the faith communities – and especially the churches – are serious in their commitments to owning the past and moving ahead into the future. The only way we will know how 'sincere' the confessions were is to observe the actions of communities in the years to come. After all, if there is one lesson from observing faith communities in South African history (as many of them admitted) it is that words are easy and accomplish little when not backed up with action.

It would be a mistake, however, to simply adopt a 'wait and see' attitude on the sincerity of the faith communities. The TRC process needs to be taken down to denominational structures on a national, regional and local level as a matter of extreme urgency and importance.

Faith communities made a number of commitments to embodying both reconciliation and involvement in the wider public. The problem is that it is easy to make promises in a public forum such as the TRC –

where no one wants to be left out. It is much more difficult to follow them through. (See also our comments above about representation.) And it is even more difficult to hold communities accountable. Precisely who will hold them accountable? The fact that they do not speak for all their members (or even perhaps all their leaders) means not only that there will be stumbling blocks, but that their own constituents will not be able to hold them accountable.

5.2.5 A note on gender oppression

It was unfortunate that a separate submission had to take place from a group representing women in religion – especially in the light of the role of women in the struggle demonstrated by the early testimonies to the Commission. Women and women's groups played a key role in supporting opponents of human rights abuses, including those in churches and mosques. Yet they were overwhelmingly relegated to secondary status in these communities.[321] Women bore the brunt of migrant labour systems and forced removals. Indeed, as committee member Seroke observed on the second day of the hearings, most of the victims who have come forth to testify before the Commission are women, and most of those testify not about their own suffering, but about the suffering of male relatives.

The speakers at the faith community hearings were mostly male.[322] There was little mention of women as victims of oppression and abuse in the submissions of the faith communities, and as little of their agency in opposing apartheid.[323] While this may have been a result of not defining the parameters of 'human rights abuses' to include gender oppression, it nonetheless stands as an indictment of the faith communities that for the most part they continue to see racial, economic and gender oppression as separate categories.

So what are we left with? Are the faith communities 'leavened through' with repentance, as their submissions and presentations would indicate? Or are their spokespersons (overwhelmingly spokesmen) merely voicing once again the mood of the powerful in society? (The comparison between the faith communities' understanding of reconciliation and that reflected in the public debate invites itself.) We may say that only time will tell. But the needs of the present (and the short-term life of the TRC) demand more immediate actions.

5.3 Recommendations

The legacy of a complicit past is still with the faith communities, and dealing with their own stories of compromise is crucial to their becoming the agents of social change they expressed the desire to be. This report wishes to speak to this need, outlining actions and commitments which are necessary to the healing process. We, however, leave it up to local communities to concretise these actions around their own specific needs. As the lion's share of responsibility amongst faith communities for the past lies with Christian churches, we shall have them specifically in mind, although some of the recommendations are more broadly applicable.

(1) We recommend, in accordance with the submissions of ICT and MJC, that faith communities initiate their own processes of healing.[324] This can be done at local church, parish, mosque, synagogue, temple or homestead levels. It can be done at interfaith levels, with different communities in the same area participating. It can be done at institutional or denominational levels. It can be done employing the language and symbols of particular traditions (see the Salvation Army's submission which spoke of the 'testimony meeting'). We furthermore urge that this be initiated before the year 2000. Not only does this year have a tremendous symbolic importance as the dawn of a new millennium (and the possibility of a fresh start), but some groups have declared it an international Jubilee year. In the Jewish and Christian traditions, the year of Jubilee is a year where debts are cancelled, land is returned and equalisation of resources takes place. What better way to celebrate it in the churches than with the initiation of a process of healing.[325]

(2) We recommend that this process of healing goes beyond a handshake and a hug (see the AFM presentation at the hearings) to address the deep pain that the wounds of the past have caused – not only at the level of race relations, but in the economy, within families, within institutions, and especially in issues relating to gender. Apartheid was 'a total strategy' that cut into all areas of life. In their legitimisation of it, faith communities infected all areas of the lives of their members. Any process of cleansing and healing must also have the character of a total strategy.

(3) The inter-institutional dimension of healing is very important. Healing institutional and denominational splits is more than simply an expression of doctrinal unity; it is the acid test for commitment to socio-economic transformation. We urge that such unity talks as are going on now be brought to a positive conclusion, and that especially the Christian church no longer be a reflection of society's economic divisions, but rather a model of a new society. We wish particularly to support the processes of unity involving the DRC and the URCSA, the PCSA and the RPC, and the BUSA and the BCSA.

(4) The question of reparations is a difficult one, especially with limited state resources. As noted several times, many faith communities suffered the loss of buildings and resources under apartheid while many others, directly or indirectly, were beneficiaries. One way that the faith communities themselves could demonstrate their commitment to healing in a concrete way, and create a model for other institutions to follow, would be for the more well-off to set up a fund to help redress the debts incurred

by their sister churches, temples and mosques that suffered from having to relocate. We recommend that faith communities, in considering what they can do to facilitate healing, consider this step and have as a goal the eradication of this debt by the year 2000 – the year of Jubilee.

(5) We recommend that faith communities allow space for the expression and articulation of pain and lament.[326] Lamentation is a process that finds resonance in many faith traditions. It is not something that is easily done in political forums. It needs smaller, safer spaces, spaces of trust. Faith communities can be such spaces. Lament can be made for very specific losses (a son, a place like District Six, personal failure). It can be personal or communal. It is capable of being ritualised and therefore integrated into the discourse of faith communities.

One way that lamentation could be ritualised is in the construction and use of permanent monuments. Vaults could be provided therein for people who see themselves as victims, as perpetrators or as guilty bystanders to tell their stories, to contribute mementoes, as well as being memorials to those who perished as a result of the policies of the past. The Holocaust Memorials in Jerusalem and Washington are an example of such a place. Another way that individuals could participate would be to sign the Register of Reconciliation in regional TRC offices – something that faith communities could sponsor or facilitate, perhaps in the form of a Book of Lament in which the necessary narratives of members could be recorded for the future.

(6) How can faith communities, with their different kinds and sources of authority, be held accountable for what they have committed themselves to? We recommend that forums or structures be created for the specific purpose of tracking healing processes in faith communities. One structure that could be created would be an annual or biannual event, like the *Kirchentag* in Germany, where all faith communities could be invited. Here comparative notes could be shared on the processes of healing in the communities. It would also be an opportunity for cross-fertilisation and debate. But even more, it would be a chance for a celebration of the hope of healing.

(7) Finally, recognising both President Mandela's and Deputy President Mbeki's call to religious leaders to take the lead in the construction of new values for society as a whole, we also urge the state for its part to protect the particular laws and values of different communities, especially those previously disadvantaged by Christian nationalist ideology, to encourage a healthy pluralism that supports the common good.

6. CONCLUSION

This report has barely scratched the surface with regard to understanding and analysing the submissions to and presentations at the faith communities hearings. Much more work needs to be done, including rhetorical and discourse analysis of the submissions, and a hermeneutical analysis of the particular languages of the different communities in relation to the language of the Commission. While we have placed particular submissions from different communities next to each other, they also need to be placed more carefully in the context of other documents produced by the same community, to identify with more nuance the different trajectories of faith communities in South Africa, past and present.

There can be little question of the historical significance of the hearings in East London for the South African churches. In many ways it brought the 'church struggle' to closure, and represents a résumé of its legacy. It also demonstrated again the similarities and differences between faith communities in terms of their treatment under apartheid, proving the possibility of co-operative reconstructive effort based on a shared history of legitimisation, victimisation and struggle. The emergence of a common story, however, must be in tension with the active promotion of smaller-scale stories – something which faith communities (in so far as they are present at the grass roots) are well positioned to promote. These smaller-scale stories need to relativise even the heroic narratives now being written into denominational histories which celebrate the struggle.

Despite the many shortcomings of the process – which included the selection of representatives of the various faith communities, the selection of commissioners and the structure of the hearings – it was important that the Commission placed on public record the significance (and responsibility) of faith communities for reconstruction, and also recorded their confessions of shortcomings and responsibilities for the past. For the first time, communities like the Church of England in South Africa and the International Fellowship of Christian Churches have come out and confessed that their silence during the apartheid years, once interpreted as faithfulness to a gospel 'above' political life, was complicity in sin and betrayal of that gospel. Moreover, it was significant that the suffering of faith communities was made public, especially in the presence of those communities that gave apartheid legitimacy.

The appearance of the Dutch Reformed Church at the hearings, after a period of speculation about whether it would appear, caused great anticipation. While the DRC submission was ultimately rather disappointing and must be judged a largely failed opportunity, the fact that it came at least gave the TRC process some legitimacy in the eyes of its constituents, many of whom continue to see the Commission as a direct attack on

Afrikaners. Likewise, although the ZCC submission refused to address the question of its own complicity and the serious allegations made about relations with the defence forces, the fact that it was willing to appear on the same platform as the other faith communities (especially the CAIC, which has many times tried unsuccessfully to involve the ZCC in its activities) is not without significance. Indeed this particular meeting may hold the possibility of a new era of ecumenical co-operation amongst the largest AICs.

The challenge for the future is twofold. First, will the communities who were eloquent in their commitments to reconstruction and development follow through on these commitments? Or will they simply be a matter of record and nothing else? We have spelt out some concrete steps that communities can take to demonstrate their seriousness, although this is only a beginning. The second challenge is that of co-operative action. The silence of the Christian churches about other faith communities who were partners during the struggle was loud. And the quest for identity was evident throughout the submissions, both from Christian and Muslim groups. If there is such a thing as 'faith communities' (and for the purposes of this report we have granted this), then collective, ecumenical and interfaith action is a keystone of their social role – not to deny their particular traditions, but to bring each to fulfilment in a healing vision of the common social good.

Opening Up
Reflective essays

1 Reconciliation in South Africa: Is Religion Relevant?

Carl Niehaus

Faced with the question of whether religion is a decisive factor in the transformation of South Africa, I am afraid that I must answer, with a certain embarrassment, in the negative. As a professing Christian I would certainly have preferred to say that indeed it was. This remark has to be seen within the broader context of the question whether the Christian religion – as it is used in the collective concept 'church' – is still today a really decisive factor for reconciliation anywhere in the world. When I look at the current state of the church, and the lack of a clear message for our time, then I fear that the answer to this question is also negative.

I think the time has come to rid ourselves of any illusions or complacency that we may still have about the real influence and relevance of religion in our society. Believers will agree that religion ought to play a central role in the quest for peace and reconciliation. This is confirmed by a practically inexhaustible source of texts from the Bible and the holy scriptures of the great world religions. For Christians the whole life of Christ was the embodiment and confirmation of that. Even so, anyone who knows something about world history knows that very little of it has actually been realised. Wars have raged, there have been massacres and genocides. All this still remains as close and immediate as Bosnia and Rwanda.

But wars are also ended and peace is made. People who have mutilated, hated and murdered one another somehow manage to live together again, and after some time their children fall in love with one another and a new generation is born ... Such are the changing tides of history in personal human experiences and contradictions, so aptly described by the masterly Russian authors Dostoevsky and Tolstoy.

Perhaps the greatest problem (or should I call it fear?) of us believers is that, in many cases, religion has had so very little to do with the real reasons why peace eventually came. The tragedy is that religion was often rather the cause of wars. From the perspective of the worldview of believers, faith should occupy a central position, but when church proclamation and ecclesiastical institutions, faith, superstition and unbelief are confused with one another, then we become bewildered, and start doubting the value of our faith, and even our own value.

It seems to me that one of the greatest fears of the church – but also of individual Christians – is the fear of not being reckoned with in the mainstream of decision-making and activity; that your religion does not really matter that much anymore, or – perhaps even more painful – that you are not so important yourself. A growing theme for authors of the period after the Second World War is the alienated, lonely human being who is trying to make sense of his or her life, while the big world around them continues without their having any real impact on it.

Are we, as Christians, not also such shadow people, who keep ourselves busy in our enormous half-empty churches with their high towers and their pomp – a testimony of times past – while the mainstream passes us by to such an extent that we cannot even make a modest contribution to peace anymore? Perhaps the greatest tragedy is not that we are not so important, and that we do not play such a central role, but that we still hold on to the illusion of our indispensably central position.

I shall let these questions rest to return to them later on. First, I would like to make a few comments on the process of reconciliation in South Africa.

I want to share two life stories. Both are from my own life. The one is more personal because it deals with an inner struggle which, I think, will stay with me for the rest of my life. The other, because it may help us Christians, who speak so glibly of martyrdom and the sacrifices we make for justice, to be less self-confident in our claim to leadership through suffering.

One afternoon, three and a half years ago, I received a telephone call in the ANC head office in Johannesburg. When I heard the voice at the other end, I turned freezing cold. It was the voice of a policeman who had interrogated and tortured me when I had been in detention. But it was not the same arrogant voice that had loudly woken me in my cell in the middle of the night, or had threatened me with clenching teeth that I had to talk, or else die like a dog. It was a hesitant, stammering voice, pleading with me to see me urgently. In a vague, incoherent discussion he told me how he had had a nervous breakdown because he could not continue with the outrageous deeds his senior officers had expected him to commit. When it had become clear that he was not of any use to them anymore, they sent him to the complaints office of a small town on the west coast, there to try and live with himself, discarded and forgotten among the dusty papers. I asked if I could call him back the next day, and struggled through that night with the question whether I should see him. Eventually I did decide to see him, and without a moment's delay, he drove the 1 500 kilometres to Johannesburg in his car. Two days later I met him in the lobby of a Johannesburg hotel. He was a mere shadow of the big, muscular man who had hit me out of the chair in his office with a single punch. His whole body was shaking and there were large drops of sweat on his forehead.

Clearly, he had an irresistible need to relate to me all the horrible things he had done to detainees. Some he had tortured with electric shocks, others he had pushed under water until that critical point just before drowning. He had done these things time and again until they talked. Of these, and many other torture methods he had used, he told me. He said to me that he wanted to bring everything out into the open and that I had to help him to do it. (When the TRC was established a year later, he did indeed appear before it.)

Towards the end of our discussion he asked me to forgive him. It was one of the most difficult requests, perhaps the single most difficult, ever made to me. No matter how much I wanted to, I could not tell him that I could forgive him. All I could say was that I would try. Now, even after he has appeared before the TRC, I can still not say that I have forgiven him but I am still trying. Not a single day passes without me struggling with this question.

A few weeks ago I visited one of the ports of Rotterdam where dredgers are built. Attached to the sides of one of the boats were pieces of shiny, unpainted metal, serving no apparent purpose. I asked my guide what their purpose was, and when he answered that they were pieces of 'sacrifice metal', meant to attract the worst rust of the salt water so that the rest of the ship could escape decay, I once again saw the face of the sweaty policeman in front of me. He is also such a sacrificial victim, drawing the attention away from those who gave him the orders to torture. But even with the realisation that he, too, is a victim, I have still not reached the point where I can say that I can forgive him.

What about the National Party politicians, then, with whom my ANC colleagues and I negotiated a new constitution – including the last clause determining that persons who have committed serious human rights abuses could be granted amnesty? (During coffee breaks and meals we sat with them and talked.) Were they not really the ones responsible, in view of the fact that they had knowingly allowed, and even ordered, torture and murder? Am I not more merciful to them than to the man whose fists I can still feel on my body? Is hate, anger and even forgiveness really so personal then? Should blame and – I hesitate to use the term, but for lack of something better – 'the administration of justice' not be calculated less emotionally, more rationally? I cannot escape these questions, but does the church in South Africa help me, a believer, to answer them?

We will return to this question, but first I want to relate the second story. I quote from my book, *Om te veg vir Hoop*:

> The cell at the end of the passage, next to the store room, was that of Denis Goldberg ... On the small bookshelf, in the closet and under the steel bed there were dilapidated little cardboard boxes filled with study notes, neatly made little wooden boxes with tiny drawers that fit perfectly, filled with thread, needles and buttons, carefully classified according to size and colour. There were precise notes of every record, book, piece of clothing or training shoe that had been bought on the recreational account during the previous twenty years. But the cell was filled even more to the brim with memories of comrades who had come in, served their sentences, and departed, while he, as always, stayed behind. There was no release date on his prison card, just a single phrase: For life.
>
> Dennis had watched his good friend Bram Fischer die slowly of cancer, after having fought together for years for every little privilege – during the beginning years of their sentences even to be allowed outside for a couple of hours, and to be allowed to talk to one another. One afternoon, while we were both taking a shower, he told me how Bram had slipped and fallen down in that shower. He had broken his hip, but the medical official maintained that it was just a minor muscle injury, and refused for more than a week to let him take meals in his cell. Denis and Jolinnie Matthews, the carpenter who made the wooden boxes, had to carry him down to the dining hall every day. When X-rays were finally taken, the hip had been splintered. In addition, Bram had prostate cancer that had spread through his whole body. He was sent back to his cell with the allowance that he could take his meals there.
>
> During the following months, Denis faithfully carried the tin plates, three times daily, to the cell where his friend was slowly languishing. When he was clearly dying, they took him away to the prison hospital, where he lay all alone until a few days before his death. Then he was taken to his brother's farm outside Bloemfontein, but first a special proclamation had to be issued to declare the house a prison, because on Bram Fischer's prison card appeared the same entry: For life.

> We had finished showering, and only the slow dripping of the last water in the shower heads could be heard. Denis was silent for a moment, then he looked at me and the sparks in his eyes resembled a white melting pot fire: 'Carl, I don't want to hate, and during my years here I have known many good prison guards, but for what they have done to Bram I can never forgive them' (Niehaus 1993, 112–113).

Bram Fischer was, until his death, the chairman of the South African Communist Party, and Denis Goldberg is a member of the party. Both of them were convinced atheists. The guards who caused Bram so much suffering call themselves Christians, and probably sat in church on the Sundays they were off duty. And yet, it was Denis – to whom I had explained that I had entered the struggle against apartheid because of my Christian conviction that apartheid is wrong – who noticed that the way some of the guards swore and cursed at us upset me deeply. He took me by the shoulders and said that I should never allow them to rob me of my faith.

It was in the surprisingly small, neat handwriting of Bram Fischer in a piece which he had written before his death, and which Denis had treasured in a hollow leg of the chair in his cell, that I read for the first time, so clearly and movingly, a plea for a negotiated settlement with the apartheid regime. Years before it eventually happened, he had described with great insight how various forms of pressure, including international sanctions and growing protest among the population, would eventually bring the country to the brink of disaster. Fischer wrote that when that situation was reached, the people of South Africa would have to realise that either they must negotiate and co-operate to save their country, or else a destructive bloodbath would follow.

Today I remember with shame how I, in my youthful arrogance, expressed to Denis my resistance against the idea of negotiations with the apartheid regime. He, in spite of twenty years of suffering in prison, insisted that it would eventually become the only reasonable solution. A number of times he said to me that my moral condemnation of 'sinful and heretical apartheid' was correct, but that, for an achievable and relatively peaceful solution in South Africa, it should not be so dogmatic that it became a 'holier than thou' luxury which we could not afford.

The split in the church during the apartheid period is reasonably well known. On one side stood the Dutch Reformed Church (DRC), which maintained, with the theology of apartheid, that apartheid was biblically justified. The most blatant racist oppression was defended and 'God's blessing' proclaimed over it. Sunday after Sunday, deeply faithful, mainly Afrikaans-speaking churchgoers were told that apartheid was good.

Many sincere, believing people, who desperately wanted to follow God's Word, uncritically supported the policy of apartheid because it had been preached from the pulpit since their childhood. To say this does not release them from their own guilt and participation in the apartheid system, but it makes of the theology of apartheid an even greater abomination. Faith was supplanted by the superstition of apartheid theology. Believing people were led on the path of unbelief by false preachers. People who, with different guidance, would not have followed the path of apartheid, were unnecessarily dehumanised.

As a footnote, for the sake of description and contextualisation, the DRC can further be described as a church that does not live from her tradition and faith, but from a superstition that interweaves and confuses ecclesiastical institutions with a narrowly racist concept of 'nation'. This was also the case with many German churches from 1932 onwards.

On the other side were the various shades of religious protest and resistance against apartheid. This aspect of the church during the apartheid period is also reasonably well known. It varied from the carefully worded letters of protest from the official organs of the Methodist, Anglican, Roman Catholic and other churches, to the much louder condemnations of confessing groups within these and other denominations. Then there was, of course, the clear witness of the Christian Institute until it was declared illegal, and the South African Council of Churches (SACC), who entered the struggle against apartheid with great moral courage. In the struggle against apartheid, the role of that part of the church deserves full recognition. In innumerable cases, church structures were the only channels available for the financing of anti-apartheid activities because a government that liked to project itself as Christian could not very easily ban churches as such.

The fact that some particularly courageous individual church leaders and theologians played an important role in the struggle against apartheid does not mean, however, that the church as such provided a clear confession. Church leaders like Archbishop Desmond Tutu, Dr Beyers Naudé, Dr Frank Chikane, Father Albert Nolan, Bishop Simeon Nkoane, Dr Wolfram Kistner and many others deserve all honour and recognition. They are people who did not step into the trap of nationalistic and racialistic superstition. But, as great as their confession was, and as much as it also found an echo in important ecclesiastical policy documents, like the Confession of Belhar, it must still not be seen as an indication that the church, in its broad dimensions, developed a clear, coherent theological basis in the struggle against apartheid, and especially an understanding of what had to come in the place of apartheid.

Ecclesiastical protest was rightly based on a moral–ethical denunciation of apartheid. And yet, when the next historical jump had to be made, with the complex challenges of the transitional phase, of negotiations, compromises and efforts at reconciliation, the church in South Africa – except for a vague call for peace and reconciliation – contributed very little theologically and substantially.

During the process of negotiation for the Interim Constitution that guided South Africa towards the first democratic elections of 27 April 1994 the church played a very marginal role. It was the leader of the South African Communist Party, Mr Joe Slovo, who – in following up on what his predecessor Bram Fischer had advocated in prison years before – suggested the most significant compromises for a peaceful settlement to the broad anti-apartheid front. He argued for it with great conviction until it was eventually accepted. If there is someone who, together with President Nelson Mandela and Mr Cyril Ramaphosa, ought to be recognised as moral and intellectual prophet of the relatively peaceful settlement in South Africa, then it is not a religious person, but the outspoken communist and atheist Joe Slovo.

One of the last decisions before the Interim Constitution was finally approved was whether amnesty would be available for persons who had committed grave human rights abuses. The National Party made it clear that they were willing to shipwreck the whole process if provision was not made for amnesty. There were growing indications of restlessness among the South African Police and the South African Defence Force. For days the ANC struggled with the difficult moral and juridical questions of how to create a possibility for amnesty – without simply making it automatic – in such a way as to let as much of the truth as possible become known. I am ashamed to have to admit, as a believer, that during that time, no significant contribution was made from the religious angle with regard to matters that address so clearly the essential questions of confession, reconciliation and forgiveness. The church was confused and silent.

It was the political negotiatiors who thrashed out the unique model of the TRC, which provides the opportunity for victims of human rights abuses to tell for the first time, with recognition and respect, what had happened to them, together with the insistence that those who have committed grave human rights abuses would have a right to amnesty only if they are prepared to tell the truth about what they had done. There was very little, if indeed any, theological input.

In the functioning of the TRC the religious convictions and spiritual strength of Archbishop Tutu played an important role. But one must distinguish between the personal role played by the Archbishop and, viewed broadly, the role of religion, in the effort towards reconciliation in South Africa. It is people like Archbishop Tutu who let one see how important faith is, but also how irrelevant the church is in the broad sense.

Many individual believers are engaged in a personal inner struggle about the fundamental questions regarding the limits and possibilities of forgiveness, about whether we can forgive offences committed against others, about what needs to be done in terms of recognition and compensation for victims. But when they look for formal encouragement, they are confronted with the confusion of the church.

In most cases the church (including ecumenical organisations like the SACC) would very much like to be of help, but the help is still limited to shallow, generalising remarks such as that God's forgiveness in Christ is infinite, and that confession must go hand in hand with the willingness to put right what was done wrong (which, in itself, is good and proper). It does seem, however, that even that part of the church that has a basically positive stance towards the TRC is not currently in a position to provide any real guidance.

An even greater tragedy is the position of the DRC. After everything that has become known during the last few years about the horrific human rights abuses taking place under the apartheid regime, the leadership of the church that had defended the apartheid regime refused to appear before the TRC, and to confess their guilt and co-responsibility.

I have already referred to the members of the DRC who, for years, supported apartheid because the minister told them from the pulpit that it was God's will. Today those church members are confronted on a daily basis with the most horrifying tales of torture and abuse, perpetrated by government structures on their behalf, and for the sake of safeguarding their privileges. They are scared and confused, they need the guidance of their church, but they do not receive it. What functioned as the DRC's written submission to the TRC was a tract with the title 'The story of the DRC's journey with apartheid, 1960–1994 – a testimony and a confession'. It is, however, no real confession, but an attempt to water down grave sins and abuses with a selective handling of history. It tries to create the impression that the basic intentions of the DRC have always been good and sincere. This little piece of writing is a betrayal of their members who long for guidance.

The tragedy intensifies because that part of the church community in South Africa that did, to a greater or lesser extent, oppose apartheid is also at a loss as to what is required of them in the face of the new challenges of the transitional phase. Very little prophetic guidance can therefore be expected from that quarter. Once again, it fell on the shoulders of individual believers, like Dr. Beyers Naudé who, together with some other theologians in their personal capacity, issued a call, in an open letter, to the ministers of all churches (not only those of the DRC) to confess their guilt before the TRC.

This brings tears to one's eyes, knowing what Dr Naudé has meant for the struggle against apartheid, and what he has suffered, and also to read how he confesses that he had not realised the wrongness of apartheid early enough, and should have done more to oppose it. When one reads that letter, one begins to see something of what the church could have meant for reconciliation, had it been less self-obsessed and more humble, had it been more willing to do some serious soul-searching, and had fewer illusions about its own value.

One of the greatest tragedies, as embodied by the church, is that we have never quite managed to stand in the midst of the realities of the world. We still tend too much to see ourselves as special, and to try to find simple, good versus bad moral solutions.

Even when we want to proclaim a prophetic message amidst the problematics of social injustice, we tend to seek simplistic, moralistic solutions. In the sixties and seventies various versions of liberation theology had an influence on the thought of many Christians who were worried about social injustice. Socialist and even communist socio-economic models were sometimes taken over quite naively. It was believed that the solution was within reach. I count myself among those who embraced the economic models of liberation theology all too uncritically. When I was working on this address, I had a look once again at what I had seen as the solution to the problems of poverty and exploitation ten years ago. It was a sobering experience.

We thought it was simple to know which was the good cause, and who the enemy. With this simple assurance we made ourselves guilty of the ideologising of faith. We did not have the courage to accept the pluriformity of Scripture, and to live in the light of its challenges. When the rigid, dogmatic economic approach began to collapse everywhere, confusion and growing silence followed among many believers who had thought along that line (among those who do not keep silent, it is perhaps even worse: more and more irrelevant explanations to which fewer and fewer world leaders pay any attention). Just think of the World Council of Churches (WCC). Not too long ago, it was a relatively small organisation with a big voice. At that time attention was paid to the positions adopted by the WCC. But today its voice becomes steadily weaker. I suppose those church leaders who are still directly involved in the activities of the WCC still know what is going on there. But who among the broad population still has the faintest idea of, or shows any interest in, what the WCC does and says? We have to admit that there is very little interest.

As with the SACC, I ask myself whether it is really still of any consequence to know what is being done. After all, does anything relevant to the needs of people in our time still happen there?

In South Africa the Biko family had to hear that their appeal to the Supreme Court could not stop the amnesty process of the TRC with regard to the policemen who had tortured and murdered Steve Biko. The amnesty process might be necessary for the sake of general political stability in South Africa, but surely we cannot demand of them, and many other victims, that they personally have to forgive! How will they be supported during this difficult period? What is the church's message to them and to the government? If the church wants to be relevant, it will have to offer something more than the well-known hymn (regardless of how touching it is):

> Make me a channel of Your peace,
> It is in pardoning that we are pardoned,
> In giving to all men that we receive;
> In dying that we're born to eternal life

The same dilemma also faces Christians on a daily basis in Bosnia and Rwanda.

I do not know what the answer ought to be. I do not even know whether there is an answer as such. But it seems to me that the way in which one deals with the problems is more important than a clear answer. Therein, I believe, faith has a role to play. But it is not necessary to strive for it to be the decisive factor.

Those of us who are believers often fail to serve because we think that we have to rule and shout orders. As I have said, the members of the DRC (in fact, of all churches) long for guidance. But most of all, they long for a servant-like guidance, which will help them to seek, which will help them to relativise, and even to doubt.

We as believers should cease to think that we have the answers. Perhaps the most important thing we can do is to struggle sympathetically and humbly, together with our fellow human beings, with the questions of our existence.

2 Right-wing Christian Groups

Roger A. Arendse

In the spring of 1978 a scandal hit the headlines of the English-speaking press that unmasked the apartheid state's 'grand design' to secure at any cost its own survival and the survival of those who supported it. This scandal, later dubbed 'Muldergate', constituted an attempt

> to influence public opinion by presenting a softer image of apartheid while in reality it became more repressive. The conspiracy also involved attempts to undermine opposition groups and especially the churches within South Africa and abroad by denigrating their leadership, their policies, and their integrity (Knight 1989, 2).

The South African Council of Churches (SACC) was a prime target of this conspiracy. Already a painful 'thorn in the flesh' of the state in the late 1970s, the SACC was at the time also gaining substantial ecclesiastical support for its anti-apartheid campaign within the South African English-speaking churches and had also successfully rallied powerful international support for its cause, especially in North America and Europe. Therefore, in a well-orchestrated attempt to discredit the SACC and its allies both locally and abroad, the South African government forged its own alliances with groups in the English-speaking churches. These independent church groups were all motivated by a strong pro-apartheid agenda that sharply opposed that of the SACC and its supporters.

Among such right-wing Christian groups (RWCGs) were the Christian League of Southern Africa (CLSA), the Catholic Defence League and the Anglican Reform League. When Muldergate broke, the CLSA and founding Methodist minister Fred Shaw were directly implicated in the 'dirty tricks' campaign of the South African government and its state security system. Vast amounts of secret government funds had been channelled into the sponsorship of the CLSA newsletter *Encounter* and its German equivalent *Vox Africana* in order to bolster the apartheid government's campaign of discrediting the SACC in South Africa and abroad (Knight 1982, 110, 114).[1]

A fuller account of the CLSA and its right-wing political and church alliances during the 1970s is well documented and readily accessible (e.g. Knight 1982). Less known, however, are the close connections between RWCGs such as the CLSA of the late 1970s and many of their successors in the 1980s and 1990s. Unlike many of the 'older' RWCGs that were largely exposed and discredited for their pro-apartheid ideology and strategy, the 'newer' RWCGs have so far managed to escape relatively unscathed from this kind of public and church scrutiny. And as their predecessors before them sought to do, so the 'newer' RWCGs have continued to cover up their own direct or indirect complicity in the atrocities of the apartheid government in a cloak of conservative Christian theological and ideological rhetoric and actions.

The TRC's hearings into the role of faith communities in South Africa during the apartheid era would have been the ideal forum to throw the spotlight on these 'newer' RWCGs. But this did not happen. The RICSA Report (sec. 5.1.1) suggests that the omission of RWCGs may be 'the most serious omission' of all. In this essay, I wish to respond to this suggestion more directly by focusing on the phenomenon of RWCGs in South Africa, particularly since 1980. Firstly, I describe the identity, character and strategy of some of the 'newer' RWCGs that emerged in the wake of the Muldergate scandal. In this way I hope to help fill the glaring gap left by the omission of RWCGs from the TRC hearings in East London. Secondly, I raise my own critical questions about the TRC process, asking specifically about the implications of the omission of RWCGs for the broader process of 'truth-telling' about our country's past. My intention here is to stimulate ongoing reflection and debate in the South African churches about the actual role and social function of the kind of Christianity that RWCGs represent. Finally, I offer some tentative recommendations for church leaders and lay members about how to undertake further critical analyses of RWCGs in South Africa in their own local churches. I also suggest that these groups should be actively engaged, and that there appear to be 'signs of hope' that even they do not lie beyond the bounds of reconciliation and healing so desperately needed in our churches and wider communities.

Right-wing Christian groups in South Africa during the 1980s

In an editorial introduction to a series of articles on the phenomenon of right-wing religious movements in the late 1980s,[2] Charles Villa-Vicencio (1989, 2) observed that

> The right wing religious phenomenon is highly complex, extremely well-funded, and appears to enjoy the support of repressive forces both in and beyond state structures in numerous countries as well as in many churches. To the extent that it is necessary for the church in both pastoral care and theological reflection to be informed about the actual situation within which it proclaims the liberatory message of the Gospel – it is imperative that right wing religion be analysed and understood.

This complexity has largely contributed to the variety of ways in which it has been analysed and understood. These analytical frameworks range from the more simple to the more complex. Only a few examples are provided here to cast some light on the identity, character and strategy of RWCGs.

The RICSA Report (sec. 3.2) classifies faith communities according to three essential roles that they played during the apartheid period, namely, 'agents of oppression, victims of oppression, and opponents of oppression'. It is careful to point out that these three roles are never completely unambiguous for many faith communities in South Africa. A single Christian community, for example, can display elements of any one, two, or even three of these roles simultaneously. However, in the case of RWCGs, the ambiguity disappears. RWCGs are undoubtedly 'agents of oppression' who propagated 'state theology' (sec. 3.2.1.1.5).

A 'Statement on the Political Abuse of Religion' issued by three church bodies in Cape Town in the late 1980s provides another example of how RWCGs may be classified.[3] It distinguishes between some RWCGs that were highly organised and produced glossy newsletters to propagate their views,[4] and others that were relatively small and operated only in single townships, although often they were brought together by co-ordinating umbrella bodies.[5] 'Christian Collaborators: Part of the Total Strategy' (in *Crisis News* 1988, 2, 6–7) further classifies RWCGs according to five main types. These include militant activist groups,[6] groups organised within specific denominations,[7] whole churches which represent the right-wing of their denominations,[8] evangelistic groups which aim to counter progressive ecumenism,[9] and state-related structures which give overt support to political actions of the state.[10]

My first analysis of RWCGs (Arendse 1989a), written from a more progressive evangelical perspective, attempted to provide a more complex content analysis of these groups.[11] I described RWCGs according to certain dominant ideological and theological trends. Ideological trends embraced the anti-communist, pro-capitalist, militarist, reformist and authoritarian nature of RWCGs. Theological trends included their largely apolitical quality, and their stress on personal and spiritual salvation, biblical fundamentalism, aggressive moralism, anti-liberation theology and liberation theologians, and prosperity teaching.[12] In a later, more detailed case study (1989b) of one specific RWCG, namely the Gospel Defence League (GDL), I focused more directly on five of its dominant ideological biases; namely, antagonistic dualisms, fanatical anti-communism, sacralised capitalism, legitimation of state militarism and limited social ethic. Dorothea Scarborough, a German emigrant and the spouse of a former missionary and dissident Congregationalist minister, was the Cape Town organiser of the CLSA in the mid-1970s. She then became the founder and leader of the GDL.[13] The GDL also had strong alliances with RWCGs in former West Germany and North America.[14]

An alternative to the research paradigms of the earlier studies of RWCGs in South Africa[15] was the analysis of Lesley Fordred (1990), which sought to provide a more complex and thorough conceptual analysis of RWCGs on the basis of their overall cosmology (worldview) and ideology.[16] Her study focused on two evangelical RWCGs in Cape Town; namely, Frontline Fellowship (FF) and the GDL, preferring to attach to these groups the label 'Conservative Christian Group' (CCG) rather than 'Right-wing Christian Group' (RWCG). On closer inspection, though, the defining characteristics of CCGs largely overlap with those that others have used to describe RWCGs.[17] Admittedly, Fordred's study seeks to reflect a far greater sensitivity to the conservative character and function of the cosmology and ideology of the FF and the GDL than previous studies, providing us with a way of understanding how English-speaking churches were 'vulnerable to the right' (Brews 1989). Her primary goal was 'not to excuse, but rather to explain' the agendas of CCGs. These agendas 'in terms of their anti-communism and pro-apartheid stances, [were] not as much a conspiracy for maintaining white power as a strategy for maintaining the "empoweredness" of their discourse of right and truth' (1990, 39).

The phenomenon of RWCGs has also been analysed by focusing more comprehensively on the state militarism of some groups.[18] Steve Askin (1989, 106–116) provides an illuminating example when he explores the missionary activity of some RWCGs in Mozambique and other neighbouring countries of South Africa during the 1980s. Askin (1989, 113–115) makes specific mention of Frontline Fellowship (FF). FF unabashedly viewed the South African army as a 'missionary force' during the height of apartheid (cited in Askin 1989, 113).[19] Initiated by a group of South African Defence Force (SADF) soldiers on a South African military base in northern Namibia in the early 1980s, FF claimed to be a cross-border evangelistic mission society, but in reality it became a front for South African state militarism in the frontline states. Askin (1989, 114) observed that

> its main work involves the sending of 'missionaries' to work with South African-backed rebel groups, including RENAMO and UNITA, and the dissemination of quasi-religious propaganda against those governments and movements which have been targeted for attack and destabilisation by the South African military: Angola, Mozambique, Zimbabwe, the South West Africa People's Organisation (SWAPO) of Namibia and the African National Congress (ANC) of South Africa.

The undisputed links of FF with former mercenaries, 'shadow' evangelical groups and pro-Nazi societies are also highlighted in Askin's study (1989, 114–115).[20]

Another striking example of the connection between RWCGs and state militarism was provided in the analysis of Worsnip (1989a, 82–94). Reminiscent of the clandestine strategies of the Bureau for State Security (BOSS) in the 1970s which the Muldergate information scandal exposed, Worsnip's study demonstrated how elements in the South African churches once again become deliberate targets and co-conspirators in the Low Intensity Conflict strategy (LIC) of the apartheid government in the 1980s.[21] At the highest levels, LIC strategy was reflected in the highly sophisticated and complex intelligence network of the State Security Council (SSC) which operated through its National Security Management System (NSMS), later called the National Management System (NMS). But the NMS also had numerous Joint Management Centres (JMCs) comprising local and national civil servants across the entire country. Worsnip (1989a; 1989b) mentioned several other RWCGs directly implicated in the LIC strategy of the South African state, some because of their very conservative theological and political agenda.[22]

Right-wing Christian groups, the TRC hearings and the churches

The analyses described in the first part of this essay, in spite of their different emphases, clearly point to the close connections between RWCGs and the agenda and strategy of the apartheid government in the 1980s. Whether overtly or covertly, explicitly or implicitly, RWCGs helped entrench South African state hegemony throughout the years of 'grand apartheid'. Given this evidence, it does appear strange and problematic that RWCGs are omitted from the historic three-day TRC hearings in East London. Indeed, the RICSA Report (sec. 5.1.1) calls this omission 'sadly ironic', when many churches and individuals which were targeted by RWCGs and became their victims made confessions of their own failures at the hearings. Equally strange and problematic is the fact that none of the mainline English-speaking churches that made submissions at the TRC hearings appear to have made any specific mention of RWCGs. Of the sixty-six persons that sat as representatives of a wide range of faith communities in South Africa at the TRC hearings, only one made explicit reference to RWCGs.[23] But no submission was forthcoming from right-wing churches or organisations themselves.[24]

Perhaps the time has now arrived to address some questions for critical reflection and debate both within the circles of the TRC and its affiliated structures and within the churches across South Africa. Does the omission of RWCGs from the TRC hearings in any way constitute an indictment of the process around these hearings? Have the interests of 'truth-telling' about the role of faith communities in South Africa during the apartheid era really been served when there remains this rather deafening silence with respect to the role of RWCGs during this period of our history? Commissioner Bongani Finca (1997, 18)[25] highlights an essential task of the TRC hearings as the production of 'a report which unmasks the official lie' of apartheid's past. But, just how complete is this reconstruction of the past with the glaring omission of RWCGs from the hearings? How satisfactorily has the 'official lie' of apartheid's past been unmasked when the role and strategies of RWCGs have avoided the searchlight of political and ecclesiastical scrutiny? These questions are not meant to detract from either the 'great challenge' or 'historical significance' of the TRC event in East London (RICSA 1998, sec. 6). Rather they are meant to stimulate a critical evaluation of the process around this event itself, and more specifically, question why it was that RWCGs were not brought into this process.[26]

Specific questions should also be addressed to the churches themselves. For example, why did representatives of the Church of the Province, the Roman Catholic Church and the Methodist Church make no direct mention of RWCGs in their respective submissions when (as mentioned above) affiliated structures in their churches had issued a joint statement about the political abuse of religion by RWCGs in 1988? Have those churches or organisations identified specifically as agents of oppression really been unaware of RWCGs in their own ranks? If so, have their confessions, apologies and self-criticisms truly 'come clean' on the active role of many of the RWCGs within their own structures and programmes? How many of these church groups or organisations are now prepared to actively and decisively engage RWCGs in order to contribute more meaningfully and honestly to a process of reconciliation and healing in our churches, as well as the wider communities across South Africa?[27] The explicit or implicit involvement of RWCGs in gross human rights violations of the past, both within South Africa and beyond its borders since the 1980s, has still not yet become the subject of serious scrutiny within the churches and the broader socio-political arena. This may explain why many of these groups continue to operate quite freely in South Africa as well as in other countries in Africa today, propagating an ideological agenda that deliberately seeks to oppose the agenda of democratisation, transformation and reconciliation.[28] Indeed, the demise of the old apartheid order has not really halted but appears to have given renewed impetus to RWCGs. The spider web of right-wing Christian intrigue and mystery continues to conceal itself behind frenzied denunciations, vitriolic attacks and narrowly conceived spiritualities.

And so the critical challenge becomes even more urgent. Are churches that are prepared to face the truth about our past, also prepared to expose and face the truth about right-wing Christianity and the incipient dangers of its theological and ideological beliefs and practices? This challenge cannot be ignored or avoided if churches in South Africa are to make a meaningful and authentic contribution to the process of reconciliation and healing in our land.

Meeting the challenge of right-wing Christianity in South Africa

The RICSA Report (sec. 5.2.4) recognises that 'the TRC process needs to be taken down to denominational structures on a national, regional and local level as a matter of extreme urgency and importance'. This will be an essential test of the sincerity and commitment of local church communities to put their words into actions, especially those that made submissions at the TRC hearings. How this will happen cannot be dictated from 'outside', but must ultimately be grounded in the concrete reflections, analyses and decisions of the local church communities themselves as they respond to the TRC process and its findings as a whole. In this important task, church communities may find useful some of the suggested recommendations in the RICSA Report (sec. 5.3). What I intend to provide now are some additional recommendations about how church leaders and lay members can reflect, more specifically, on the phenomenon of RWCGs in South Africa in their local church and community contexts, and so decisively meet the challenge that these groups present.

Firstly, church leaders and members should commit themselves to the study of the phenomenon of RWCGs as part of an ongoing process of reflection, analysis and debate about the meaning of Christian identity and faith in South Africa. A starting point for this process could be the various descriptions and analyses of RWCGs already provided in this essay. Church leaders may prefer to explore these studies further for themselves before engaging their own members in discussion about RWCGs. Rather than getting bogged down in the many smaller and often divergent details of RWCGs, it will be an essential first step to obtain a 'big picture' of these groups in terms of their overall character, agenda and strategy. It is vital to be very clear about the kind of Christianity that RWCGs represent and propagate, as well as the social function of this kind of Christianity.[29] The larger majority of leaders and members in the mainstream tradition of the church are not openly or consciously right-wing, but they may nevertheless still be helping to spawn the reactionary ideas and activities of RWCGs. The first step is to become more aware of the variety of ways in which RWCGs manage to exaggerate and exploit 'the reactionary dimensions of the Judaeo-Christian tradition' (Villa-Vicencio 1989). The next important step is to find definite and creative ways to transcend and overcome these dimensions.

Secondly, church leaders and members should have a critical awareness of how the past and present agendas of RWCGs connect with one another. What is important to recognise here is the fact that RWCGs are seldom ever willing to give up their brand of Christian theology or ideology, even when their dominant political or religious support base is exposed and eroded. In fact, they are usually very adept at finding ways to survive. For example, as I pointed out earlier, the discrediting of the Christian League of South Africa in the wake of the Muldergate scandal gave rise to the Gospel Defence League, a clear case of 'new name, same old ideology' (Arendse 1989b).[30]

Thirdly, the literature of RWCGs requires careful and critical analysis. RWCGs usually disseminate vast amounts of literature in churches and other public forums. Distribution of this literature is customarily in the form of handbills, newsletters, pamphlets and books, and usually under the guise of 'missionary' work (see Askin 1989). Often literature is distributed at church or public meetings to propagate their views on a particular topic.[31] Church leaders and members should be especially aware of how RWCGs promote their views on these topics. Usually words with deep Christian associations such as God, Christ, gospel, righteousness, truth, cross and church are readily appropriated, but in reality they help to conceal the real ideological agenda of these groups. Most often, the primary strategy of RWCGs is to use the Bible to ensure unquestioning support for their views among many unsuspecting Christians. Even a casual survey will reveal how biblical texts punctuate every piece of literature that RWCGs put out. The intention is clear. Christians must believe that what RWCGs say is really what the Bible says, and vice versa.

RWCGs, of course, are not alone in this abuse of the Bible. But they are most typical of groups that deliberately exploit the Bible to legitimise a conservative or ultra-conservative ideological agenda. Biblical scholar James Dunn (1987, 107) warns us about this kind of Christian fundamentalist approach to the Bible, describing it as 'exegetically improbable, hermeneutically defective, theologically dangerous, and educationally disastrous'. Christians in South Africa would be wise to heed this warning, especially when they confront what RWCGs claim to be the 'truth' about God's Word for our situation.[32]

Fourthly, RWCGs should be actively engaged. This should never be the first step that church leaders or members undertake, but rather should follow other preliminary steps such as those already mentioned. The reason for this is that the direct engagement of RWCGs will usually prove to be the most difficult step of all, especially for lay members who may easily be intimidated by the seemingly sane, rational, persuasive and self-confident arguments that proponents of RWCGs present. Most often, these proponents also resist meaningful engagement or dialogue of any kind, and desire instead to enforce their views upon others. Therefore, it is important that those church leaders or members who are better prepared for the task of engagement with RWCGs should offer support to those who may struggle or be hesitant to do so. RWCGs may present some of the greatest challenges to churches that are committed to the important task of reconciliation and healing in our country. This is because most RWCGs appear to have placed themselves outside the boundaries of any reconciliatory embrace. Yet there have been definite 'signs of hope' that a change of heart and openness to broader reconciliation and healing can become a reality, even for church communities presumed to have been right-wing in their theological and political agenda. The examples of the Church of England and Rhema Church at the faith hearings come to mind. Another 'sign of hope' is the prestigious and highly influential DRC in Lynnwood, Pretoria, historically a stronghold of conservative Afrikaner ideology and nationalism, and the spiritual home of many National Party government leaders during the apartheid era. Recently, Archbishop Desmond Tutu, chairperson of the TRC, was invited to preach in the church for the first time. At the end of the sermon it became clear that the congregation had opened not only their church doors, but also their own hearts to Tutu, once believed to be a staunch enemy of everything the church and her members stood for. Reconciliation and healing has started to become more of a reality here.[33]

These 'signs of hope' should provide enough incentive for churches in South Africa never to abandon completely the power of the Christian gospel and the love of God to open up avenues of reconciliation and healing in South Africa, even in the most unlikely of places!

Conclusion

This essay has been an attempt to fill the rather unfortunate 'gap' left by the omission of right-wing Christian groups (RWCGs) from the TRC hearings in East London. Consequently, little can be explicitly known about RWCGs from the church submissions at the TRC hearings, or from the RICSA Report. The first part of this essay therefore has tried to introduce church leaders and members to the phenomenon of RWCGs. It has become clearer that RWCGs have, particularly during the last two decades of the apartheid era, offered direct support to the propaganda machinery of the state, both inside and outside the borders of South Africa. Yet most RWCGs, especially those that have operated since the 1980s, have so far managed to escape any direct complicity in or responsibility for the clandestine and oppressive strategies of the apartheid state or its reactionary partners locally and abroad.

On this account, the second part of this essay has challenged the TRC process for its omission of RWCGs from the hearings, and has raised some critical questions about what this may imply for both the TRC and the churches in South Africa. Finally, some steps were suggested about how local church leaders and members across South Africa may proceed with their own critical reflections and analyses of RWCGs in South Africa, and also how these groups may be actively engaged. RWCGs represent a great challenge to the churches as they commit themselves to the urgent task of reconciliation and healing in our land. But there are at least some positive 'signs of hope' to indicate that even these groups have the potential to embrace positive change and join with other Christian and religious communities to bring about meaningful transformation in our land.

3 The Truth and Reconciliation Discourse: A Black Theological Evaluation

Tinyiko Sam Maluleke

> ... in seeking to develop a hermeneutic of good news to the poor in the Third World, the question is no longer on which side God is. That was a good question for its time. Now however, the relevant question is how to interpret the eloquence with which the poor are silent and the absence through which they are present ... It is in struggling with these silences and absences that a new creative re-appropriation of the liberation of the gospel takes place (Mosala 1994, 147).

The starting point of black theological reflection on the truth and reconciliation process in South Africa must be the silence and absence of black thinking (and thinkers) – beyond acting as mere informants for mainly white male researchers and commentators – from the discourses that are shaping and assigning meaning to the 'New South Africa' project. This is the main point advanced by this essay. But a necessary prior step must be an account of the shape of reconciliation discourse in South Africa, especially as shaped and contested by black voices. Historically there have been six strands. I begin by outlining them briefly, before examining the silence of black voices within the current reconciliation process.[1]

Black thinking on reconciliation: a retrospect

First, within the black consciousness movement there was a strong rejection of superficial integrationist reconciliation – especially when touted as the only and best method of combating white racism. This conviction was usually operationalised through the creation of several multi- or non-racial groups, ideologies and theologies. Black theology, like black consciousness, rose out of a basic disagreement with this dangerously and sometimes deliberately superficial notion of reconciliation, which amounted to a sporadic, temporary and palliative integration of 'non-whites' and 'white liberals', posited as the method of fighting white racism.

Secondly, while the most influential sections of the South African churches theologically and practically mirrored the idea of complete separation, liberal enclaves within the churches tended to seek a 'third way'. In his penetrating analysis of South African 'third-way theology' and its understanding of reconciliation, Balcomb (1993) highlights the seminal idea of the church as 'an alternative community', standing, in David Bosch's words, 'neither to the left nor to the right ... at home nowhere' (in Balcomb 1993, 68). Practical attempts at such alternative communities included Koinonia, founded by Nico Smith in Pretoria, and the National Initiative for Reconciliation (NIR). Like Steve Biko's 'black-white mixed circles', such multiracial or integrated groups sought to constitute a 'reconciled alternative community' which transcended and thereby undermined social divisions. In a sense, even though they were clearly not meant to be established as permanent 'third-way communities', ecumenical movements, notably the South African Council of Churches (SACC), did sometimes operate as third-way communities – though generally with slightly more radical theologies and ecclesiologies. Black theology has been rightfully critical of both third-way theologies and third-way communities as expressions and legitimate goals of reconciliation.

Closely related to certain third-way theologies is the contrasting of reconciliation with revolution and liberation. Here black people continue to be seen as inferior: *only* equal human beings can ultimately be reconciled (cf. Tutu 1976, 10). Otherwise what passes as reconciliation is nothing more than a few 'black people becoming white' (cf. Boesak 1977, 107ff.) – and often only for a moment. For this reason, Mofokeng (1986, 172) insists that 'there is no possibility of reconciliation between black and white people ... until the oppressive structures and institutions, be they black or white, are transformed'.

Fourthly, though a product of para-church ecumenism, the *Kairos Document* has been seen as expressing radical theology. Its view of reconciliation resonates with aspects of those above. It distinguishes between 'true reconciliation' and a type of reconciliation 'that allows the sin of injustice and oppression to continue [which] is a false peace and counterfeit reconciliation'. The document also rejects an absolutised notion of reconciliation which 'must be applied in all cases of conflict and dissension', even in 'conflicts that can be described as the struggle between justice and injustice, good and evil, God and the devil' (Kairos Theologians 1986, 9–10). However, not all black theologians have given it unqualified endorsement, and its view of reconciliation has been criticised for 'erroneously admitting [to] a division between reconciliation and liberation ... [and for adopting] a ruling class definition of reconciliation as the harmonisation of attitude between persons, especially blacks and whites' (Mosala 1987, 23). Another cause for concern has been its utter silence on black and African theologies. Mosala (1995, 81) expresses anger at 'the fact that this potentially empowering document was careful not to mention the word "black" once – despite its Sowetan origins'.

Fifthly, though fairly recent and rather frail, reconciliation has been discussed against the framework of gender issues as reconciliation between men and women (cf. Maluleke 1997c).

Finally, borrowing from the Marxist notion of alienation, some black theologians have sought to transcend both race-bound and people-bound reconciliation:

> Reconciliation must have something to do with the reversal of our alienation; and our alienation is not alienation from white people first and foremost. Our alienation is from our land, our cattle, our labour which is objectified in industrial machines and technological instrumentation. Our reconciliation with white people will follow from our reconciliation with our fundamental means of livelihood (Mosala 1987, 22).

Viewing alienation from 'means of livelihood' rather than alienation from white people as being the primary 'ailment' from which blacks need to be 'cured', this view of reconciliation extends to and includes the need to be reconciled to black history, culture and religious traditions.

Hearing the silences and seeing the absences

Its shortcomings notwithstanding, the advent of the TRC has opened up some space for serious discussion of 'truth' and 'reconciliation' in South Africa. While there is a growing literature on its work among white journalists and academics – especially in-depth, book-length reflections (e.g. Krog 1998a; Hay 1998; Nuttall & Coetzee 1998; Pauw 1997; Boraine, Levy and Scheffer 1994; Boraine and Levy 1995) – solid, extensive and critical commentary by black thinkers has been scarce. By 'critical' I do not mean a negative oppositional regard, either for the ideal of national reconciliation or the instruments currently in place to promote that ideal. Of this kind of reconciliation discourse there is no lack in South African newspapers. I speak rather of a lack of probing, structured analyses of the processes through which the ideal of national reconciliation is being promoted or hampered.

Failure to recognise the pregnancy of the absence or silence of black voices with respect to the TRC will lead to a situation where an ostensibly 'one-sided' and circuitous discourse is (inadvertently) 'blessed' as an authentic starting point for all (further) discussion on reconciliation. The absence and silence of blacks in both the TRC discussions and discourse about national reconciliation is an eloquent absence–presence. It is an absence and a silence that 'speaks', illustrating not only the marginalised positions of blacks, but especially the grinding and continued marginalisation of black women.

Given the rhetoric, status, stature, personalities and symbols involved and invoked in reconciliation discourse (see Maluleke 1997a), it is possible to either disregard the significance of the absence–silence of blacks or perhaps simply not to notice it. Has not space been made for victims to tell their stories? And who are the symbols of the reconciliation rhetoric if not the very 'champions of the oppressed', such as Nelson Mandela and Desmond Tutu? On top of all that, all the 'right words' are being used in reconciliation discourse. Who in their right mind would oppose the pursuit of national reconciliation? Is 'national reconciliation' not the best deal for the poor? Is reconciliation not a central concept in most if not all religions? Yet the debate largely excludes blacks (especially black women), the poor and the marginalised.

Problems in critical discussion of the TRC

Almost all those who oppose the TRC benefited from apartheid. It is interesting to note that most of the victims, black and white, have largely been supportive of the TRC process (Tutu 1997).

Several problems bedevil critical discussion of the reconciliation process in South Africa. The first is the tendency to confuse the ideal of and the process towards reconciliation with the competencies and successes (or lack thereof) of certain instruments set up to promote national reconciliation, most overtly the TRC. While claiming that the TRC should not be regarded as, nor allowed to become, the 'owner' of reconciliation, I am not thereby suggesting that its immense influence in reconciliation discourse can or should be wished away simply by means of verbal protest. Sometimes what appears as serious debate around the issues of reconciliation, its cost and its implication in South Africa tends to be little more than a debate between TRC supporters and its detractors – lending support to the idea that this small, temporary and ambiguous body is the be-all and end-all of reconciliation in the country.

Mahmood Mamdani, in a public discussion in March 1998,[2] suggested that the TRC was being both legally and wilfully narrow in its investigation of apartheid as a crime against humanity (cf. Maluleke 1997a), and that it was thereby missing a unique opportunity to initiate a radic debate around issues of reconciliation and justice in broader terms than those suggested in the Promotion of National Unity Act. In his reply to Mamdani, Charles Villa-Vicencio, head of the TRC's Research Department, referred to the 'very narrow' though not 'insignificant' task of the TRC. While acknowledging the need, Villa-Vicencio was unconvinced that it was the duty of the TRC to become involved in promoting such a debate because it 'was given a specific task to do'. But it is the apparently 'exterior' matters which are so central to what the TRC is trying to achieve. At stake here is not the sheer image, performance and conduct of the TRC as an instrument but the ideals with which it is bound to dabble. Its focus has not prevented some of its supporters and staff members from assigning it superlatively positive, grand-narrative significance and implications. Note this not-so-subtle praise-song for the TRC and its grand implications for national healing from none other than its charismatic chairperson, Desmond Tutu:

> This is a crazy country; if miracles had to happen anywhere, then it's here that they would have to happen. No other country has been prayed for as much as this one. You remember the white woman victim of the APLA attack on the King William's Town golf course? She was so badly injured, her children had to teach her to do things we take for granted. She still can't go through the security check points at airports because she has shrapnel. She said, 'I would like to meet the perpetrator in a spirit of forgiveness.' That's wonderful. She goes on, 'I would like to forgive him', and then quite incredibly she adds, 'and I hope he will forgive me.' Crazy. Or the Afrikaner father whose toddler son was killed in the ANC Amanzimtoti Wimpy Bar bomb attack. He said he believed his son had contributed to the coming of the new dispensation. Or the Afrikaner woman in Klerksdorp who testified about the abduction of her husband by liberation army operatives, who spoke about how her grief and loss were just a drop in the ocean in comparison to what other people have suffered in this beautiful traumatised land. Or the daughter of the Cradock Four after hearing all the gruesome details of how her father had been killed, who said in a hushed East London City Hall, 'We would like to forgive, we just want to know whom to forgive.' . . . Who couldn't be moved by such exchanges? Who would doubt that a significant contribution was being made to healing, to reconciliation? (Tutu 1997)

According to Tutu, the TRC is at the helm of a grand miracle. And there is nothing 'narrow' about it. The carefully selected events which

Tutu catalogues are presented not as isolated, 'local', individual cases, but as exemplifying a miracle which is 'sweeping the nation', as it were. Others have joined Tutu in granting these healing powers to the TRC (cf. Botman 1996; Hay 1998, 59f.).

The confusion of the temporary commission called the TRC with the ideal and the process of reconciliation can be, and often is, done both by those who 'worship' it and by those critics who nevertheless retain a belief – however subtle or unconscious – that the current TRC, with few nudges and adjustments here and there, ought to be capable of producing a grand-narrative of reconciliation for the benefit of all. The dishonesty and error of the former groups is that, while they hold that the TRC can, has and will unleash a 'big story' of truth and reconciliation, they foreclose any seriously critical discussion of that story by appealing to the narrow and contingent nature of the tasks of the TRC. Tutu (1997) reminds those who 'have made it their business to denigrate, vilify, ridicule and misrepresent the TRC and its work' that 'the TRC is required not to achieve unity and reconcile our nation – it is required to promote, to contribute to it'.

Most of the time such appeals to the 'narrowness' of the TRC's brief are rhetorical strategies in the perceived onslaught on the TRC by its so-called 'detractors'. 'What have our detractors done to contribute to reconciliation? Absolutely nothing,' declares Tutu (1997) almost triumphalistically. What is denied is not the wider significance of the TRC but rather an open and critical debate about what that significance ought to be beyond the confines of its life and competencies. All the while, its hegemony and monopoly as the manufacturer of both reconciliation and reconciliation-discourse are being asserted. This must at least be challenged, if not altogether dismantled. The TRC is not synonymous with 'truth and national reconciliation', but is one small instrument, among many (possible) others, aimed at promoting these ideals. What is more, it is a flawed instrument, some of whose shortcomings are given while others are self-created.

Only an honest recognition of these flaws will initiate, for Mamdani, a 'reframing of the social debate so as to bring to the surface, to bring to light the truth the TRC has obscured; a commission which would put centre-stage the experience of apartheid as a banal reality: the reality of Pass Laws, forced removals, Bantu education, the reality of racialised poverty alongside racialised wealth – both undeserved, equally'. Sheer cheering or rebuking, however 'loud', will not cause the current TRC to deliver. Only a hard-nosed look at its genesis, competencies and performances can initiate a valid search for reconciliation.

It needs no statistical ingenuity to assume that the majority of the victims who have testified before the TRC have been black, many of these being women (cf. Ross 1996). This is not to suggest that only blacks are victims; rather, that blacks (and in particular black women) form the majority of the victims and that this is not an accident of history. Therefore their absence–silence in TRC discourse – where meaning is sought and assigned to events in which blacks were largely at the receiving end – is highly significant.

Current reconciliation discourse as a silencing mechanism

Not only are certain voices absent from current reconciliation discourse but the very project of national reconciliation in all its manifestations could in itself risk functioning

> . . . as a silencing and censoring discourse. This devalues the experiences of the thousands who have been forcibly uprooted from their homes, displaced into hostile environments which could not sustain life, forced to carry passes, as well as those who endured torture and human rights violations in the name of legitimate opposition to that system (Grunebaum-Ralph).

A crucial point is being made here, namely, that the absence–silence of the black and the poor are not matters merely and only external to the truth and reconciliation process. The process may itself be part of the silencing process. In this way, and without timely intervention, reconciliation discourse as it is being conducted may have the silencing of the poor, the black and the victimised either as an aim or as a wilful implication. Grunebaum-Ralph also warns that the manner in which the notions of reconciliation and healing are privileged and foregrounded over and above notions of justice, culpability and restitution tends to (and is meant to) obscure and minimise the differences between the victimised on the one hand and the perpetrators and beneficiaries on the other. Unless care is taken, reconciliation can (if it has not already) become 'a fetishised discourse, a claim, a right, which devalues the experience of those who have been wronged' so that all are regarded as being equally victimised. A statement made during the aforementioned public debate by commissioner Wynand Malan, who was a politician during the apartheid era, echoes this very distorted view:

> Trying to posit perpetrators versus victims in this country is an over-simplification which simply does not reach the reality of the totality. South Africa does not consist of only perpetrators and victims. There has been a debate and I made this note before some of the observations here; there is an effort to extend it in a sense,

> to look at victims versus beneficiaries, but again it's by definition the seeking for a more simple or simplex understanding of the problem. I refuse to be put into a box. I am both perpetrator and victim, I am both beneficiary and victim in different ways and I think that goes for the majority of people when we talk about the subject matter of the Truth Commission.

Something in the basic assumptions of the current TRC makes it possible for everyone in South Africa to consider themselves victim, beneficiary and perpetrator all at the same time. While on the surface it would appear that this great equalisation should facilitate healing, since everybody is everything (victim, perpetrator and beneficiary), the truth is that while some beneficiaries and perpetrators (especially in the white community) have much to show for their status, many others (especially in the black community) have little. Herein lies perhaps a severe shortcoming of the (Nuremberg- and Latin American-inspired) victim–perpetrator model which has been adopted for the South African TRC. However, even within this model it is still possible to question the morality and practicality of the great equalisation. Thus 'the TRC invites beneficiaries to join victims in a public outrage against perpetrators. "If only we had known we would have acted differently. Our trust has been violated, betrayed." So beneficiaries too are presented as victims' (Mamdani 1996). The equation of beneficiaries and perpetrators with victims, and vice versa, is a great sleight of hand, effectively displacing and silencing the claims of the black and the poor by refusing even to acknowledge their existence, let alone their significance:

> What is displaced is the acknowledgement that survivors and victims of trauma very often do not heal or that the healing involves processes that exclude the possibilities of reconciliation: that reconciliation is a choice and the sole prerogative of the victimised with all the conditions of remorse, material reparation or even social exclusion that it may require, and this remains in the domain of the victimised. As a beneficiary of that system I need to reconcile to this truth: that I have a moral obligation to acknowledge the criminality of apartheid, not in its aberrations or its excesses, but in its banality and in our complicity with that digestible banality to acknowledge the right of the victimised not to reconcile. So perhaps we need to explore the notion of reconciliation in other terms, becoming reconciled to the notion that healing and forgiveness can never be on the terms of the beneficiary or the perpetrator, nor should they be. We have no moral claim on the victimised (Grunebaum-Ralph).

Grunebaum-Ralph's observation that the victimised have a right to refuse to be reconciled is crucial. Indications are that the choice of victimised people for or against reconciliation – at least as defined within the framework of the TRC – is being severely undermined, if it is recognised at all. One way in which this happens is through the repeated claims that the reason blacks have been silent and uncomplaining is that they are an amazing, forgiving lot with *ubuntu* (cf. Maluleke 1997a). But do poor black people have any real choice on the matter? What alternative do they have? To rise against Mandela, 'our reliable father', and Tutu, 'our naughty uncle, the one who carries all the family's emotional baggage, weeping for us when we grieve, dancing when we celebrate' (Gevisser 1996, 12)? Black people will rise up against the powers that be, though all indications are that this will happen only after the time of 'our father' and 'our uncle'.

It is an open secret that the reconciliation process as it is being conducted by the TRC, and indeed the TRC itself, are products of compromise (cf. Maluleke 1997a; Maluleke 1997b). This presents the need and possibility for the 'great equalisation'. But this is only a novel instance of an older silencing strategy. Once the struggle for liberation was abandoned in favour of a 'negotiated revolution' (Sparks 1994), poor blacks were left with little space for dissent. While the need for compromise is appreciated by all – including poor black people – as Mamdani points out, the necessity must not be made into a virtue. 'I am not opposed to the compromise,' he says, 'I am not opposed to the amnesty. What I am opposed to is turning the political compromise into a moral one, letting it become the boundary of truth telling.' When this compromise is granted a form of permanence and a moral high ground (whereas by definition compromises ought to be temporary and contextual), at that moment the 'marginalising [of] the victimhood of the majority' is effected. In this way the TRC 'stifles the social debate in the name of maintaining peace, or in the name of maintaining social peace. In the name of maintaining social peace it turns the political boundaries of a compromise into analytical boundaries of truth seeking, and by reinforcing the political compromise with a compromised truth it turns the political compromise into a moral compromise.' To the extent that the TRC process marginalises poor black voices, it partakes in the silencing process.

Confronting apartheid as a legalised crime

Most illustrative of the danger of extending the political compromise into a compromise of the truth and a compromised reconciliation discourse is the extremely narrow focus of the TRC within so-called 'gross violations of human rights'. Mamdani puts it this way:

> . . . the TRC has displayed a systematic lack of interest in the crime which was institutionalised as the law. It has been interested only in violations outside the law, in benefits which are corruptions, but not in the systematic benefit which was conferred on beneficiaries at the expense of the vast majority of people in this country. It is also a fact that most beneficiaries are not conscious that they are beneficiaries. Most beneficiaries believe they are not. They believe exactly as the TRC researchers do, that the beneficiaries of apartheid were only those who benefited through corruption, who were given privileged impartial treatment as businesses. I would have called every ministry before the TRC, and I would have asked them, 'Who did you supply electricity to and who didn't you supply electricity to? How much did you spend on education for the minority and how much on education for the majority? Where did you build the roads and where didn't you? Where did you build the houses and where didn't you?' This is the structural benefit which you do not choose, which you are born into; and this is the benefit they have systematically hidden from public view by defining benefit in [such] a way that very few seem to have benefited.

This statement aptly identifies the extent to which current reconciliation discourse excludes both the discussion and investigation of the most crucial and most widespread aspects and effects of the apartheid regime. Instead, some veneer of legality is forced upon the apartheid system when and as the TRC seeks out the illegal activities of perpetrators – to be precise, those illegal activities which can be proved to have been political in motivation. Apart from minimising the role of systems and institutions in the apartheid crime against humanity, this approach also reduces the apartheid evil to the acts of its worst perpetrators as well as forcing an artificial 'equality' between beneficiaries and the victimised. Confining reconciliation discourse within the framework of both the Promotion of National Unity Act and the way in which the TRC has so far interpreted this law is therefore severely limiting. It is for this reason that observers such as Mamdani have suggested (though I wish he had made the following suggestion in less tongue-in-cheek terms) that only a different commission from the present one would deliver what South Africa needs:

> The way out, I think, would require a different commission. It would require a commission committed to re-framing the social debate so as to bring to the surface, to bring to light the truth the TRC has obscured; a commission which would put centre-stage the experience of apartheid as a banal reality: the reality of Pass

> Laws, forced removals, Bantu education, the reality of racialised poverty alongside racialised wealth – both undeserved, equally ... It would be a commission whose purpose would be to teach beneficiaries not only of the abuses for which they bear no personal responsibility but also of the structural injustice of which they have been direct beneficiaries, and therefore bear direct responsibility to redress. And it would be a commission which would now forefront the question of justice, not as criminal but as a social justice, as the only morally acceptable way of living with a morally unacceptable truth.

Despite making this radical critique of the current TRC's operational framework, Mamdani appears to harbour a belief that the TRC could have brought the truth to surface and that it has wilfully missed 'the opportunity of framing a social debate'. He believes that

> the Act invites the Commission not only to explore the gross human rights violations but to explore the context, and I tell you context means linking the violations to that which is critical in explaining them. That to me means you are not only free but obliged to link power to privilege, racialised power to racialised privilege, perpetrator to beneficiary.

I think Mamdani is being too optimistic in suggesting that the current TRC on the basis of the legal and political scope given to it could 'frame a social debate' and explore the link between race, power and privilege. I do not think that the present TRC has enough scope or will to initiate these tasks. Its contributions to reconciliation or the lack thereof must be evaluated within the confines of a severely limited understanding of justice borne out of a political compromise.

The TRC phenomenon in global perspective

One of the bases on which the South African reconciliation process has been promoted has been its 'uniqueness' and 'exemplary' nature (cf. Maluleke 1997a) – at least in the eyes of its proponents:

> We are going to succeed. Why? Because God wants us to succeed for the sake of God's world. We will succeed in spite of ourselves, because we are such an unlikely bunch. Who could ever have thought we would ever be an example, except of awfulness? ... God wants to say to the world, to Bosnia, to Northern Ireland ... look at them. They had a nightmare called Apartheid. It has

> ended. Your nightmare too will end ... We are a beacon of hope for God's world and we will succeed (Tutu 1997).

Many have extolled the 'global significance' of TRC-type processes, often (though not in all cases) with the South African experiment taking pride of place (cf. Shriver 1995; Baum and Wells 1997; Bronkhorst 1995; Müller-Fahrenholz 1996; Schreiter 1992; Harper 1996). The myth that South Africa, through the TRC process, is pioneering previously uncharted territory needs, however, to be exploded in order to instil a sense of sobriety in South African truth and reconciliation discourse. The South African experiment is not unique in the world, and not even on the African continent. Ironically, the first African country to institute a TRC-type official commission of inquiry was Uganda under the rule of the infamous dictator Idi Amin (Bronkhorst 1995, 85), who went on to oversee the killing of even more people. While the appointment of a commission of inquiry may be part of a new government's purging of its predecessor, thereby hoping to enhance its own standing, it is no reliable indicator of a government's commitment to the protection of human rights.

Between 1971 and 1995, no less than thirty countries (including twelve in Africa) instituted TRC-type commissions of one kind or the other. Naturally, the terms of reference have differed from country to country and commission to commission. However, quality is not always the main or only indicator of difference between the commissions. While cautious in his assertions, Bronkhorst (1995, 69) 'suggests' by way of a rhetorical question that the South African TRC constitutes a significant 'step forward in international model-building'. Subtly underlying his historical review of TRC-type commissions is a progressivist view wherein later commissions are supposed to be better structured and prepared than earlier commissions. This kind of progressivism is precarious. Without the benefit of hindsight – which benefit we may have with regard to earlier commissions – we have no way of determining the 'quality' of later commissions, such as the South African one.

However, the basic point I want to make here is that the South African TRC process is part of thirty years' experimentation in an ever-growing number of countries in the world. Without seeking to take away from the distinctiveness and subsequent controversial nature of the African Charter on Human and People's Rights (cf. Mutua 1995), otherwise known as 'the Banjul Charter', these experiments must be seen against the background of the intensifying Euro-American human rights campaign within which the 'third' or 'developing' world has been caught. Ever since the Second World War, the 'third world' has been the ideological playground of the superpowers. Viewed from the perspective of the third world, the human rights campaign of this century, its positive contributions notwithstanding, was also caught up in the Cold War. The rise of TRC-type commissions all over the world may be directly linked to such campaigns. However, Mutua expresses dissatisfaction with their individualist and liberal democratic roots, which tend to pit the individual against the state and vice versa. 'The cultures and traditions of the world', he suggests, 'must, in effect, compare notes, negotiate positions, and come to agreement over what constitutes human rights' (Mutua 1995, 346). One of the unfortunate realities of TRC-type commissions in the third world has been a failure to interrogate the human rights framework upon which they have been based. Superimposing the notion of human rights upon apartheid, seeking out isolated and specific violations, can degenerate into a rescue operation for apartheid – if it has not done so already. More than just a feature of human rights campaigns, TRC-type commissions have also become a feature of the politics of the so-called 'new world order'. Without taking away from the immensely positive possibilities in attempts to make peace with the past, TRC-type commissions, like 'democracy', can easily degenerate into some of the 'requirements' expected of developing countries by so-called developed countries.

The prospects for black theological reflection on truth and reconciliation discourse in South Africa are vast and varied. I suggest that black absence–silence is the crucial point of departure for such reflection. Furthermore, black theology has at least four decades of black discussion and reflections on reconciliation to build on. Whereas Mamdani seems to think that the current TRC has missed the opportunity to frame a social debate about truth and reconciliation, I would suggest that the present TRC does not have the (political) will nor the legal and political space to initiate such a debate. We must therefore maintain a strict distinction between the TRC as an inadequate instrument on the one hand, and the ideal of reconciliation and truth-telling on the other. It is this ideal which we must probe and discuss fearlessly and radically – not allowing anyone (including the TRC) to 'father' or monopolise it. If we are agreed about both the fact and significance of black absence–silence, then it is not what happens in the official channels and instruments of reconciliation discourse in South Africa that matters. It is the silences and the absences that should arrest our attention.

4 The AICs and the TRC: Resistance Redefined

Robin M. Petersen

This is not the place to enter into the interminable terminological debates on naming. Let AIC suffice.[1] What is more important is the sometimes equally interminable debate about 'reading', a debate that this chapter must enter, as indeed does the TRC Faith Communities Report. How are the AICs to be read, to be understood, to be interpreted? Quite clearly, any analysis of the submissions of the AICs to the TRC must perforce undertake its own 'reading'. A warning, however: does not this very act of 'reading', of seeking to interpret from the outside, perpetuate the colonial gesture of appropriation and control that gave birth to the AICs in the first instance? These are the dangers, this is the challenge.

There is a long history to this 'reading' and it is a history that is not neutral. It is a history which the AICs themselves have contested, either directly or indirectly (mostly by a gesture of refusal, to which we will return).[2] It is clear from an investigation of scholarship on the AICs during the last three decades – much of which was done from within Afrikaner missiological circles – that much of the 'fascination' with them was linked to an (unconscious?) political agenda which saw in many of these churches a 'politically safe' black voice. Here, supposedly, was found not the radical and 'angry' face of black protest, black theology, black struggle, but the compliant, 'happy' and respectful black face of 'traditional African values' and respect for (government) authority. Clearly more subtle than the crass political parading of AIC leader Isaac Mokoena before the international media to denounce sanctions and attack Archbishop Tutu, this academic enterprise nevertheless often had similar intent and effect.[3]

But even within the circles of 'prophetic theology' and scholarship, readings of the AICs have by no means been unproblematic.[4] On the one hand, there has been the positive desire to affirm the AICs as the necessary starting point for any theological reflection which is contextual, which draws from black and African experience and which reflects the interests of the poor. On the other hand, the AICs have been reluctantly dismissed as being 'unreliable', 'apolitical' and even 'reactionary' and 'conservative'.

The leading black theologian Bonganjalo Goba provides, in his work on black theology and hermeneutics, perhaps the best example of this double, contradictory evaluation of the AICs. In the mid-1980s he wrote: 'The Black Independent Church movement represents the future of the black Christian community in South Africa out of which a relevant theology should emerge' (Goba 1988). On the previous page of his text, however, he had almost wistfully concluded,

> ... the Black Independent Church movement has become apolitical. The dynamic and often unreliable type of leadership characterised by internal conflicts relating to power makes it impossible for them to offer any significant political contribution. This would also be true of their theology, which is couched in a kind of supernaturalism which makes it difficult for them to interact creatively with their social environment or provide the kind of political direction which the black community needs at this time.

Within prophetic theology, three strategies for dealing with this problem of the double (positive and negative) evaluation emerged. The first was to dismiss the AICs as irrelevant and reactionary, in effect, therefore, undermining the credibility of the positive assessment. The second strategy was more common, and consisted in the sometimes disingenuous tactic of simply ignoring the challenge posed by the AICs, or even their existence altogether. While this had the same effect as the first strategy, it was somewhat less honest. The former strategy at least addressed the problem and chose a position. This second strategy simply did not address the problem at all. For instance, the original version of the *Kairos Document* contained not one reference to the AICs, reflecting perhaps both the composition of the authorship of the document, and, more significantly, the attitude that the AICs are simply to be ignored in the construction of a 'Challenge to the Church'.

The third strategy for dealing with this double evaluation had the appearance of taking the AICs very seriously, and was seen in the writings of Itumeleng Mosala who, more than any other of the black theologians, argued for the importance of the AICs for South African black theology (see Mosala 1985; Mosala 1989a; Mosala 1989b). Mosala situated his positive evaluation of the AICs within a rigorous class analysis of black culture and history. He deployed this class analysis of African society and a periodisation of African history around the changing forms of the means of production and the consequent conflicts within African society at both the political and ideological level. The Zion–Apostolic AICs emerged in his analysis not only as 'authentically black' and 'authentically African', but as 'authentically black working class'.

Having advanced this more nuanced assessment of the AICs, in particular of the Zion–Apostolics, Mosala nevertheless ended up undermining his positive assessment as he too attempted to address their perceived lack of political engagement. They might well be a church of the 'authentically black working class', but their politics, for Mosala, was certainly different from those of, for instance, the trade unions. He tried to resolve the conflict by arguing that the AICs represented a 'political potential', both in terms of their numbers and, more importantly, in terms of their structural position as the church of the working class and peasantry. But it was a potential that was inadequate, and needed 'interventionist structures, based externally in the parent culture of the black working class' for transformation to occur (Mosala 1989b, 17). In his analysis, therefore, the challenge the AICs posed to prophetic theology was important, but important only inasmuch as their 'potential' could be realised by means of dialogue, education, involvement, conscientisation and common action, so that they would no longer, in the rhetoric of class analysis, be simply a 'class in themselves' but become a class 'for themselves'. As such they would become involved in the racial and class struggle against oppression.

Mosala's 'reading' had many merits when compared with the first two. It purported to take the AICs very seriously, at least on the surface. But despite this, his argument was fundamentally flawed. It was premised on a disguised theological and intellectual imperialism which asserted, implicitly, that the AICs were important only as they became more like 'us', that is, only as they were transformed (often by 'our' pedagogical and strategic intervention), into a slightly more exotic clone of ourselves (the prophetic black church). In his reading, the AICs did indeed express, in their religious practices, their social structures, their teaching and their healing, an implicit criticism of domination. But this, according to Mosala, is inadequate. What was implicit must be made explicit. Dwight Hopkins, a black American analyst of the South African prophetic theology scene, expressed this attitude perfectly: 'Therefore, the question for the emergence of a South African black theology of political-cultural liberation is: how can the Independent Churches' efforts to dissociate from European culture be transformed into conscious steps against apartheid's white supremacist theology, policy and practice' (Hopkins 1989, 177).

These 'readings' are clearly inadequate. In my own work I have sought to find another, more adequate reading of the AICs from the perspective of a prophetic theology, one which neither ignores the AICs nor reduces them to the categories of prophetic theology. The contours of the reading involve a reconsideration of the notions of resistance, struggle and 'the political'. This involves breaking the peculiarly 'enlightenment cast' in which these terms are generally understood, a position that accords credence only to self-conscious and overt forms of resistance and struggle and ignores the force, power and intensely political nature of ritual practice and symbolic action in and of itself.

So much for the history of 'reading'. What is now necessary is a new 'reading', this time based on the testimonies and stories, the apologetics and apologies, of the AICs themselves in their presentations to the TRC. It goes without saying that those groups that did indeed testify cannot be assumed to be representative of all AICs. Their numbers are too great and their structures too diverse and disparate for any group to claim to represent them. Nevertheless, the submissions are important, embodying as they do the voices of two of the oldest and largest AICs in the country (the Ibandla lamaNazaretha and the Zion Christian Church), as well as that of some of the smaller yet influential groupings of AICs that are a part of the SACC, including the Council of African Instituted Churches (CAIC).

There are, indeed, significant differences in the three submissions. That of the latter grouping (the CAIC grouping) begins with asserting the links these churches have had with the SACC and other prophetic forces in the country. In particular they thank persons like Archbishop Tutu and Beyers Naudé for the support they have provided in the emergence and support of the CAIC. They also unequivocally confess that they did not do enough in the struggle against apartheid. As Archbishop Ntongana testified at the hearings: 'We ask forgiveness for not having fought in the struggle, for not having been beaten up, detained and killed ... We should have stood up for our people. We are cowards and we admit it. We are cowards because we did not stand up and fight.'

The submissions of the Ibandla lamaNazaretha and the Zion Christian Church (ZCC) are more alike, stressing as they do their commitment to strict moral codes and economic self-reliance, and only under examination addressing the question of the perceived lack of participation in 'the struggle'. They also emphasise the history of their respective churches and the constant attacks and misunderstandings that they have had to endure, from church and state.

What all the submissions force us to do, however, is to rethink notions of resistance and struggle. For the amaNazaretha and the ZCC in particular, their perceived lack of active resistance to apartheid is contested by them on a different terrain. They refuse to be trapped in a modernist logic that seeks to understand these terms solely within the framework of self-conscious political action. In answer to the probing on this point, they respond by contesting the categories in which the questions are posed. For instance, Immanuel Lothola, the ZCC spokesperson, is pushed on this point by TRC commissioner Mgojo. 'I would have liked to have heard about what programmes were those which your church was involved in, in fighting against apartheid.' Lothola replies: 'as a church, the Zion Christian Church did not lead people into a mode of resistance against apartheid. But as a church the ZCC taught its people to love themselves more than ever, to stand upright and face the future, to defy the laws of apartheid.' This, clearly, is not the language of political struggle as Mgojo understands it, but it is undoubtedly struggle language, a remapping and a remaking of the conceptual tools of resistance. 'Loving themselves' might seem facile in comparison to the heroic struggles of black political leaders, but it is, as Steve Biko, Frantz Fanon and others have reminded us, a revolutionary act of defiance against a system that is premised on inculcating a sense of black inferiority. Lothola goes on to state that the ZCC had not 'stood up and said let's go and fight the white government', and that this might be construed as an omission by some. But, he argues, 'we thought genuinely [that] we needed to teach our people to be able to stand upright and not to hurt others, but to refuse to be hurt by others'.

'Refusing to be hurt by others.' What a statement of profound resistance. For apartheid's intent (along with that of its colonial predecessors) was to colonise the hearts and minds of its black subjects, to make them believe that they were not fully human, not capable of full citizenship, that they were inferior and deserved their subjugation. To this domination, such a philosophy of self-love and self-reliance, of refusing to allow the dominator to 'hurt', is supremely resistant, albeit at another level to that of direct political action.

There are a number of places where this reconceptualisation is necessary for us to analyse properly what is at stake in the submissions. For purposes of the analysis, I have grouped these around various themes.

Speech and silence

Perhaps the most dramatic moment of the faith hearings occurred when Bishop Edward Lekganyane of the ZCC was asked to address the Commission. A reading of the transcript of the proceedings conveys much of the drama. Archbishop Tutu calls the Bishop to the stand. He introduces him as 'one of the outstanding leaders, religious leaders, in our country'. He acknowledges that the Bishop has 'significant influence on a very, very large section of the population', and states that this was demonstrated by the 'fact that a former State President has been to see you ... and other political leaders'. Given that his introduction is extempore, it is extremely interesting (and significant) that the Archbishop refers directly to the controversial visit by P. W. Botha to the ZCC Easter celebrations at Moria in the midst of the 1985 uprising and resistance, and refers to the more politically acceptable visits of Nelson Mandela and F. W. de Klerk in 1993 and 1994 as those of 'other political leaders'.[5]

Despite his graciousness and praise of the Bishop, therefore, it is clear that Tutu wants to hear some explanation for this political act (symbolic, perhaps, of so many other understandings and critiques of the ZCC). His next few sentences indicate that he is aware that he is treading on extremely thin ice, wanting to affirm the Bishop, but also wanting to hear how he will explain this and other politically sensitive issues:

> We are looking forward to hearing from you the submission that you are going to be making to the TRC as we look to what happened in the past [Botha's visit?] and in what manner you may have suffered [is this going to be the justification?] and what contributions you believe you may be wanting to make, or able to make to the healing and reconciliation of this beautiful country we all love so much. Thank you, Ndade.

One can picture the Archbishop, whose moral authority in the proceedings to this date has been universally acknowledged, leaning forward in anticipation to hear the Bishop speak, perhaps for the first time. And then, the drama. Two others take the stand, and the Bishop remains seated, smiling benignly and not saying a word. Tutu is taken aback: 'Is it Bishop Lekganyane who is going to testify, or are you going to do so? Just switch on – now I'm not quite certain. Bishop, are you going to say anything?'

Tutu is thrown. He sounds almost desperate, pleading. The ZCC representative, Immanuel Lothola, takes the microphone and states that the Church Council has decided that he, Lothola, is to make the submission. Tutu attempts to recover: 'Yes, your council is free to determine how you want to do this ... but if at the end of this we are asking questions, is the Bishop going to reply?'

Now verbatim:

> Lothola: Chairperson, the speaker Thomas Mahope will reply to the questions.
>
> Tutu (desperate now): Only he?
>
> Lothola: I will reply to the questions as part of this panel.

> Tutu: We want to know who, you see, if it is the two of you are going to be spokespersons?
> Lothola: That is correct, yes.
> Tutu (really desperate now): Now I don't know, some of your congregation are here. I don't know whether they will be happy to go away without hearing a word from their leader.
> Lothola: Chairperson, thanks for your concern, but that has already been addressed, the congregation is aware of the situation and I can assure this commission that they are more than happy.
> Tutu (game, set, match): Yes, all right, I wish I had such a congregation. Thank you very much and will the two of you then please stand.

The power of silence. In a commission constituted by words (submissions and testimonies), it is silence that is ultimately the most dramatic. It unsettles and disconcerts even the usually unflappable Tutu. It is a gesture of refusal which frames the testimony of the ZCC in a powerful way. It is a statement which says, 'I will not be reduced to your categories, even to your language. I do not have to justify myself to you in your terms.' It is an act of resistance, of 'independency' at its most dramatic.

Speech and silence also frame the other two AIC submissions. Mr Mpanza of the amaNazaretha states that 'Even though my speech is prepared in English I will speak in Zulu, because most of my congregation consists of people who cannot speak English.' There is a double gesture in this: 'We are able to do things on your terms, but we choose not to.' Ntongana of CAIC tropes another refusal: 'My ancestors, my clan, refused that I write down a submission.' Not only is resistance asserted in the present, but the invocation points beyond to another authority, one equally resistant – the ancestors.

Speech as resistance is also seen in another form, that of the mystical destabilisation of power through prayer. Mpanza argues that Shembe taught his people to respect the authorities, 'but promised that through our constant prayer and supplication to God, one day God will answer our prayers'. He then elaborates on how this becomes a form of resistance and struggle:

> In 1920 [Shembe] composed a Sabbath liturgy, which he instructed the Nazarites that it would be read before God three times every Sabbath day from generation to generation. In the introduction of the liturgy he wrote that it is the hymn of the Sabbath, the hymn of remembrance from generation to generation and the hymn of fasting in order to remind God of our suffering. Isaiah Shembe also taught that the Nazarite must lead a simple life and

> that every year they must walk on foot to Mt. Nhlangakazi, to worship God and report all their suffering. So, for amaNazaretha, whenever they were confronted by the government, or other missionary churches, all they had to do was to ask the congregation to kneel down and have Isiguqa, which is a special prayer to God.

Sites and locations

It is not only speech and silence that shapes resistance in a different key. It is also the interplay of space and place. The space of the AICs is that of the margins. As Michel de Certeau (1984) has argued, the ability to mount overt struggle implies possession of a secure place from which to mount a strategic offensive. This is the mode of struggle usually understood within the discourse of prophetic theologies. De Certeau draws a distinction, however, between this stable place of strategy, of overt struggle, and the more marginal, fluid space of tactic, that hidden, mobile foray of 'thrust and riposte' utilised by those who do not possess 'place'. Tactical resistance is the only possible mode of resistance for those who inhabit the margins. It is the mode of resistance of the poor, the marginal; the 'weapons of the weak', as James Scott (1985) calls them. It utilises the 'cunning logic' of struggle, which is able to turn the trick on the powerful at the moment, at the *kairos*.

Given De Certeau's analysis, it is interesting but not surprising that all the submissions emphasise this positional marginality: 'we are . . . a group of small churches under the bridges of our country, under the trees of our country, in the dining rooms, in the sitting rooms' (Molisiwa, CAIC); 'it therefore came to pass that the Nazarites developed a culture of worshipping God whilst seated under the trees and calling people to the church service by shouting loudly' (Mpanza, amaNazaretha). It is from the margins, therefore, that resistance is shaped as tactic, as the creating of space to be human, to construct a communitas in the face of devastating destruction and oppression. It is resistance that in the face of a system determined to squeeze the humanity out its victims, refuses to accede to the logic of domination.

Simplicity and self-reliance

'The secret lies in its simplicity' (Mpanza, amaNazaretha).
'There is no secret at all. It is the basic teaching of pride in our people, self-reliance to appreciate that their future lies in their hands' (Lothola, ZCC).

Simplicity and self-reliance: hardly notions of extraordinary moment. But in a context marked by the market, shaped by the incessant production of consumptive desire through the commodification and reification of life under the domination of capital, and constituted by the extension of its capillaries of power in the making and shaping of the construction of the self as consumer and as dominated object, simplicity is a resistant moment.

The solid core of this simplicity is seen in the moral codes which mark the AICs as different. For the amaNazaretha, the code is linked by Mpanza to the simplicity of life, and includes prohibitions on alcohol, smoking of any kind, pre-marital sexual intercourse and the use of medicine for healing. These restrictions, he notes, should make them 'very popular' with the Health Minister, Nkosazana Zuma. (I am not so sure about this!) The ZCC echoes this code, but significantly adds the notion of 'peace'. The consequence of this personal ethic is immediate: 'the amaNazaretha are among the most hardworking, trustworthy and reliable people in the black society.' The goal of the church is to 'promote decency, hard work, and self-reliance in developing our country'.

It was Max Weber who noted the connection between a deep sense of personal morality and what he called the 'Protestant work ethic'. It has rarely, however, been stated as eloquently as it was in these hearings, by both the amaNazaretha and the ZCC. Again, is this resistance or is it simply functional to the forces and powers of capital and the emergence of a black bourgeoisie? In the 1980s the latter might have been the common understanding. In the 1990s, it suddenly has become the discourse of liberation. Of course, it could be argued that the 1980s simply got it wrong, that it reduced everything to overt and highly self-conscious political action. Another reading might look through the lens of a reclaimed understanding of the black consciousness philosophy of Steve Biko. In fact, developing self-reliance and independence through disciplined hard work could be seen as the most resistant act of struggle against white domination.

The payoff of this ethic of simplicity and self-reliance comes in the creation of economic independence. As Lothola puts it, the secret of its ability to sustain itself lies in the

> basic teaching of pride in our people, self-reliance to appreciate that their future lies in their hands. That if we want to start a project, we are not ... going to have a God dropping a Calvin Klein from heaven to us on earth, we've got to stand up and work and I can tell you Archbishop Tutu and the panel, or all these people who are listening here, the Zion Christian Church raises funds from its own people and nothing else . . . This bursary fund we are talking about which spends R2 million per annum to educate African children comes from these people who sweep the floors,

comes from these people who dig manholes, come from these people who paint walls in the suburbs (Lothola, ZCC).

Culture and theology

A fourth site of resistance and reconstruction in the submissions can be seen in the arguments that are made by the various AIC presentations concerning the issues of culture and theology. These can be seen clustering around a number of themes.

Firstly, there is the issue of tradition and authority. As H. Richard Niebuhr (1951) has pointed out in his classic text on the relation between Christ and culture, at stake in this relationship is the question of authority. Is authority ultimately derived from Scripture (Christ against culture), or culture (Christ of culture), or is there some dual authority that structures the relationship more dialectically or dialogically (the various combinations of Christ above culture)? The submissions of both the ZCC and the amaNazaretha situate their understandings of this issue in the context of a discourse of resistance. It is resistance to the domination of Western culture, signified primarily in resistance to 'the missionaries': 'when the missionaries came from overseas, trying to change and trying to force the people to abandon their culture and tradition, . . . we resisted. Instead we continued to worship God using our own culture and tradition' (Mpanza, amaNazaretha). And

> Bishop Agnus Barnabas Lekganyane had by then (1910) become acutely aware of the attempt by missionaries to erode African value systems and cultural beliefs. He realised that unless Christianity was interpreted in a context suitable to the African lifestyle, cultural and political development, Africans would, in due course, find themselves as a nation alienated from its roots, rich history and religious foundation (Lothola, ZCC).

Cultural resistance, as Amilcar Cabral has argued, is crucial in the contesting of identity and domination. From the submissions, this is stated with great force and tremendous insight. Given contemporary debates around inculturation and contextualisation of Christianity, the ZCC submission points to its local origins in the AICs. As the ZCC submission puts it: 'we believe that we have got a specific missionary work to preserve what we guard closely as what belongs to us Africans.'

In Niebuhr's typology, it would be, however, simplistic and quite incorrect to see this mode of inculturation simply as a radical synthesis of Christ and African culture. The issue is far more complex. Both submissions indicate that at crucial points, the founding prophets of the two churches departed significantly from African cultural traditions. After a restatement of the sensitivity of the ZCC to African culture, seen in their reaffirmation of the 'African chieftaincy', the submission states that 'From the beginning, our church viewed habits such as drinking liquor, smoking tobacco or dagga and violence as against the gospel of Christ' (Lothola, ZCC). Mpanza of the amaNazaretha likewise states that they follow such a code of practice but adds, perceptively, 'albeit they [smoking and beer drinking] are part of African tradition'. Likewise he argues that Shembe outlawed 'the use of medicine as a form of healing' (resistance to Western domination) and 'the practice of divination or sorcery, the use of mediums or spirits, although these form part of African traditions'. Why? 'For such practices are repugnant to biblical teachings.'

Here the locus of authority sways towards biblical teachings. But immediately Mpanza states that Shembe allowed polygamy, and, when 'confronted by Christians', appealed to a different authority, that of his own calling and personal revelation: 'I was not sent by man, but by God and God did not tell me of a sin called polygamy. Those who sin are the ones who divorce and thereafter take another wife.' Mpanza states this dual authority directly: 'Although amaNazaretha use the Bible in their teachings, Isaiah Shembe as a prophet did not regard the Bible as his sole authority of his teachings, but as a reference to his main authority, which is God . . . the Bible was there to support and confirm his authority.' Likewise, however, the divine authority also allows Shembe to challenge and confront African tradition: 'whilst traditional religions based their teachings on 'Izwelabantu' which is the voice of the people, Ibandla lamaNazaretha bases its teaching on "IzweleZulu," which is the voice of heaven which came to the prophet.'

This stress on the ability of the church to reach the heart of the people, located as it is within the fabric of African life and culture, and embodying its code of discipline and self-reliance has, Mpanza argues, significant power to transform peoples lives in the face of the tensions and traumas of modernity, on the one hand, and retrogressive traditional responses, on the other:

> In KwaZulu-Natal and Gauteng, where the Nazareths are in big numbers, this church has converted many hostel dwellers, thus able to unite the most . . . sophisticated township people with the rural people. Because the church addressed the hearts of the people, I have seen many warlords not throwing away their sticks but changing their sticks into staffs, and using these staffs for healing instead of beating. The shields used for fighting are then used for dancing for the Lord. The war cry is then changed into praise of the Almighty.

Quite clearly, if it is possible to squeeze these churches into Niebuhr's mould, it would best be situated in the 'Christ the transformer of culture' position, which takes culture with intense seriousness and yet establishes a critical and ultimately transforming position in respect of it.

There is one final issue that connotes an understanding of AIC theology as resistance, and that is the incipient black theology expressed in the early Lekganyane's statement that God, for black people, is black. Some fifty years after Lekganyane, this rethinking of the 'colour of God' caused much theological controversy, as a profound statement of theological resistance to the domination of 'white' theology.

Conclusion

'Reading', as I ventured earlier on, is a hazardous, politically laden enterprise. It is not, and can never be, neutral. What makes the TRC faith community hearings important in terms of the AICs is that it is one of the few occasions where they do, indeed, speak for themselves. I have in this chapter problematised the terms in which the debate concerning resistance is generally construed. I do so because this is precisely what the AICs in their presentations do as well. There is in their submissions little or no defence of their actions or inaction. As I have already pointed out, it is only under questioning that they respond to these concerns. But they do so in a manner which rejects the simple either/or of involvement in the struggle, or the lack of it, in which the question is generally cast. They instead turn the question on its head, and demonstrate that their teachings, practices and engagement were in fact profoundly resistant to the domination of not only apartheid, but the ideology of white superiority, which is the bedrock underlying the racism of both colonialism and apartheid.

Finally, in a contemporary political and social climate where the most intense political debates revolve around the notions of African Renaissance and the renewal of the moral fibre of the nation, it is clear that the AICs should move from the margins of 'struggle discourse' to its centre. Whether this occurs, of course, is yet to be seen. The dismissive attitudes of most of the so-called 'mainline' churches, the lurking vestiges of white fear against such visible assertions of black independence and self-reliance, and the lingering suspicions of past inactivity or active complicity with the apartheid structures among certain black church leaders, all conspire to marginalise the AICs from the 'mainstream'. Their own 'stubborn' refusal to enter dialogue and even alliance with these mainstream structures certainly contributes to the problem. But while the former attitudes prevail, it is unlikely that the latter will change. Quite simply, the mainline churches need the AICs more than the AICs need the recognition and acknowledgement of the churches.

5 The Offender and the Church

H. Russel Botman

> The society and the religious or ideological community or cultural group which has contributed towards shaping the mind of the offender shares in the responsibility of the offence and is in need of repentance on its part and forgiveness on the part of God and the victims with the view to facilitating a process of healing and taking precautions against a repetition of the offence. (Kistner 1994, 16).

One of the great ethical dangers of South Africa's process of reconciliation is that it may leave us with the impression that the atrocities of apartheid were the deeds of 'the disturbed few'. The most crucial acts, however, were done in public, and under the approving eyes of many Christians in the Afrikaans- and English-speaking churches. Perpetrators were also members of these communities. But the TRC faith hearings did not adequately explore the way the consciousness of the perpetrators was shaped therein.

The law which gave rise to the TRC defined the perpetrator as an individual who has committed (a) human rights violations, (b) of gross dimensions and (c) with a political motive. The perpetrator could qualify for amnesty should he or she make full disclosure of gross human rights violations with a political motive for which they were responsible. The focus was, therefore, on the human rights violator, the extent of the violation and the motive. Duties and obligations to political parties or liberation movements took centre-stage in so far as the violator was concerned. And so people could argue that they received orders and acted honourably as functionaries of their superiors.

Although violators must indeed be held politically and individually responsible for their dastardly acts, the faith communities which formed the perpetrators' minds must also be helped to come to terms with their part in the offences. As the testimony of Craig Williamson in his amnesty hearing in September 1998 made clear, even perpetrators of the violence of apartheid seem to need the recognition that communities have also contributed to the formation of their minds. While accepting their own responsibility, they also speak of a broader frame for responsibility. Kistner, in the quote above, seems to suggest that the religious community played a part in this broader frame.

This essay takes the example of the Dutch Reformed Church (DRC), exploring ways in which that church played a formative role in shaping the mind of perpetrators, using the idea of 'desirability choices'. It critiques the 'dispositional ethic' characterising the DRC's appearance before the TRC, calling on the DRC to embrace an ethic of responsibility.

Forming common values in the DRC[1]

Communities form values. These values take the form of norms. But they are also understood as choices for what is 'desirable'. These choices are often informed by class struggles (as proposed by Marxist philosophy), motivated by needs (as proposed in Maslovian psychology) and subjected to race and/or gender ideologies (as proposed by cultural theorists). The DRC has made a choice for the value of 'separateness', which has become its norm. This orientation was based on contextually experienced desirability. The famous decision of the synod in 1857 to exclude non-whites from communion created a situational orientation based on a value choice for the desirable. The word 'desirable' is, in the text of the initial decision, in favour of church apartheid.[2]

The importance of the 1857 decision emerges when one considers that issues of integration and segregation were debated in churches long before they actually emerged in political institutions. Gerstner (1997, 25–29) shows that Christian status and European descent were identified in the minds of the people of the seventeenth-century Cape Colony, with the term 'Christian' used to denote an ethnic identity. 'Christian' became a synonym for 'settler'. The sacraments were also essential to the construction of this ethnic identity, with the celebration of communion instrumental in forging ties among settlers. While their home worship provided the focus of their piety, their group identity was forged in this experience of taking the sacraments. Khoisan converts were not included in communion until the nineteenth century. Christians identified the black peoples of South Africa as 'heathens'. The term 'heathen' thus also denoted a racial as well as a religious category.

In 1831, a DRC congregation was founded among the Khoikhoi people near Grahamstown. Some white congregants who had joined the church after moving to the area then petitioned the local church council asking for the separate celebration of communion. Now we come to the 1857 synod:

> The Synod considers it desirable and according to the Holy Scripture that our heathen members be accepted and initiated into our congregations wherever it is possible; but where this measure, as a result of the weakness of some, would stand in the way of promoting the work of Christ among the heathen people, then congregations set up among the heathen or still to be set up, should enjoy their Christian privileges in a separate building or institution (Translation by Loff 1983, 17–19).

In this decision, the DRC affirmed first that what is scriptural is more desirable: the unity of the races in one religious institution. However, this biblical position would no longer serve as the ultimate orientation of the church because of the 'weaknesses of some'. The reference to the 'weakness of some' is a metaphor for the attitude of over-againstness and the value of separateness among the majority of members. The majority of the Afrikaner people as members of the DRC had, then, successfully internalised separateness as their personal and tribal core value.

Although the formal missionary policy of the DRC only came into being in 1935, the value choice of 1857 established the institutional framework and the official value pattern by which the policy of separate development was delivered. Driven by the value of separateness the DRC could make the following claim in 1948, the year of the election of the apartheid government: 'As a church, we have always worked purposefully for the separation of the races' (*Kerkbode,* 22 September 1948).

The DRC has, therefore, shaped minds with a powerful value of separateness and a parallel value of over-againstness among whites in relation to blacks in South Africa. They have further strengthened this value-orientation by institutionalising and developing a tradition of separateness. Its embodiment arises from participation in the practices of apartheid. Through such practices, members of the church experienced the goods internal and external to separateness and over-againstness. Over a period of time, a 'common sense' of apartheid was developed which contributed to the formation of the mind of the perpetrator.

In its introductory remarks, the DRC's most recent policy document, *Church and Society* (1990), confirms the issue of racial difference as the main contextual problem for the DRC. According to this document, 'the unique composition of the South African society out of different groups and peoples and a variety of languages and cultures' is the essential social problem. The DRC can therefore claim that, 'knowing what has been done in this respect in the past, however faulty and full of shortcomings it may have been, [it] is nevertheless convinced that everything was not without significance, but was of service to the kingdom of God' (DRC 1990, par. 3). This positive evaluation is based on the false belief that separateness would promote 'the work of Christ among the heathen people'. This central historical problem 'places the church of Jesus Christ before great and exceptional challenges concerning the kingdom of God' (DRC 1990, par. 1). This concrete problem was and remains the historical *kairos* for the DRC as perceived through their experience. To their mind it is therefore 'unreasonable to brand as wrong and bad everything which took place within the political structure of apartheid' (DRC 1990, par. 208). This remains the official position of the DRC.

Martin Marty (1981, 33) suggests that a church can be captive to the value of separateness, which leads to 'pluralistic ignorance'. This, in turn, gives rise to psychological 'patterns of constriction' that reinforce boundaries instead of breaching the walls of separation. The value of separateness ultimately leads to 'dismemberment', with some members developing 'wholeness hunger' (Marty 1981, 28). The presentation at the TRC faith community hearings by the Rev. Freek Swanepoel, Moderator of the DRC, says more about him than about the church he represented. He has a 'hunger' for wholeness and unity. However, this is not shared by the majority in his church. Such personal hunger for wholeness can, with subtlety, be held hostage within a church that has institutionalised the value of separateness. Separateness, with its parallel attitude of over-againstness, drives the church.

The journey from Cottesloe to the TRC

Except for Swanepoel's brief statement at the faith community hearings, the DRC has not gone any further with the process of truth-telling than its document, *The Story of the Dutch Reformed Church's Journey with Apartheid, 1960–1994*. In its 'statement of confession and witness', the DRC now acknowledges 'past mistakes' (1.1.1); that apartheid was 'church policy' (2.4.5); that the church pushed hard to get the National Party regime to enact laws against mixed marriages (2.5.1), to establish group areas (2.5.2), and Bantu education (2.5.3); and that it received secret funding from the apartheid government for propaganda purposes (4.6). The church even acknowledges that it provided a theological and biblical justification for apartheid in its 1974 document, *Race, Peoples and Nations in the Light of Scripture*. The statement further emphasises that, since 1986, the church has been moving away from the vestiges of apartheid. It regards the biblical justification of apartheid as an error to be rejected. The 'journey with apartheid', the statement claims, is over.

Is this adequate? The DRC would argue that the Commission required only full disclosure, and that is what they have done. Fair enough. However, the statement of the DRC was not written as a TRC submission,[3] and only served this function subsequently. This is their 'message to the people'. But for the DRC to say that it has made an acknowledgement of guilt, thereby ending its journey with apartheid, is extremely problematic. Jon Sobrino (1994, 83–88), the Latin American liberation theologian, points out that recognition forms one of the most important building blocks of reconciliation. Indeed, reconciliation depends upon recognition. But acknowledgement does not constitute recognition. The DRC's statement does not display recognition of the inherent gross violation of human dignity which is in every act of apartheid.

Unity as acid test[4]

The DRC's *Journey* statement could not bring itself to an unequivocal rejection of apartheid – which was, according to the statement, a good idea gone wrong; a well-intended system which 'degenerated' into an oppressive one. Those who had the responsibility for the political management of apartheid, are to blame for the atrocities. The DRC has thus not recognised its own role in the making of the mind of the perpetrator, or even the inherent evil of apartheid.

The submissions of the DRC, the Uniting Reformed Church, the Apostolic Faith Mission and others referred to church unity as a constitutive part of reconciliation. The DRC's representative expressed strong, positive support for church unity with the black Uniting Reformed Church. His support for this is well known. It is also well known that his church is not ready to follow him on this course. But this is the acid test of whether the DRC has formally broken with the racism of apartheid. Church unity between the Dutch Reformed Church and the Uniting Reformed Church is an essential element of truth-telling, reconciliation and reparation. It could be that those who resist church unity understand only too well that the practice and value of unity lies in its political, economic and social dimensions.

Religious notions of reconciliation expect from perpetrators an ethical commitment to making redress, restitution and reparation. No confession is complete, at least not as far as the Bible is concerned, unless the person has converted in the broad and the narrow sense of the word. Neither does reconciliation preclude compensation and reparation as acts required of the perpetrator. It is in the nature of confession that the confessed wrong be redressed by the violator.

From a dispositional ethic to an ethic of responsibility

The DRC's statement is embedded in the dispositional ethic that undergirded its notion of guardianship. The reference to 'good intentions' and the good principle of apartheid comes from this background, and makes it clear that the DRC still wants to be seen as 'guardian'. Instead of a dispositional ethic, the DRC should consider remaking the minds of its people in terms of an ethic of responsibility. A dispositional ethic is founded in a 'high anthropology', while an ethic of responsibility finds its foundation in the principle of justice as seen from the side of the victim. Drawing upon the insights of Max Weber, Hans Jonas and Dietrich Bonhoeffer, Wolfgang Huber (1996, 135–157) has characterised the quest for an ethic of responsibility in three ways. First, we cannot hide behind good intentions or other personal or corporate dispositions, but rather we should look at our deeds in terms of their results. These must then be seen in the light of our human responsibility for others. Second, when we become aware that our actions have hurt our relationship to others, we must make self-sacrifices. At that point, we do what an ethic of responsibility requires. Third, the ethic of responsibility is connected to the notion of substitution. Responsibility thus calls us to stand-in for one another, to act selflessly for others, in particular for the poor and oppressed.

The DRC's insistence on a dispositional ethic has driven it into a corner where it cannot bring itself to accept full responsibility for the inherent evil of apartheid, both in intention and application. Reorienting its journey by taking the step towards an ethic of responsibility will serve the future of the DRC's own children and the children of its victims. This leads it into 'the way of Christ', who is 'the centre of history' (Bonhoeffer 1966).

6 Stories, Fragments and Monuments

David Chidester

At three in the morning I was standing outside my house talking in the moonlight with a former officer of one of the notorious death squads of the apartheid regime. 'I did all those things because of my Christian faith,' he explained. Under the guidance of his church, his school and his national leaders, he had been led to believe that his work was fulfilling a Christian calling. All the killing, kidnapping and torturing, all the secrecy, deception and lies, served to advance a Christian crusade against the demonic evil of communism. 'You have to understand', he insisted, 'I really believed that I was being a good Christian.' Earlier that day at a hearing before the Truth and Reconciliation Commission, we had listened to one of his former death-squad colleagues giving some indication of what it might have meant in that context to be such a good Christian. After describing how his unit had detained, tortured and killed a man on a deserted mining dump, this witness said, 'I was sickened.' At the prompting of one of the commissioners, he clarified the reason for his revulsion. 'You see, we shot him in the face. That's just not right. It's cruel. We should have walked up behind him and shot him in the back of the head.' Although these scruples do not appear to have been explicitly Christian, they do suggest a kind of horrible morality in the midst of murder. Recently, however, my new acquaintance had turned state's evidence to testify against his erstwhile death-squad colleagues. He had rejected both the ideological rationale and the political authority he had once served with such dedication. 'So what happened?' I asked. 'What made you change?' In all seriousness, he looked me straight in the eyes and said, 'You see, I'm a devout Christian. I was changed by my profound Christian faith.'

A few days later I was speaking with a former Umkhonto weSizwe (MK) commander who recalled that during the 1980s they had devised a plan to blow up the Voortrekker Monument. As they did in all operations, MK leadership had undertaken a thorough and careful political analysis to identify the Monument as a strategic target. Deciding that an attack on that memorial to Afrikaner nationalism was politically justified, they had worked out the logistics, determining the quantity of explosives and the number of cadres that would be necessary for the operation. In keeping with the morality that generally governed MK operations, they had determined that blowing up the Monument could be effectively accomplished with minimum loss of human life and maximum symbolic impact. As ANC leadership had often insisted during the 1980s, armed struggle was also 'armed propaganda,' a forceful medium for addressing the state and mobilising the masses. However, when the proposal was put before Oliver Tambo, the ANC president turned it down. Reportedly, Tambo gave two reasons for not blowing up the Monument. First, the ANC was involved in a struggle against a state that had consistently and systematically destroyed the sanctity of the land, the lives and the human rights of the people of South Africa. In opposing that desecrating state, the ANC had to maintain a moral position in which it would never descend to destroying something that anyone held to be sacred. Even the monumental shrine of a triumphalist Afrikaner nationalism, therefore, could not be a legitimate target because it would implicate the ANC in an act of desecration. Second, Oliver Tambo advised, the ANC had to look forward to the possibility that in the future South Africans might be involved in a process of national reconciliation. In that event, reconciliation would only be made much more difficult if the ANC were to destroy a nationalist monument that was held to be sacred by a segment of the South African population. For these two reasons, therefore, the president of the ANC in exile denied permission to proceed with the operation.

Two stories: one framed in terms of Christian faith, the other in terms of the political dynamics of the sacred in South Africa. What are these stories about? Obviously, the first story, which invokes the motivating power of Christian faith, can only remind us of the profoundly ambivalent character of Christianity in South Africa. As a double-edged sword – legitimising oppression, mobilising liberation – Christianity has been a mixed blessing. All Christian churches in South Africa stand within that dilemma. No matter how much they might apologise, confess or testify to their innocence, they actually have no way out of that history. It is their location. Accordingly, since they cannot get out of it, not even by saying, 'I was changed by my profound Christian faith', they can only go through it. The second story, however, points to a radically different religious sensibility. In refusing to give his presidential sanction to the plan for blowing up the Voortrekker Monument, Oliver Tambo certainly demonstrated a fundamental respect for human values and an extraordinary insight into the South African future. But he also demonstrated a profound insight into religion. Without necessarily bestowing 'prophetic' status upon him, we can still recognise that Tambo had a thorough understanding of the political economy of the sacred that was at work in South Africa. He understood the inherently religious character of political strategy, a religious dynamic that he recognised running through South African society that was not contained in churches, mosques, temples, synagogues or other religious institutions. Beyond the scope of 'faith communities', he negotiated on the political terrain of the sacred and the sacred terrain of politics.

It is possible that I have made up these two stories. Perhaps I was not awake at three in the morning, perhaps I was not privileged to plans about blowing up the Voortrekker Monument. Who knows? How do we adjudicate truth in the midst of so many stories, in the midst of so many accounts that claim to be 'full and complete disclosures', in the midst of so many obvious and blatant lies. How can we possibly know?

Stories

Launching the Truth and Reconciliation Commission on 16 December 1995, Archbishop Desmond Tutu announced that the commission was charged with the awesome responsibility of facilitating a process of national healing in South Africa. Healing depended upon truth. In making that story about healing and truth convincing, Tutu invoked two analogies from the Christian tradition. On the one hand, the medieval Christian inquisition was an institution set up for producing a certain kind of truth. As Tutu clarified, however, the Commission was not an inquisition designed to expose heretics or hunt witches, 'hell-bent on bringing miscreants to book'. On the other hand, in contrast to the Christian inquisition, Tutu posed another Christian institution that was designed for the production of truth: the sacramental ritual of confession. 'We will be engaging in what should be a corporate nationwide process of healing', he declared, 'through contrition, confession and forgiveness.' At its inception, therefore, the Truth and Reconciliation Commission was presented as a Christian liturgical process of confession. Trying to broaden the sacramental scope of the Commission's work for a religiously diverse country, Archbishop Tutu called upon all of the religious communities in South Africa to participate in this national ritual of confession. Calling upon all of the faith communities of South Africa, he expressed his hope that 'our churches, mosques, synagogues and temples will be able to provide liturgies for corporate confession and absolution.' Informed by his own profound Christian faith, however, Archbishop Tutu established the narrative framework of the Commission as an essentially Christian story of contrition, confession and forgiveness.

As Desmond Tutu knows better than any of us, the Commission has heard stories that could not easily fit into that ritualised model of contrition, confession and forgiveness. He has listened to countless stories of perpetrators of gross violations of human rights in which there was no evidence of remorse, no full disclosure, no hope of absolution. But he must also know that the Commission's mandate to facilitate national healing and reconciliation has not always adequately served the stories that he has heard. For example, when a woman related her horrible account of being tortured by the South African Police, she concluded that she only hoped that her tormentors would be brought to justice. 'Thank you', one of the commissioners responded, 'for contributing your story to the national process of reconciliation.' Whether calling for justice, retribution, or even revenge, a witness could easily be absorbed into the master-narrative of reconciliation that governed the commission (Franz 1996).

During the hearings in November 1997 that were devoted to written and oral submissions from representatives of South African 'faith communities', more stories were told. From the transcripts of the hearings, it appears that these stories were told in a particularly congenial and collegial atmosphere. Perhaps on no other occasion was the Commission's religious character more evident. Certainly, the 'faith communities' had to understand these hearings as a ritual process. In some cases, as in the appearances of representatives from the Dutch Reformed Church (DRC) and the Zion Christian Church, their mere presence seemed sufficient to validate the ritual. Following the direction of Archbishop Tutu, however, this was their moment for contrition, confession and forgiveness. On behalf of their various churches, Christians did apologise and confess. Even representatives of the Dutch Reformed Church showed a degree of remorse, although they apparently persisted in distinguishing between 'good' and 'bad' apartheid. When Jews, Muslims, Hindus, Baha'is and adherents of African traditional religion were included in the hearings, Archbishop Tutu apologised for the history of 'Christian arrogance' in South Africa. Apologies were heard all around.

But representatives of faith communities also seemed concerned with vindication. RICSA's Report (sec. 3.2) attempts to distil from all the diverse stories three subject positions – perpetrators, victims and opponents of oppression – that can be located in a broad narrative of national liberation. Certainly, this analysis grows out of the church struggle in South Africa that was most closely associated with the work of the South

African Council of Churches (SACC). Essentially, the history of the SACC defines the relevant periodisation of Christian opposition to apartheid. Its doctrinal statements represent the basic terms of engagement. In particular, the theological analysis that was advanced in the *Kairos Document* of 1985 is applied to the submissions of the various faith communities. As a result, faith communities that developed a 'state theology' or a 'church theology' are found to have been complicit in apartheid oppression. By adopting a 'prophetic theology', however, some faith communities identified with the victims of oppression and actively opposed the apartheid state. From that vantage point, the truth of submissions can be assessed – one exaggerated, another misrepresented the facts, a third avoided responsibility, and so on – in ways that place the various faith communities in the narrative of church struggle. As the authors recognise, however, this 'prophetic' narrative poses problems for shaping a shared memory of the role of religion under apartheid.

First, the term 'prophetic' itself emerged at the hearings as a contested term. While the SACC and the Institute for Contextual Theology claimed prophetic status for liberation theology, the Dutch Reformed Church also claimed to be fulfilling a 'prophetic' mission. Asserting that it played that role in the past by advising the state behind closed doors, the DRC promised to continue performing a critical function in relation to the new democratic government. Significantly, therefore, the DRC submission embraced the prophetic mandate of opposition to the state that had been the province of the SACC in the 1980s. Both of these prophetic claims, however, were challenged by the presence of Bishop Lekganyane, whose role as prophet of the Zion Christian Church was interpreted by his spokesperson as providing spiritual leadership in personal morality and community formation. Instead of 'speaking truth to power', this prophet did not have to say a word during the faith community hearings. His mere presence seemed sufficient. Clearly, these different constructions of the prophetic role – critical speech, powerful silence – were left unresolved at the hearings. However, it is possible that the term 'prophetic' does not provide adequate grounds for reconciliation. When he was released from prison on 11 February 1990, Nelson Mandela seemed to recognise this problem. 'I stand before you not as a prophet,' he told a hundred thousand people gathered in the streets of Cape Town, 'but as a humble servant of you, the people' (*Cape Argus*, 12 February 1990). Not the prophet but the servant, therefore, was the potent symbol that Nelson Mandela invoked to suggest the way forward.

Second, the 'prophetic' narrative assumes that certain faith communities were effective agents of political struggle. During the 1980s, concern about this claim was expressed within the ANC. In a cautionary critique, for example, John Lamola (1988) warned that the new, radical involvement of organised Christianity might create the illusion that the church was leading the revolution. If the church were to be regarded as a leading force in the political struggle, then people might think that all they had to do was support the church. As Lamola observed, however, the church is not a force of struggle but a site of struggle. Like schools or factories, the church presented both a gathering point for mobilising people and a target to be captured and liberated. According to Lamola, no theology, not even a 'prophetic theology', could provide a firm basis for deriving political principles and practice because theology itself was 'one of the most disputed among human areas of enquiry'. However, by means of 'consultation between the religious structures and the people's political structures', Lamola concluded, the church could play an important role, not as a prophet, but as a 'servant of the revolution' (Lamola 1988; see Chidester 1992, 130–132). Although this revolutionary rhetoric must now seem strange, like the voice of an exile who has remained in exile, the resonance of the term 'servant' still echoes with possibilities for a different kind of narrative about faith communities in South Africa.

Fragments

This attention to alternative narratives, however, makes the submissions to the TRC faith community hearings sound entirely too coherent. The RICSA Report leaves the lingering impression that we have not heard genuinely coherent narratives. Instead, we have heard broken fragments, bits and pieces, unfinished sentences, words hanging in the air. We are left with 'flashbulb memories' of disconnected events. Psychologists have defined 'flashbulb memories' as images that 'suggest surprise, an indiscriminate illumination, and brevity' (Brown and Kulik 1982, 24). Like a shocking photograph, they freeze an extraordinary moment in time. Although they seem to capture everything about that moment, 'flashbulb memories' are only fragments. Their sudden illumination can also be blinding. Nevertheless, these brief, luminous fragments of memory are often assumed to represent the whole truth.

Submissions and testimony before the faith community hearings evoke many 'flashbulb memories'. Their impact is derived not from verbal confession but from startling visual images of damaged bodies, destroyed buildings and firefights in a war zone. Fragmentary images of bodies represent the most enduring 'flashbulb memories'. According to Christian tradition, the church must understand itself as the body of Christ. However, as a member of the Gereformeerde Kerk confessed at the hearings, Afrikaner churches 'acted as no more than limbs ... of the volk and state'. While this metaphoric image of the Christian church as a deformed body is startling, more powerful images are provided by physical bodies that bear indelible traces of the past. In the case of Father Michael Lapsley, whose body certainly bears such traces, the Church of the Province of South Africa found a 'living icon of redemptive suffering'. As a basis for memory, however, the body is more than a verbal metaphor for the church or a visual icon of redemption. The body is the primary site of memory. While the fragmentary character of embodied memory resists the imposition of any single, coherent narrative, it nevertheless provides the most basic material of memory.

Like damaged bodies, destroyed buildings feature prominently as 'flashbulb memories' in the hearings. These buildings represent important sites in an architecture of memory. As the representatives of the DRC explained, they had advised ministers of the apartheid state 'behind closed doors'. Inside that architectural enclosure of power, they used their access for their church to 'express its doubts' and urge that government policies be 'applied with compassion and humanity'. Beyond those closed doors, however, a different architecture of memory was taking shape. In the Northern Cape, the stone church at Majeng, which had stood for a hundred years, was bulldozed by the state in 1975 as its congregants were declared to be 'trespassers in their own home'. The submissions refer to the destruction of other buildings. Churches, missions, schools and seminaries were closed. Hindus were forcibly removed from religious sites, which were reportedly bought up by Christian churches. In these and many other instances, fragments of memory are housed in buildings, even when those buildings no longer exist.

In one of the most enduring 'flashbulb memories' of the fate of a building, Khotso House was blown up in 1988 on the orders of State President P. W. Botha. Ten years later, Botha could argue in court that blowing up Khotso House did not violate human rights. At worst, it only violated property rights. From 'behind closed doors', however, Botha and his legal advisers seemed to have no sense of the architecture of memory in South Africa that connected people to specific places – a home, a school, a church – that were not merely 'property' but sacred sites where memory gathered. Apparently, ten years after its destruction, Khotso House was a site of memory that even informed the composition of the faith community hearings. As Archbishop Ntongana remarked at the hearings, when he saw the commissioners on the panel he thought he was back in Khotso House. Linking human beings with place, therefore, the architecture of memory can reconstruct even what the state destroyed.

For modern memory, fragmentary images of war have been particularly powerful. In blazing 'flashbulb memories', we see the bombs bursting, the soldiers running, the refugees crying and the corpses rotting. Surprisingly, submissions at the hearing did not dwell on such images from the battlefield. Perhaps in the spirit of reconciliation, representatives of faith communities for the most part did not tell war stories. Although one submission referred to the state's 'holy war' and another recalled the church's tradition of the 'just war', these observations seemed rather abstract. Removed from the battlefield, these statements about war served to clarify relations between church and state, correcting what the representative of the South African Catholic Bishops' Conference called the 'unhealthy alliance of altar and throne'. Certainly, the alliance between church and state during the apartheid era must be remembered. While the DRC was 'blessing weapons of terror', the South African Defence Force presented every soldier with a New Testament inscribed with a message from P. W. Botha that identified the Bible as their 'most important weapon'. Generally, however, the submissions failed to evoke the vivid and horrifying images of warfare that so many South Africans retain in memory.

The most dramatic exception to this general avoidance of the imagery of warfare was the 'flashbulb memory' of the sudden, shocking transformation of St James Church from a church into a battlefield. In its submission to the hearings, the Church of England in South Africa reflected on lessons that had been learned from that traumatic experience. Recognising that even an apolitical religious group could become caught up in the politics of war, the church went further in confessing that it had been 'misled into accepting a social, economic, and political system that was cruel and oppressive'. Certainly, these lessons of war are important. As the leaders of the Church of England recognise, however, they do not begin to address the visceral trauma of survivors. If bodies, buildings and battlefields provide the basic materials of memory, then the work of memory – even the work of producing a shared, collective or national memory – must begin with the material fragments of a painful past.

Monuments

Efforts to forge a shared memory of the past are by no means new in South Africa. During the early 1940s, for example, while Anton Lembede was working out the constitution, manifesto and statement of 'Our Creed' for the ANC Youth League, he invoked the aphorism of Paul Kruger, 'One who wants to create the future must not forget the past.' In support of the 'new gospel of Africanism' that he proclaimed as South Africa's future, Lembede called for the erection of monuments and memorials to the great heroes of African history that would create a national memory of the past. Significantly, he rejected the commemoration of narrowly defined 'tribal' or 'ethnic' histories by insisting that the heroes of all 'tribal' histories were the common possession of Africa. Monuments to a shared African past promised to support a future in which Lembede saw people 'converted from tribalism into African nationalism, which is a higher step or degree of the self-expression and self-realization of the African spirit' (Gerhart 1978, 61). Memory of the past, therefore, was essential to the process of opening Africa to that spiritual future.

As students of cultural memory have argued, a collective sense of the past is produced through specific 'technologies of memory,' those material objects, images and representations through which a shared memory is shaped and reproduced. The 'technologies of memory' that are located at national monuments have often provided particularly potent means for transforming individuals into what Lauren Berlant (1991, 20) has called 'subjects of a collectively held history'. When a national monument is effective in shaping cultural memory, Berlant has suggested, 'its traditional icons, its metaphors, its heroes, its rituals, and its narratives provide an alphabet for a collective consciousness or national subjectivity'. The monument, therefore, can mark the intersection of personal and national identity.

During the apartheid era, however, South Africa became a kind of laboratory for the study of failed nationalisms. For example, take the nationalism of the Republic of the Ciskei. Impressed by the monument to Israeli heroism at Masada, President Lennox Sebe established his own holy mountain, Ntaba kaNdoda, where all citizens of the Ciskei were supposed to 'swear their oaths and allegiance to the nation before this National Shrine' (Hodgson 1987, 30). When Sebe was deposed, people danced in the streets. Or take the traditional village constructed in the Republic of Bophuthatswana by President Lucas Mangope that was designed as a memorial to the history and culture of South Africa's 'tribal' nations. An adviser on the project, Credo Mutwa, praised Mangope by declaring, 'Anyone who gives me the opportunity to rebuild the African past knows what he is doing' (Bophuthatswana, Rep. of 1987). A decade later, as anthropologists Jean and John Comaroff observed, this 'tribal' village had fallen into disrepair. No longer a national monument, it had become an informal settlement (Comaroff and Comaroff 1997). These examples of failed national monuments could certainly be multiplied. At the very least, they demonstrate that a national monument cannot actually make a nation.

In Anton Lembede's terms, these nationalist projects only represented fragments of a unified African nationalism. Because they went against what he called the 'divine destiny' of a unified Africanism, Lembede certainly would have seen these projects as doomed to failure. Many of the submissions at the faith community hearings expressed the desire to unify what apartheid and separate development had fragmented. In both church and society, new grounds for unity are being sought. Among their recommendations for ways in which faith communities might facilitate reconciliation, the authors of the RICSA Report call for the construction of permanent monuments (sec. 5.3). They imagine these monuments as sacred spaces for the expression of pain, loss and lament. By contrast to the monuments of triumphalist nationalisms, therefore, these monuments would be sites for shaping a national memory of suffering and solidarity.

Although Holocaust museums and memorials have been cited as precedents, we might also consider the examples of two sites of cultural memory in the United States – the Vietnam War Memorial and the AIDS quilt – that have memorialised pain. These seem to have reduced representation to its most minimalist form, a list of names. Nevertheless, they have provided rich and complex occasions for what cultural analyst Marita Sturken (1997) has called ongoing 'conversations with the dead'. More than focal points for private recollection, these public memorials have both been crucial sites for productions and counter-productions of national memory in America. Whether anchored at the nation's capital or travelling around the country, these memorials have given national scope to different formations of cultural memory. Not necessarily affirming shared values, social continuity or national healing, these memorials continue to define a shifting field of relations with the past at the intersection of personal subjectivity and national history.

How will South African faith communities fit into new national narratives? After the first democratic elections, building a new nation seemed as simple as one, two, three – one flag, two national anthems and three sporting teams. But the work of the TRC has certainly shown the intractable difficulties faced by South Africans in forging national unity out of the historical conflicts and struggles of the past. Generally, the faith community hearings made the task of achieving national unity seem too easy, as if it could be facilitated by the mere fact of many different religious groups coming together in the service of the common national interest. Certainly, communication across religious divides is important. But the national question remains. In an insightful discussion of his own struggle to reconcile personal memories of his family's suffering and loss in the Holocaust with national narratives of the modern state of Israel, anthropologist Steven Robins (1998, 123) resolved 'to live with fragments and silences rather than embracing totalising narratives of collective suffering, national redemption, and destiny'. While they might tell stories, build monuments, and identify with new national goals, religious communities in a changing South Africa are particularly faced with this challenge of finding ways to live with the fragments and the silences.

7 The Question (of) Remains: Remembering Shoah, Forgetting Reconciliation

Heidi Grunebaum-Ralph & Oren Stier

Apartheid is not the Holocaust.[1] The Holocaust was not apartheid. And yet the comparison is often made. Why? One reason is that, since World War Two, the Holocaust has become the benchmark of 'gross human rights violations'. In Lyotard's (1988, 56) words, the Holocaust may be an earthquake of such magnitude that it destroyed all instruments of its measurement. But at the same time it is also possible to see the Holocaust itself as the new instrument of measurement against which all other cases of atrocity are compared. In a certain sense this is a mistake, not only because it often leads people to create a hierarchy of human suffering (my holocaust is better/worse than yours), nor only because human suffering allows for no arithmetic of atrocity, but mainly because it takes away the specificity of one case by comparing it in this way to another.

But the mind works by comparison, and compare we must – only without judgement, without establishing a hierarchy. Therefore we recognise that we can learn something about one case in the context of another, and together they tell us more than we knew about the single case in isolation. This is especially true when we are dealing with the aftermath, with memory and, yes, even with reconciliation. It is in this context that we will speak here of the Holocaust.

In South Africa, this comparative mode has had a somewhat turbulent history since the start of the TRC hearings in 1996. In *Reconciliation Through Truth*, Kader Asmal, Louise Asmal and Ronald Suresh Roberts lay the ground for such work:

> If one leaves aside the systematic and technologically adept extermination of Jewish people that intensified under the Nazis in

> 1941, and which really has no parallel, there is a striking overlap between early Nazi German solutions to the Jewish Problem and apartheid's way of dealing with the Black Threat . . .
>
> It is as wrong to assert that every defining aspect of Nazidom was unique as it is wrong to assert that apartheid amounted to a duplication of Nazi policies. There was substantial overlap; but the one was not a carbon copy of the other (Asmal et al. 1997, 132–133).

This position therefore suggests that the Holocaust is a useful signpost on the road towards placing apartheid in its own context. But Mahmood Mamdani, in a critical review of the book, suggests that such an example is not so easily translatable to the African case. In the first instance, this is because, in his view (1996, 3), the Holocaust here is no more than a metaphor for apartheid's institutionalised oppression – a metaphor that is misleading because the reference point for the Holocaust is a Eurocentric one and apartheid is more appropriately localisable in a history of European colonialism in Africa. Moreover, the metaphor is inapplicable because it establishes a false parallelism between historical actors: 'it highlights as key to the injustice of apartheid the relationship between perpetrators and victims, not beneficiaries and victims' (Mamdani 1996, 5).

On the other end of the political spectrum, Hermann Giliomee has challenged the apartheid–Holocaust comparison. In his presidential address to the South African Institute of Race Relations (Giliomee 1996), Giliomee objected to this comparison in order to challenge apartheid's international status as a crime against humanity, largely by casting doubt on the moral rights of the states who supported the UN resolutions establishing the criminality of apartheid. Then he contributed to a series of leader page articles in the *Cape Times* which appeared intermittently throughout 1996, specifically in response to the Asmal book. In these articles, Giliomee invoked the uniqueness of the Holocaust in order to distance the Holocaust from apartheid, essentially decriminalising the latter and isolating each in its historical specificity. In our view, Giliomee thus rejects the process of comparison in favour of a 'forgetful' line of South African historiography, in which the criminality of apartheid is devalued.[2]

But Asmal and his co-authors have been misunderstood. They clearly do not equate apartheid and the Holocaust. They do, however, acknowledge the historical links connecting Nazi policies with National Party ideology. The National Party were Nazism's 'modernisers, bobbing and weaving so that Nazi ideals of race hierarchy would survive in another place, and also, translating Nazi policies and programmes for local conditions' (Asmal et al. 1997, Afterword, 8). Furthermore, they recognise that the work of comparison lies neither in simplistically equating apartheid with Nazism, nor in rejecting the work of comparison out of hand, but in carefully sketching out the terms and conditions by which valid and valuable comparison can be made without doing violence to the specificity of each case in its own right.

In this, Asmal and his co-authors succeed, in our opinion, because they deal with apartheid and Nazism as historical realities, not as metaphors. It is this point that is lost on Mamdani, who fails to see the actualities of the legacy of Nazism and therefore rejects it as a basis for comparison. The 'key metaphor', he writes (1996),

> is that of the Holocaust. It is a metaphor that is politically inappropriate and misleading for a variety of reasons. Key to these is that it abstracts from the real problem: whites and blacks in South Africa are not akin to German[s] and Jews, for Germans and Jews did not have to build a common society in the aftermath of the Holocaust. There was Israel.

We find this a disturbing misreading of both *Reconciliation Through Truth* and of the socio-historical aftermath of World War Two. To simplistically suggest that Israel automatically stands in, in a redemptive way, to solve the Jewish question without any real post-war engagement is to miss the point and read history with hindsight (Bernstein 1994). Mamdani forgets that Israel was, for many, more necessity than choice, with continuing pogroms after the war only one of the many factors in the decision to emigrate.

In any case, we wish to go further. Reading the Holocaust as a benchmark means that we know now what human beings are capable of – we are all living in a time 'after Auschwitz' (Rubenstein 1992) – and thinking about national traumas forces us to think about such collective suffering against the Holocaust. This is why Asmal's comparison is so valuable. But it is not the historical events as such that interest us here so much as their legacy in memory. We suggest, therefore, that not only is the Holocaust – and particularly the Nazi system – instructive for the South African case, but the manner in which the collective trauma of World War Two has been memorialised is even more relevant.[3]

In our view, there are different ways of speaking about the Holocaust, particularly in terms of its memory. While one sees memory as redemptive (a modality we will not take up here), the other calls on memory as anti-redemptive, challenging the notion that people can heal, that the memory of events becomes more distant, that the past passes. It suggests that the past haunts the present, in a manner described by Lawrence

Langer (1993) as 'durational time', where the experience never relinquishes its hold on the individual long after the traumatic events recede in history. Here, memory does not redeem, it does not save, and it does not render the past as meaningful in favour of a reconstituted whole that is the present.

In this context, it is therefore crucial for us to point out that the term 'Holocaust' itself is problematic, coming as it does from the Greek *holokauston*, the Septuagint translation of the Hebrew *olah* – the whole burnt sacrificial offering in the Jewish Temple of old. We are wary of using a term with such an overt sacrificial connotation here because it too easily allows for a redemptive teleology that is built into the unfolding of the events themselves. We prefer to use the term Shoah which, though also linked to biblical notions of cataclysm, resonates in a much less sacrificial way (see Young 1988, 85–89).

This kind of attention to language is actually central to our approach here. It is vital, in our opinion, to engage seriously with the nature of TRC language and discourse, especially in the context of the faith communities hearings. We maintain that such a focus can illuminate the appropriateness of the memorial language of the Shoah in the discussion here. Take, for example, Archbishop Desmond Tutu's opening remarks at the faith communities hearings:

> It is almost trite to say that this country is possibly the most religious country. It certainly is a very religious country. Let me not be engaged in comparisons. Now that doesn't say a great deal because religion is not necessarily a good thing, not necessarily a bad thing. It can be a good or bad thing. It was, after all, German Christians who supported Hitler, but then it was also Christians in the confessing church who showed that wonderful resistance to the awfulness of Nazism . . .
>
> And so we have a peculiar responsibility as members of religious communities, for we have, I think, still a great deal of influence if we wished to exercise it. I hope that it will be clear to the world that this particular hearing has a different quality to it from all the other hearings we have heard so far . . .
>
> [W]hat are we going to do for the healing of this land? That is going to be the major challenge. What are we going to do to carry out the ministry of reconciliation that has been entrusted to us?

Aside from the notion that we do not want to 'be engaged in comparisons', Tutu's language evokes Nazism and the Shoah as reference points for these hearings. Perhaps it is through this retrospective gaze that the distinctiveness of these hearings emerges – a difference that we read as the mandate, once the faith communities undergo their own TRC trial by fire and are purged of their guilt, to pick up the torch of national healing and establish a 'ministry of reconciliation' after the TRC disappears from the national stage.

But this position itself is problematic: the language of the TRC faith communities hearings, and perhaps of the TRC as a whole, strives for a kind of wholeness and completion in its zeal for reconciliation. As such, it presents both a hermetically sealed space for remembrance, which limits the memorial field, and a discourse which obscures the individual remembrances (rooted in individual bodies) that may disrupt or otherwise contest the closed master narrative of national reconciliation expressed as Christian forgiveness and healing. And it is the imagery of organic healing – of healing wounds, crossing bridges, making whole historical divisions – which sets the tone for a continuous and seamless shifting from a collective project of nation-building, through the construction of a 'shared memory', to individual attempts to deal with the past. So the TRC is described in the media as a truth 'body'; the Promotion of National Unity and Reconciliation Act envisages the TRC process as an 'historic bridge', and even the Constitutional Court judgment handed down upholding the constitutionality of the amnesty provisions of the TRC's mandating act refers to a 'country [that] begins the long and necessary process of healing the wounds of the past'.[4]

This kind of imagery shifts the focus from individual to collective in ways that cover over the differences and needs central to both individual and collective claimants to the legacy of the past. By conflating the process by which a collective heals (and we would also like to question this assumption) with the process by which the individual comes to terms with loss, death, torture and atrocity, not only is the individual memory co-opted into the mythological founding moment of the collective, not only are those memories which contest the possibilities of wholeness and healing silenced, but the memorial process itself becomes endowed with a coherence, continuity and linearity which belie the unexpectedness, fragmentation and complexities of memory and its memorialisations.

It is here that the memory of the Shoah becomes instructive. While there certainly are as many ways of remembering the atrocities of World War Two as there are individual rememberers, and while there certainly have been numerous attempts to utilise the memory of Nazi persecutions for national ends (most notably in the memory paradigm of 'catastrophe and redemption' institutionalised in the early years of the state of Israel – see Friedländer 1994), we would like to focus here on ways of memorialising the past that allow the questions of healing and forgiveness to remain open. We can therefore identify two distinct modes of invoking the Shoah in the context of the faith communities hearings. Thinking about these leads us to a reconsideration of the lessons to be learned from Shoah memory. One such way endorses reconciliation, perhaps at the expense of remembrance, while the other reserves the right to resist reconciliatory closure in favour of a more focused engagement with memory.

Chief Rabbi Cyril Harris, for example, in his testimony at the faith hearings invokes the Shoah not as a reference point for comparison but as an explanation and apologetic for Jewish silence:

> And this was a very small community . . . in numbers, it's a post-Holocaust generation. Do you know what the Nazis did to the Jewish people? So therefore, Jewish people all over the world have a sensitivity, one would say a hyper-sensitivity, to survival. At all costs they want to survive. I am not condoning the silence of the Jewish community in the apartheid era, I am attempting to explain it and I am asking for your understanding.

It is in the context of this plea for 'understanding' that Harris therefore asks for forgiveness on behalf of the community:

> The Jewish sources tell us . . . that the reason [Job] was punished by G-d, was that he failed to speak out against the injustices of his own time. So the Jewish community in South Africa confesses a collective failure to protest against apartheid . . . Because of the evil of indifference which so many in the Jewish community professed, we confess that sin today before this commission and we ask forgiveness for it. The pivotal issue of this commission is to turn the inequities of the past towards advantage for the future.

We therefore understand Harris's 'confession' as being fuelled by his reference to the Shoah: because of what Nazis did to Jews, Jews can, at the very least, explain their silence and their 'collective failure' in the past. They nevertheless confess their 'sins'. This confession allows for, and perhaps almost predetermines, forgiveness and reconciliation, which in this case are projected into the future, in a way which appears to erase the present.

Thus, the way we understand memory to be invoked within this submission is as a tool for reconciliation in the service of an as-yet-to-be-reached future, which reveals how memory, disengaged from the present, can actually promote forgetfulness. Harris's submission therefore feeds into the 'script' for this special hearing (reconciliation, wholeness, healing) in which, in order to carry forward the ministering flame of reconciliation, the faith communities, through their confessions, are granted what can be understood as a non-legalistic kind of amnesty, as institutionalised forgetting (see Braude 1996, esp. 64). Curiously, Harris is also therefore feeding into a Christian teleology of forgiveness, whereby reconciliation is a foregone conclusion in the same way as Jesus has already died for humanity's sins.

But what happens when a representative of a 'faith community' does not subscribe to reconciliation as a foregone conclusion? The testimony of Mr D. K. Koka at the faith hearings, representing the African traditional religious community, suggests a different way of reading memory. In his opening statement, configured initially as a confession, but which is more poignantly reminiscent of an essay by Shoah survivor Primo Levi (1986), Koka says this:

> I must here submit the truth that I tried my best to scrape the bottom of the barrel in search of the drops of my guilt by my goals, not me as an individual but in a collective single plurality, and I failed to find one in the course of the struggle. This puts me to a point where I say, we can remark that the guilt of the oppressor and the oppressed shall never be the same and shall never be faced from the same angle, for they are operating on different levels and therefore the structuring of forums where the two sectors can express themselves sometimes needs to be reconsidered.

Koka's anti-confessional here thus draws our attention to the fundamental disparity in the memorial discourses of oppressed and oppressor. We see this as establishing an understanding of memory in opposition to reconciliation, memory as fragmented rather than whole, as warning and witness rather than redemptive and reconcilable. Our understanding of what we would like to call this 'right not to reconcile' is not presented here as a defence of retribution or vengeful action, but as the assertion of the right of the victimised to define both the limits of dialogue and the configurations of the memorial landscape. Grounded in an understanding of remembrance in the present, Koka's testimony becomes an assertion of the right to deferred closure.

This assertion is articulated in Koka's close attention to the legacy of the past in the present. Invoking the Shoah in a very different manner from that of Harris's testimony, Koka depicts the contemporary impact of a long history of genocidal oppression:

> Sound social-cultural, ethical and spiritual values have been destroyed by the evangelised policies of apartheid without any replacement. As a result, we find ourselves ushered into an age filled with the ruins and fragments of morality. Hence our intellectual landscapes are littered with . . . tales of deterioration in

> human relations, rather than dramatic narratives of humanness, reconciliation, justice and peace. This reality has been brought out to us clearly in the deliberations of the Truth and Reconciliation Commission. The most inhuman institutions and ideological hierarchies ever recorded in the pages of human history are nothing but slavery, Nazism, apartheid, and others . . . Apartheid should not be seen in isolation, but must be seen as a final product of the Eurocentric spiritual thinking and faith that separated divinity from man . . .
>
> We are here today to look at the actual living products, we are here to look at the protagonists of Nazism and fascism, the rapists and murderers of Bosnia, the genocidists of Rwanda, and the epitomes of apartheid in South Africa, these including the third force gangsters who terrorised, maimed, and slaughtered thousands of innocent train commuters in Soweto and other places. In those who raped women and killed innocent children, all these including the Gestapo murder squads of Vlakplaas, the Mamaselas, De Kocks, Coetzees, and those of the killing fields of Natal . . .

By grounding memory in the present, Koka subverts the reconciliatory master-narrative of the TRC. In placing apartheid in a historical trajectory with slavery and Nazism, all leading to the here and now, Koka's version of memory is not the vehicle by which we rush headlong into the future.

As we understand his testimony, Koka suggests that we are living in a time of fragments and the ruins of morality: the time of the aftermath. Through the grounding of memory in the present, we therefore understand how Koka sees the disparity in memorial discourses of oppressed and oppressor as implying a difference in the very claims that each may make on the meaning of the past in the present, and thus on the very concept of reconciliation itself. Rather than supporting a Christian concept of reconciliation as a blanket thrown indiscriminately over all participants in the TRC process as equivalent parties to that reconciliatory process, Koka suggests that the roads to reconciliation and healing are multiple and diverse. And this means that the very ways in which different parties to the reconciliation process work through their memories must be given the necessary time and space to unfold.

The advantage of allowing memories to unfold in this way, what we call the assertion of the right to deferred closure, is twofold. First, it preserves the fragmentary nature of individual processes of coming to terms with the past, outside of an imposed reconciliatory narrative; and second, it leads to a mode of remembrance that is more open-ended and inquisitive. Such a memorial process especially protects those of the victimised who are still unable even to speak about their experiences in the past, who may yet be silent for many years. The history of the memories of the Shoah, for example, reflects this claim: many survivors either could not speak in the initial years following the war or discovered that there was no one who wanted to listen (Wieviorka 1992, 161–190; Laub 1992a; Laub 1992b).[5] Such a recollective mode, really a self-reconciliation, does not close off memorial space, but rather allows it to remain accessible for a long time. This is especially important when considering the imminent end of the TRC's mandate. It would be wise for those who take up the torch of the 'ministry of reconciliation' to keep this future of memory in mind.

One way this mode of open questioning has played itself out has been in the search for, and restitution of, the remains of the bodies of countless activists and other 'disappeareds'. A common refrain in the human rights violations hearings was the request for the return of the bones of the missing and answers to questions regarding a victim's disappearance. Note the testimony of Ncediwe Mfeti:

> I have an interest in the commission making a thorough investigation ... even if it is his remains, if he was burnt to death, even if we can get his ashes, the bones belonging to his body, because no person can disappear without trace. If I could bury him, I am sure I could be reconciled (Minkley et al. 1996, quoted in Grunebaum-Ralph 1997).

Not only does this remarkable testimony speak to the issue of potential self-reconciliation, but it couches it in the language of questioning and literally embodied restitution. In light of the success of the TRC's Investigative Unit in discovering and exhuming the remains of many of the disappeared, we see the reclamation of human bones not only as a metaphor for the need to grieve but as the initiation of a memorial process that can now begin to take place. Not only the end of a search (an answered question, a provisional closure), the return and reburial of the bones of the beloved is furthermore the beginning of a process of memorial integration and personal reconciliation.

Even when there are no bones, no recourse for actual reburial and restitution, the legacy of the Shoah reminds us of both the need and possibility for symbolically creating the site for memory and mourning. For example, participants in the March of the Living, a memorial pilgrimage involving a visit to the epicentre of Nazi atrocities in Auschwitz-Birkenau, plant memorial plaques as symbolic grave-markers throughout the former death-camp grounds, making of the undifferentiated mass death space a marked and individualised memorial graveyard (see Stier 1995).[6]

We understand such reconstitutive memorialisation, especially in its articulation, as a kind of interrogative mourning process, as elegiac.[7] In an article which traces the aesthetic possibilities of the concept of elegy in a post-TRC cultural milieu, Ingrid de Kok (1998, 62) cites Peter Sacks's notion of elegiac construction as aesthetic reconstitution, which we read as memorial reconstruction: 'In effect [elegy] brings back into our presence the disappeared, in a newly refigured form.' Furthermore, De Kok (1998, 71 citing Sacks 1985, 22) sees the possibilities of elegiac questioning as the setting free of 'the energy locked in grief or rage and . . . [the] organis[ing of] its movement in the form of a question that is not merely an expression of ignorance but a voicing of protest'.

The voicing of protest, and the solace it provides, is the mediating ritual of renarration, the recontextualising of the past. As an alternative memorial paradigm, that voicing of protest may offer other opportunities towards integration and healing that challenge both a master reconciliatory narrative and empower individuals in their quests for modes of memorial expression. Thus, the act of questioning becomes essential, expressing as it does the symbolic force of the continual reclamation of memory (see, in the Shoah context, Jabès 1991). Members of the clergy who may wish to orchestrate rituals of reconciliation, a mode of memorial engagement we endorse, should nevertheless encourage the expression of this interrogative mode.

We remain, therefore, with questions, the question of remains: the open wounds, open questions. Our concern is that the discourse of reconciliation, expressed in forums such as the TRC faith communities hearings, can be used to displace precisely the trauma that this discourse seeks to ameliorate. What is displaced is the acknowledgement that survivors and victims of trauma very often do not heal, or that healing involves processes that exclude the possibilities of reconciliation. We find Shoah memory instructive here in that, in many cases, the institutionalisation of remembrance has also proved to threaten the autonomy of survivor memories – whose legacy nevertheless extends beyond the first generation. In other words, a museum, monument or memorial may, in reconciling the past, displace the process of working through trauma, a working through which continues for and remains with subsequent generations.

When the Israelites left Egypt after generations of slavery, they took with them the bones of their ancestor Joseph, in order to honour his request to be buried in the promised land. This image is a powerful one in this context: the remembrance of collective trauma, in its translation from the individual to the national, the personal to the public, cannot so easily shift into the reconciliatory mode. The remains of the past must be borne into the present before they can be laid to rest in the service of a still deferred future. The performance of national memory must not be allowed to elide the questions and the remains of the traumatised. The image of Joseph's bones reminds us, not of the yet-to-be-reached promised land (with its own problematic redemptive political resonances), but of the portage of the remains of the past through the wilderness on the way to the hoped-for future. The Israelites spent forty years in the desert; it is now only a little over fifty years since the Shoah: in the here and now of post-apartheid South Africa, we cannot forget to bring along those bones of the past.

8 Going Public, Building Covenants: Linking the TRC to Theology and the Church

William Johnson Everett

The Truth and Reconciliation Commission (TRC) emerged out of the constitutional negotiations between the African National Congress (ANC), the National Party (NP) and other parties in 1992–3. While it began as a compromise between NP delegates who wanted blanket amnesty for their past actions and many ANC and other delegates who wanted trials and retributive justice, it soon developed its own logic as an essential ingredient for building a new political order. The logic of the TRC process is shaped primarily by its legal definition in the Constitution and in the parliamentary Act which established it. However, its logic goes far beyond this legal frame. It extends first of all to the reconstituting of a civil society and, beyond that, to the religious and deep cultural anchors of people's lives.

In this brief reflection I will follow the connections among these three fields in order to link the work of the TRC to the ongoing work of the churches. In order to do this, I will briefly reflect on similar efforts in the history of modern constitutionalism to lift up the centrality of respect for higher law and participation in public life for the development of constitutional democracies. Then I will draw out a way to link these theologically to the work of the church through the concepts of covenant and publicity.

Modern constitution-making and democratisation

South Africa is only the most recent country to seek to repair past wrongs in order to establish a new constitutional order of democratic participation.[1] The US Constitution of 1787 emerged out of an established political culture among the farmers and merchants of the British colonies. The questions of slavery, of the enfranchisement of women and the expropriation of native lands were all swept aside, to be confronted later – in the case of slavery, in bloody terms in the American Civil War. The efforts at reconstruction following that war, in spite of the constitutional amendments ending slavery and guaranteeing civil rights to black males, were soon extinguished, leading to a century of segregation before the modern civil rights movement could begin to repair the ravages of slavery. The trail of broken treaties between the US government and the American tribes has led to legalised paternalism, fictional sovereignties and casinos. Denial of atrocities has given way to fawning nostalgia for Native American ecology, but neither apology nor reparation has ruled the day. As with women, the most that has occurred in a gradual process of moral growth are fitful programmes of affirmative action.

Because of the age of its sacrosanct Constitution and the slow pace of social development in the country, the nation has not experienced a compressed time of national atonement, save perhaps in the wake of the Vietnam War. Coming to terms with the past is left to the slow trickle of information from government files and to occasional acts of reparation, as with the Japanese Americans interned during World War Two and the victims of medical experiments at Tuskegee, Alabama. The churches, often wrapped up in the American flag, have only grudgingly helped reveal past government atrocities. Only occasionally, and with the usual notable exceptions, have they begun the process of apology, atonement and repair.

It was only with the German and Japanese defeats in 1945 that the modern era of judicial appeals to higher law along with an honest effort to rebuild the nation (rather than punish it) begins to take shape. While both countries began the process of anchoring fundamental human rights in their democratic constitutions, the relative homogeneity of their population, gained through genocide in Germany's case, delayed the issues of cultural pluralism encountered by India and, now, South Africa.

Because of its profound plurality and history of caste discrimination, India separated out the affirmation of fundamental human rights from constitutional 'directives', which would guide the country in repairing the legacy of caste and developing a democratic culture. This included a directive to equalise the position of women through marriage law reform. The trauma of partition in 1947–8 paralysed the nation's will to disturb further the explosive lattice of religious traditions in which caste and female subordination were entrenched. The programmes of 'compensatory discrimination' to reduce discrimination and economic disparity, while not without some success, have intensified caste, ethnic and tribal consciousness. The effort to give women marital equality in a common civil code has foundered on intense religious suspicions as well as radical differences among religions organisationally and culturally. Any efforts at national reflection, reparation and atonement are short-circuited by the way religion, culture, kinship, caste and even language are all intertwined.

More recently, Germans have had to reopen the questions left unanswered by the surgical intervention of the Nuremberg trials and the amnesia produced by mere 'denazification'. The unification of the former zones of Allied occupation brought a new history of exposure of personal betrayal between party operative and dissident citizen. The opening of the security police files has been a quasi-public process, but its revelations of wrongdoing have led only to ordinary civil trials in which people are held responsible solely for what the applicable law required at the time. Legality has taken precedence over healing. Reparation has not been personal and individual, except for personal acts of apology and forgiveness. Rather, it has occurred through a massive programme of economic rehabilitation. While the evangelical churches of the old German Democratic Republic provided pivotal publics and leadership for the transition, they now languish in the throes of economic struggle and drastically declining membership.

More recently, the countries of Central and South America have struggled in a variety of ways to repair the injustices of their past and build a more democratic society.[2] In each case efforts at public procedures for finding the truth of past enormities have been stifled or reduced to *in camera* proceedings by military and near-feudal ruling elites anchored in a traditional culture of personal rule. Some direct prosecution of military officers has occurred, as in Argentina where the military was discredited by the Falklands War. Uruguay, however, has had virtually no judicial process against perpetrators of state violence. Chile's National Commission on Truth and Reconciliation was tightly constrained by the agreement with the Pinochet government and its continued military domination of the political process. In all these countries, the people experienced more a change of regime than a fundamental break in the pattern of government. Repair and rebuilding has occurred within, hopefully, a gradual evolution of political forms.

The Catholic Church in these countries, while supplying a culture legitimising the personal rule that hinders the development of democratic life, has also acted to open up public processes, as in Guatemala or El Salvador, often with heavy loss to its episcopal and priestly leaders. The recent assassination of Monsignor Juan Gerardi for his leadership in exposing human rights abuses in Guatemala only dramatised the fragility of that country's efforts to expose and repair the damage caused by its own government, along with linkages extending back to US complicity in fostering the systems responsible for these human rights abuses.

The 1993 South African Constitution was a fundamental break with the country's past form of government. It replaced the tradition of parliamentary sovereignty with that of constitutional sovereignty, interpreted by a constitutional court. It embedded a developed catalogue of human rights in that higher law and redistributed powers more evenly among the branches of government. While the issues of the nation's federal structure and the relation of the constitutional order to 'traditional leaders' and a putative Afrikaner Volkstaat were left unresolved, this constitution clearly demanded a commitment to governance through open, participatory publics and an adherence to constitutional requirements. These fundamental commitments to full publicity and constitutional obligation stood over against traditions of personal and patriarchal power and elite or secret collusion that run all through the country's cultural past.

The TRC's official purposes have been to promote 'national unity' and 'reconciliation'. It was to do this through uncovering the truth about gross human rights violations under apartheid and deciding on amnesty and reparations for individuals. Its findings would then be used to formulate government policy and even constitutional changes to prevent such future horrors. Thus, it served not only to enable the process of negotiation to move ahead in 1992–3 but also, hopefully, will serve to strengthen and refine the constitutional republic that emerged from those negotiations and elections.

In putting the public discovery of truth at the centre of its work, the TRC tried to concentrate on the task of building the basis for a new public and democratic culture. While limited amnesty through individual case proceedings and reparations based on individual victimage are important, these are cast within the wider task of building a political culture and society where such enormities are less likely to happen.

The TRC can therefore be seen as a crucial means for developing the fundamental political principles of public life and constitutionalism. From the standpoint of constitutional development the TRC's work has heightened popular awareness that all governance must exist within a higher frame of justice to which all are directly responsible. The members of the society are to act with this higher law written in their hearts, rather than to claim innocence because they were obeying orders or lesser authorities. The TRC has sought to do this, however, not through retribution but through fostering public truth-telling. The TRC has thus been part of the necessary process of establishing trustworthy publics and a sense of accountability to higher law. It is these two themes – of 'publicity' and 'higher law' – that I want to develop in order to draw out the implications of the TRC for the churches.

The TRC, the renewal of publicity and the higher law

By publicity I simply mean the activity of forming and continually nurturing public life. It means the work of enabling people to move from a life of fear, secrecy, hiding, denial and lies to one in which they can speak the truth as they understand it, among others who can then argue with them in the search for common agreement. This means that a public has to exist within the framework of non-violence and the capacity for persuasion. It necessarily presumes a plurality of voices, each contesting for his or her own understanding about the common good as well as their minimal needs to participate in it. The doctrine of human rights needs to be seen as an effort to construct the prerequisites for participation in public life. The TRC, in bringing what was hidden into the public light, has been an important effort to model the procedures for public life, from encouraging fearful witnesses to providing for reasoned cross-examination in pursuit of the truth.

It also, from early on, has had to deal with the acute plurality of the country's population. Finding the 'truth' requires a labyrinthine scramble through languages as well as religious and cultural assumptions about words, texts, gestures and rituals of reconciliation. Cultures of personal command clash with those of legality and records, while the truth of interpersonal confirmation runs up against the truth of transcendent 'fact'. The truth itself becomes a process of negotiation and renegotiation within a variety of frameworks of meaning.[3] The lack of national 'unity' is mirrored in the suspicion between formal panels of law and education and the grizzled veterans of violence or the disoriented and silenced victims of unconscionable attacks.

The TRC's search for truth in public reminds us that publics cannot exist without common commitment not only to lawful process and a minimal cultural consensus but also to a 'higher law' that underlies the claim of publics to precede and judge the governments they establish. Republican governance has always sought ordered means to subject government to open public judgement, whether through regular elections, referendums, popular constitutional amendment, independent judiciaries and professions, or clearly independent media, churches and cultural associations. Establishing this rich network of public associations – what we often call civil society – is indispensable for democratic government.

Commitment to a higher law transcending these publics and governments is also indispensable, for without it members of the free publics cannot develop genuine consciences by which to inform and judge each other or the governments and policies they establish. This is one reason why the lack of remorse among perpetrators angers so many. It shows that they have unformed public consciences. This higher law, however, is not an irrational compound of arbitrary decrees from tradition or charismatic founders. It is accessible to public reason and elaboration. Publicity and higher law thus require each other. Constitutional government requires both. The TRC can be seen in the light of its effort to develop people's consciences about this higher law and the deeper covenants that bind them together as human beings.

Understanding the work of the TRC in terms of publicity and constitutional loyalty helps sharpen its own public meaning. Contrary to the TRC's official aims, 'unity' is not the primary goal of public life. Like the related concept of 'solidarity' it can overemphasise agreement about specific government policies, rather than simply the fundamental mutual agreement to manage conflict within a constitutional framework. Similarly, the notion of reconciliation can lift up a vision of cultural, linguistic, economic and religious blending or homogeneity rather than a commitment to civil argument among clearly different groups and individuals. Thus, the symbol of a 'rainbow nation' has been contested by those who want to resist its harmonistic aspirations. While the basic commitment to nonviolent dispute resolution is indispensable, the concepts of unity and reconciliation may actually reinforce popular suspicion of the plurality, argument, tempered conflict and negotiated compromises that public life assumes. What in fact political 'unity' means is agreement to work within the constitutional framework to advance the common good. The work of the TRC should then be evaluated in relation to this task.

Interpreting the TRC theologically

By seeing the significance of the TRC in terms of publicity and higher law we can see the limits of using the concept of reconciliation for a theological interpretation of its work. Naturally, the understanding of the TRC in terms of reconciliation has deep resonance with religious traditions. Christian and Jewish tradition provides at least two approaches to this concept – confession and Jubilee.[4] The most widespread has been to see the TRC in terms of contrition, confession, absolution and penance. From this standpoint theologians might see the TRC as a legal and secular form of confession (without contrition), absolution (amnesty), and penance (government reparation). The TRC's neglect of contrition and personal reparation is then seen as a shortcoming which the churches might pick up as their peculiar task. Thus, churches would try to foster some personal sense of contrition, without which forgiveness will not bring about reconciliation. Moreover, without contrition there is probably little motivation for personal acts of reparation. The limit of this approach, as some have pointed out, is that it easily becomes legalistic or individualistic. It can become caught up in the dualism of victim and perpetrator. It does not lead us to the need for systemic repair of the country.

This systemic approach appears theologically under the concept of Jubilee. Jubilee does not rest on our contrition or forgiveness but on God's demand to reconstitute the conditions of original justice, namely that each family would have the basis for a dignified life. We are to respond to that higher law of original justice through common action. Biblical Jubilee includes the welfare of the land as well as its distribution for use by the people. It is God's Sabbath, in which the whole creation is harmoniously complete. With regard to the work of building up a new constitutional order the Jubilee enjoins a common effort to provide everyone with the necessities of life in community. In the light of the systemic destruction brought about by apartheid and its predecessor policies, Jubilee concepts perform an important task.

The limit of the Jubilee model is twofold. First, the biblical model, especially its land ethic, may not be easily adaptable to a world where information is the basis for economic power. Secondly, and more seriously, it may sidestep the important work of building publics that depend on conscientious commitment to arguing and negotiating about the common good – in short the virtues of citizenship and constitutionalism.

Both of these received theological models fail to pick up on the crucial and peculiar challenges of building up a constitutional republic; that is, the work of publicity and constitutional citizenship. While the churches have a valid responsibility for promoting personal forgiveness and restitution of the land, these two purposes have to be related to this third field of responsibility. To make this connection requires both a theological and an ecclesial move. At this point I move from analysis to the construction of a theological proposal. I move from theological and political analysis to some possible theological norms for relating the TRC experience to the life and mission of the churches.

Theologically, the work of publicity and constitutionalism has to be seen in terms of the biblical concept of covenant and the formation of the ecclesia itself.[5] Let us first turn to the connection between constitutionalism and covenant. South Africa's religious traditions have not brought to the fore models of relationship among humans, or between them and God, that would reinforce constitutionalism. Either they bear traditions of communal counsel to chiefs and kings, or outright images of patriarchal authority and personal privilege. The most resonant religious symbol for constitutionalism has been the biblical image of covenant. Unfortunately, the Reformed traditions bearing this image, as Dirkie Smit (1996) and André du Toit (1983) have pointed out, have used covenant to reinforce ideas of national calling, church withdrawal from society or personal salvation, rather than those of free association and mutual agreement. The concept of higher law rooted in Hebrew covenant seems not to have been rehearsed in this tradition.[6]

Covenant as a mutual agreement among free parties about their common life and profound commitments does engage the principles of constitutionalism. The famous thirty-three principles that structured the agreement among the negotiating parties for South Africa's Constitution mirror this kind of covenant-making in which a common life is built on solemn mutual promise rather than biological ancestry or sex. Even these principles reflect an earlier covenant-like document – the Freedom Charter, which served to guide the ANC and other groups throughout the long struggle for a new political order. Commitment to and dependence on covenant-like agreements have emerged out of the very experience of this struggle for democratic life. Deep immersion in the practices, values and religious tenor of covenant-making, whether or not it assumes this name, is indispensable for creating a culture of constitutional loyalty and mutual trust.

Thus, the question a covenantal theology would pose to the TRC would be whether the truth and the practices it employed to get at the truth have cultivated a covenant-making culture. Has it, for instance, transformed religious notions of God's providence to point to the historically mediated grace by which people begin to trust the processes of mutual agreement? Have people been enabled to begin making solemn promises with old adversaries about their possible common future? Have they been able to begin to set aside a governance model based on personal power for one based on constitutional authorisation? To the extent that the TRC has not been able to do this, or simply was not empowered to do so, the churches and other religious organisations have a role to play in filling in this deep covenantal culture necessary for constitutional loyalty and mutuality. From this standpoint it is not truth that leads to reconciliation, but the capacity to entrust oneself in covenantal mutuality.

Constitutions of the kind we are talking about here are an indispensable feature of republican governance. They are created by publics and they serve to preserve these constituting publics. Unfortunately, most of our religious traditions bear models of governance based in the patriarchal household, in feudalism, personal bonds and the ordered hierarchies of birth status. These models are preserved in the liturgies of practically all our churches, whether they are rehearsed in elegant finery or enthusiastic chants. They are deeply entrenched in the models of pastoral leadership, which often oscillate between paternalistic care and authoritarian command.

There are, however, also subordinated but crucial traditions in Christianity (and other deep cultural traditions) that resonate with the effort to create genuine, free publics. They appear, for instance, in the traditional councils, even when this public is circumscribed by exclusion of women or the silencing by the chief once consensus is reached. For Christian memory the struggle for publicity is symbolised in the church's choice of self-definition as an *ecclesia* – a public assembly. This peculiar public emerges most forcefully in the pentecostal experience of free communication among people otherwise separated by language, culture and religion. This barrier-transcending public, in which Christ's spirit presides, is a mark of the church. It resonates with the human drive for full publicity as well as pointing to its fulfilment beyond the ordinary limits of human life.

From this standpoint it is not the traditional concepts of sin and forgiveness which come to the fore but those of privation and publicity. It is the movement from lies and secrecy to public profession and confirmation that constitutes the logic of salvation. Forgiveness is not the act of a stern but gracious father toward an erring son but the action of being accepted into the arguments and negotiations of the people. This is the work of new beginning and new creation that constitutes a life of forgiveness. From a New Testament perspective, forgiveness occurs because God offers a new creation – a new public – which people are invited to enter and by which their past privations are 'forgiven'. In this reversal of the usual way of looking at these connections we see some elements of the Jubilee tradition, now transformed not into the return to some imagined 'original position' but into a fully new public order, which brings with it its own demands for undergirding people's capacity for publishing their lives.

Again, in looking at the TRC, we can see that it has done much to create and expand people's publicity. It has brought memories and artefacts out from the darkness into the light where a wider public can begin to form a consensus about their validity. It has helped people voice their silent pain and give expression to their inarticulate traumas. It has created a peculiar public that is both formed by the law authorising it but also presses beyond those limits, whether through media coverage, books or public conversation. Indeed, there is much that still lies in darkness and some realities will forever be known only to God. But a model of publicity has emerged which now appears in other efforts to give people a hearing about poverty, crime and education.

The role of the church

Because it is my own faith tradition, let me carry this argument further by considering, specifically, the role of Christian churches. I trust that those of other faiths may see parallels or analogies for themselves.

As a peculiar public grounded in Christ's spirit of openness, civil courage and hope, the church needs to keep creating and extending these fundamental publics. It is not simply an 'extension' of some individual 'salvation'. It is the very essence of God's saving work. Thus, churches have an opportunity to be the nonviolent centre of the people's fundamental publics. They can also nurture these publics wherever they occur. This is the work of building 'civil society'. This work of publicity is quite different from collusion with formal government. It seeks to create the fundamental publics to which all governments are accountable. These are publics where God's higher law – God's covenant for a new creation – becomes the norm of speech, of judgement and of new beginnings.

It should be clear by now that the primary work of the churches, though focused on publicity and loyalty to higher law and covenant, is not governmental or political in the ordinary sense. Rather, it is focused on the fundamental publics in which people can actually find their lives in open conversation with one another as equal citizens. This is not only a social activity of vitalising the institutions of civil society; it is also a deeply cultural matter. It involves shaping people's deepest models of authority, power, governance and relationship.

The church's primary way of doing this is through its worship practices. At this point we have to ask whether the dispositions, models of governance and conceptions of ultimate authority it rehearses in worship are able to engage the fundamentals of a constitutional republic or are simply the repetition of traditional images of kingship, fatherhood, monolithic authority and monarchical omnipotence. Much of Christian worship still revolves around the language of patriarchal monarchy rather than that of democratic constitutionalism. It may well be that no matter how socially active the churches are, they are actually cultivating models of ultimate authority that undermine the very principles of constitutional government for which so many have suffered and died. At the very least these archaic images are subliminally reduced to psychological categories of self-discipline – something every citizen surely needs. At their worst, however, they simply cultivate models of patriarchal privilege or monarchical rule that have always corrupted republican polities. How the churches will transform their worship life so that it actively engages South Africa's new constitutional order is a profound challenge for the churches, one they have hardly begun to address.

Apart from the struggle for a worship life that can speak creatively to constitutional governance, the churches can also engage the task of reconstructing the civic culture of the country around its new ideals. Most churches seem to have rejected such a task as a return to the idolatrous reinforcement of the state experienced in the early days of apartheid or as inherently irrelevant to religion.

It is, however, possible that the churches can critically but constructively accompany this process of building up a new 'civil religion'. As

John de Gruchy (1994a) has pointed out, Christians can take deep satisfaction in the civil symbols of a new political order without taking them into the church's sanctuary. Monuments to new patterns of covenant-making, such as the Belhar Confession as well as the Freedom Charter, can be created. In the TRC's framework, this is the work of 'symbolic reparation' which forms part of its mandate. Celebrations of the renewal of the land, blessings at the transferring of land to rightful owners and freedom walks to bring people together in public can all vitalise public life and constitutionalism without creating an excessive entanglement with governments and political parties. It is a task for which the church has rich resources and one that can help shape the deeper cultural values to sustain the new constitutional order. However, it is also a task that will require fundamental reconstruction of the church's worship life and of the conception of its role in the wider publics to which government must be accountable.

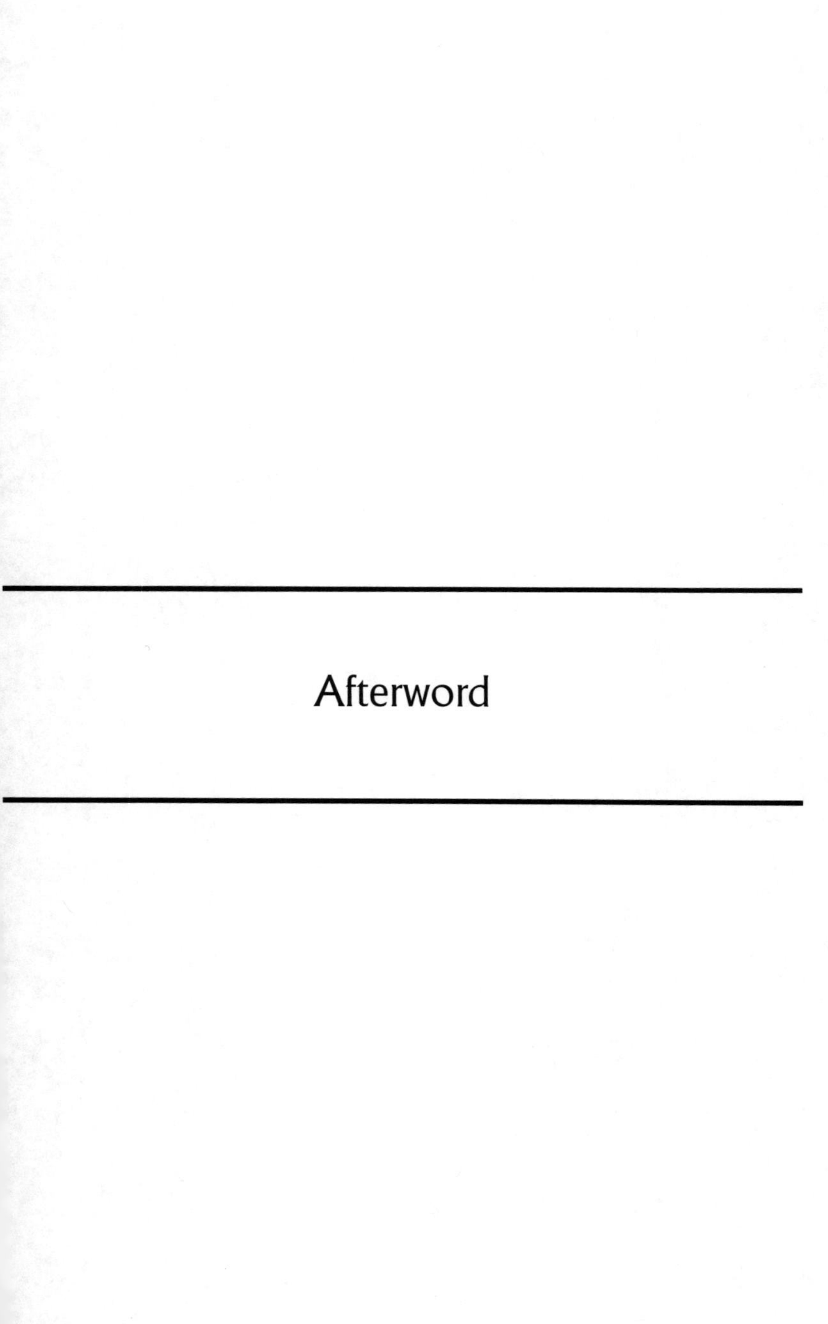

Afterword

9 Hearing the Truth

Charity Majiza

One of the most difficult things to do in life, for people and for nations, is to face the truth about the past. Hearing the truth is often unpalatable and uncomfortable, provoking feelings of guilt, defensiveness or a desire to forget. 'Openness to the truth' is going to be necessary for the churches and other faith communities in their quest for healing within themselves and for the community at large. This of course cannot be forced upon individuals or groups. There has to be a willingness to 'wake up' in order 'to hear the truth' (Ackermann 1996, 51–52).

Faith communities have played an important role in South Africa's history. After the closure of the TRC it is their responsibility to continue to listen to people's stories and to exercise pastoral care in order that healing of memories may take place. This is true of the Christian church.

The overall purpose of this book is to deepen analysis and to foster debate within the churches and other faith communities on the TRC process. The church especially must come to terms with the part she played during the apartheid period in order to effect meaningful and convincing pastoral care to the people of our nation. There remains much denial in some quarters of the church about what has taken place; partly because of revelations of gruesome acts performed by people who are known and unknown, partly because some church members knew exactly what work people they knew were engaged in, and who colluded by their silence. Others feared for their lives if they spoke up, or were benefiting from what was happening, or, even worse, felt that the evil done actually expressed the way they felt about their fellow South Africans, confirming what they were taught in their homes and churches to believe about them.

Members of faith communities might have been 'agents', 'victims', 'opponents' or, more subtly, beneficiaries of oppression. And any person may have been more than one of these. Different denominations have to internalise this information and find ways of dealing with it if the process of healing is to be realised. It is these complexities that the church has to face and address if our nation is to move forward in the spirit of reconciliation or, failing this, the authenticity of her mission will be severely compromised.

The church and other faith communities in South Africa have a significant role to play post-TRC. The challenges we face during this period of transformation require different strategies and call for new ways of doing things. We need to work together and at the same time confront within ourselves those things which have damaged our credibility with our members and with society at large.

The principalities and powers that brought about division, alienation, dehumanisation and destruction in our past history have been partially revealed to us during the TRC and are still very much with us. This requires a determined effort on our part to change the way we viewed and treated each other in the past. Both the victims and the perpetrators of violence cry out for the restoration of their human dignity. Those who knowingly and deliberately became accomplices in the oppression of others should be made accountable for their actions.

Not everyone who wished to tell his or her story was able to convey it at the TRC's hearings because of the limited space, time and human resources. It may be that there were expectations raised that this single organ would enable the nation to find out about what has happened in the past in order for us to grapple with the truth, and these expectations were exaggerated. One wonders whether some of those who came to confess their actions would have done so if the dangling carrot of amnesty was not provided and whether what the commissioners heard was the whole truth. Having said that, it is important to realise that the nation had to start somewhere in order to begin to uncover our unflattering past.

It is fitting that this kind of work be continued by religious communities. Each may effect reconciliation according to its own particular rituals, practices and forms of confronting those things which have created barriers within and between communities and families. While there will indeed be a great need of trauma counselling with psychological expertise, there will also be a need to mobilise traditional restorative methods so as to integrate those who feel alienated. Here is where faith communities can play an important role.

Although much writing has been done concerning the stories and accounts of those who attended the TRC hearings, there is still a gap to be filled by black theologians for the articulation and appropriation of what has happened especially in the black community. Women have suffered much during the dark days. It was mostly they who kept the home fires burning, who took care of the aged, infirm and the young whilst their loved ones were away. They were the ones who organised funeral services for their loved ones. Many stories of courage have yet to be told. At the TRC hearings women featured prominently, still carrying their pain with them yet accompanying others in their search for the truth. Faith communities have to minister to them as they seek to articulate and to deal with their pain, even while fulfilling their responsibilities of enabling their families and neighbours to pick up the pieces after the reopening of the wounds at the hearings.

Perhaps the truth does set us free. But this does not always translate itself into real life. Many who have found out about how their loved ones died may experience a greater burden and less freedom as they feel the pressure to forgive and to reconcile with those who have perpetrated acts of violence against them. Some may even feel guilty for not wanting to forgive those who have taken such actions towards their loved ones. Faith communities will have to be sensitive in their exercise of care. We will be engaged in this particular ministry for a long time. We may further need to confess how we misled our members in our teaching, preaching and communication.

Lastly, faith communities will have to revisit the statements of confession made at the TRC and monitor themselves and each other in order to ensure that they change their ways and work towards living out their promises.

10 Wounded Healers

James Cochrane, John de Gruchy and Stephen Martin

If the faith communities at the TRC seemed eager to take on the role of facilitators of healing and reconciliation in the post-TRC context, the essays in this book have raised the question of the credibility of faith communities with reference to their facing of the truth and their concrete, practical commitments to processes of reconciliation. These two themes are of a piece. However much guilt they have incurred in the past, faith communities must not abandon their role as facilitators of healing in the present. But neither must they use that role to mask their own complicity in the past. Facing the truth, likewise, involves an imperative to become involved as agents of healing.

The RICSA Report classified faith communities according to three essential roles that they played during the apartheid period; namely, 'agents of oppression, victims of oppression and opponents of oppression.' This volume has shown that it is not, however, a simple matter of saying 'we were (unambiguously) this or that'. Indeed, even the so-called 'progressive' churches, mosques and other centres of religious life were as much sites of struggle as they were agents of struggle or, perhaps, oppression. Faith communities were often places where the broader social forces of repression and transformation were in conflict; they were a terrain of battle in themselves. Within the same faith community there were victims, perpetrators and agents of change.

The typology of 'victim, perpetrator, agent' hides another reality, however. Many people were 'beneficiaries' of apartheid, of oppression and exploitation. This too is a crucial element in facing up to the past and constructing a healed future. Beneficiaries might have had no direct role in the acts investigated by the TRC, but they certainly carry some moral responsibility too for what happened, however 'knowing or unknowing' they might have been about the true state of affairs. Many faith communities are filled with those who benefited in the suffering caused to others, those whose stable and materially comfortable lifestyle was ensured by the activities of perpetrators of abuses. This fundamental reality poses a particularly difficult challenge to transformation, filled as it is with ambiguity and largely closed as it is to any redress in formal legal or social institutions. The question of the bystander remains. This challenge to faith communities is placed before us by several of the essays here.

Christian churches in particular, and other faith communities too, have thus emerged from the apartheid years scarred and compromised. As such, faith communities are, in Henri Nouwen's words, 'wounded healers'. Awareness of this alone should help mute any promotion of triumphalist narratives which some of the contributors to this volume warn against. Contextualising healing and reconciliation means drawing upon particular restorative practices. The question of responsibility must be raised strongly, even as it is tempered with the humility required of the wounded healer.

The wounds of the past are not only within, but also between faith communities. The RICSA Report, for example, mentions the need to address specific 'church apartheid' divisions. This must take place, especially where those divisions are along socio-economic lines. Apartheid was, if nothing else, a way of guarding the privileges of the minority by keeping the majority in economic bondage. This, in turn, expressed itself in geographic marginalisation, at the national, the regional and the local levels, with all the implications this had for access to, or lack of access to, material and social resources. It is a scandal of faith when these are replicated in the way the church and other religious institutions are set up.

Let us for a moment focus on the specific wounds of apartheid that have divided Christian churches, perhaps the most poignant of them all being the strong backing given both to the state and to forces of liberation from the apartheid state by Christians. These wounds lie also within the broader ecumenical church, which implies that the activity of healing is also an activity that must take place ecumenically. The TRC faith hearings, in some ways, were a cue for this, gathering a constituency broader than any church-sponsored gathering in memory. Especially significant was the inclusion of the AICs, and in particular the ZCC and the Ibandla lamaNazaretha. It may prove true, as Petersen points out in his essay, that 'mainstream' churches (fast becoming a minority) need AICs more than AICs need the mainstream churches. At any rate, ecumenical activity must include them, even as it now embraces the once self-declared enemies of the ecumenical church like the DRC and the Rhema Church. This may also require churches to revisit the terms not only with which they view the past, but with which 'prophetic activity', a description of social engagement characteristic of Christian struggle against apartheid, is understood.

While it is well known that the DRC provided the biblical foundation for and a sophisticated theological justification of apartheid, and that the SACC was a fierce opponent of it, the role of right-wing Christian groups, which operated within various English-speaking denominations, was more subtle. Many of these groups, as Arendse points out, are still operating. The church needs to be aware of the way in which its proclamation has been (and perhaps continues to be) contested and subverted; after all, such groups were similarly using the language of 'salvation' while acting as conduits of government propaganda.

But this vigilance goes beyond simply addressing specific groups who have abused the message of the church in the past. Careful discernment of the name (or names) in which the church speaks is required as its message of reconciliation enters the public sphere. Such awareness must be owned for the sake of the authenticity and credibility of the church's witness in the present and the future. It also involves taking seriously the churches' role in providing, in Russel Botman's terms, the fundamental value-orientation of their members. This means further self-examination, particularly by the 'English-speaking churches' (as Botman implies) with reference to the past. But it also signals a possibility of playing a more positive role in the future.

To what extent may similar things be said of other faith communities? At least two points become pertinent in this respect. First, no other faith tradition was as compromised by apartheid as was Christianity. This is a particularly difficult reality for Christian communities to come to terms with. It also affects the credibility of the Christian presence in the public sphere. Some of the essays in this volume indicate clearly that its credibility crisis might become even more severe under a 'secular' constitution where Christianity no longer has the privileged role it had in the past. Other faith communities will face the issues in somewhat different ways. Yet some of what may be said about the fractured, contested and compromised nature of Christian faith communities in South Africa will be true for most, if not all, other faith communities.

Second, as Everett reminds us, faith communities take different organisational forms, some of them incompatible with the way in which democratic institutions and processes work. In order to be heard in the public sphere under a democratic dispensation, a community must be organised in a formal, institutional manner. Only thus is one able to have recourse to legal and judicial instruments such as the Constitution and the Bill of Rights, as well as the various commissions and the parliamentary processes it establishes. Who do you represent? becomes a key question.

If the answer is 'an undefinable community', as would be the case for several faith community traditions in South Africa, then clearly one is less likely to be heard and more likely to be marginalised.

This reality was in many respects reflected both in the way in which the faith community hearings were constituted, and in the way in which presentations were made and received. Some voices were simply much more marginal than others. Essays in this volume also reflect on this reality, and we may say that the ongoing interaction of faith communities across traditions, and from within particular traditions towards the wider public sphere, will continue to evidence this pattern of domination and marginalisation. If reconciliation is to include a coming to terms with the plurality of faith traditions and the relative imbalance of power and participation in our society between various traditions, then the TRC faith community hearings have only begun to meet the need. The huge diversity of the South African public is mirrored in the religious diversity of people, a diversity as strong as anywhere in the world. How we come to terms with this in building a healed and healing society may well be indicative of both the possibilities for and constraints upon reconciliation between peoples of faith anywhere in the world.

Finally, all of these points have significance beyond the specific, limited realm of particular faith communities in themselves. However faith communities address these issues at local, regional, national or even international levels – and all of these present challenges and opportunities for a specifically South African contribution – whatever happens has not only religious, but also political significance. It has to do with how we regulate our lives together, with how we engender and practise virtues and values, of the kind of citizenry we produce and of the kind of vision we bequeath to future generations. It has to do with the *polis*, with our common life together as citizens in a land for which each of us is in part responsible. If anything, this is the challenge that the TRC presents to faith communities, with their extensive reach into the localities, the minds and the emotions of the vast bulk of our people. The challenge of the TRC concerns not the Commission itself, nor the particularities of the faith community hearings as such. It concerns our life together at this time and in this place. Thus the role of faith communities in the future, and their reponse to the issues raised in this book, must be taken seriously by others in the public sphere.

The RICSA Report identified 'healing' as an appropriate image for the activity of faith communities in South Africa's transformation. The Report, and the essays above, have also demonstrated the first-hand experience within these communities of the brokenness of the society. As 'wounded healers', therefore, members and representatives of faith communities are called to enter into processes and to develop practices which will take what was begun in the TRC a great deal further. There is an urgency in this, and a moral and spiritual imperative behind it. The RICSA Report, and the subsequent essays which make up this book, are aimed at nothing more, in the final analysis, than prompting that realisation and encouraging appropriate commitment.

Appendix 1: Extracts from the Submissions and Testimony of Faith Communities to the TRC

In what follows it is not our intention to try to represent the spectrum of faith communities that made submissions to the Commission, nor to put forth what we considered the most important contributions. Rather, we wish to allow readers to sample some of the flavours of the submissions and testimony. This is therefore a highly selective, deliberately restricted compilation. It is aimed at concretising what was said in some of the essays above and at pointing to some of the gaps in the hearings themselves.

The inclusion of the submission of the Messina congregation is, for example, not intended to single out that particular congregation, but rather to present an experience typical of many faith communities during the apartheid years, and present in the representations of other black churches before the Commission. The extract from the testimony of Methodist Bishop Dandala gives another dimension to this, displaying the dilemmas churches in the so-called 'bantustans' faced, caught between the need to resist and thus risk losing their 'legitimate' space on the one hand and the need to minister to congregants on the other.

Of the many statements that were supplied or given, we have decided to include the submission of Lesley Morgan, a poignant display of the fragmentation that remains a challenge, as well as the letter of Nico Smith. The Salvation Army submission demonstrates the way symbolic resources and practices within a tradition (the 'testimony meeting', for example) may be redeployed in addressing the need to work for reconciliation. The extract from Rabbi Cyril Harris's testimony at the hearings exemplifies a concreteness which shows how members of some faith communities may act positively within society.

We have also included the submission of the Western and Southern Cape Synod of the DRC, as of all the materials given the TRC by the DRC this was the only 'submission'. As mentioned in the RICSA Report, an account of gender oppression was all but absent in the submissions. Because the Report was an account of the submissions, there was little opportunity to mention gender oppression (see sec. 5.2.5). The inclusion of extracts from the women's submission thus fills a significant gap in the Report.

Submission to the TRC by the Uniting Reformed Church of South Africa, Messina Congregation, not dated

We, the congregation of the Uniting Reformed Church in Southern Africa (former NGKA in Messina) hereby represented by the church council, wish to submit to the Truth and Reconciliation Commission as follows:

1. In 1977 the congregation lost a house in Messina Town. Rev L. E. Matsaung, our first black minister, could not stay in our mission house (parsonage) in town white area because as the white N. G. Kerk put it: 'The Group Areas Act did not allow it.' They even rented the house to someone else. This Act no longer exists, but we do not succeed in re-owning our house. The situation continues to torment the congregation. Several times we approached the white N. G. Kerk, but no response comes through.

2. During the period 1977 to 1991 our parsonage at Messina-Nancefield was frequently raided by police and the army. At one stage it was attacked and window pains [*sic*] broken. Up to date nobody has been arrested.

3. Our church building at Nancefield where also the paralegal office is housed, was also attacked and window pains [*sic*] broken.

4. We lost also a plot at Harper of about 6 hectares . . . which was granted to the congregation by Messina Investments Limited. We had already made three boreholes and plans for conference centre and irrigation schemes where 50 people were on standby about to start to work.

5. Another parsonage we lost with the same reasons is at Tshipise 35 kms from Messina Town.

6. Our congregation was horribly persecuted by both the police, the army and the white congregation of the N. G. Kerk in Messina.

6.1. In 1982 the congregation lost the subsidy which was withdrawn because our minister was labelled a 'terrorist'.

6.2. In 1985 the N. G. Kerk in Messina blocked the subsidy from Pretoria which was coming to our congregation through them.

7. During this period the church council members were now and then taken to Belbridge police headquarters and terribly interrogated.

8. During the Messina Terror Trial where Mthetheledi Ncube and Nondula (MK cadres) were tried by the Supreme Court their parents stayed at our parsonage at Nancefield Township with the family of Rev. L. E. Matsaung. This resulted in the persecution of our pastor's family by the police, army and the N. G. Kerk congregation of Messina. The pastor's sermons were now and then confiscated by the army.

9. At one stage a planned bombing of our church building was aborted as congregation members pounced upon one government agent who was found taking fotos [*sic*] of our church building while the congregation was busy worshipping.

10. In 1991 our pastor and other church leaders were detained under section 50 of the Security Act and put in different police station cells. Rev. L. E. Matsaung was put at Duiwelkloof police station cell. 'On my arrival I was pushed into a big ice cold room. From 18h00 to 4h00 my bowels were cold frozen. After I was taken out for 2 days I could not eat nor drink. I nearly died. This was a horrible torture I will never forget in my life.'

11. The congregation suffered for many years because of our involvement in the struggle against the oppression of the Black community in Messina. The white government saw us as the enemy that was misleading the people, while the people saw us as carrying a light of hope in their lives.

Requests

We hereby humbly request the commission to help us in the following:

1. To repossess our congregation parsonage, the mission house from the N. G. Kerk congregation which they registered in their name for the reasons that the Group Areas Act did not allow us to register it in our name.

1.1. We claim also the monies they got from its rentals. Also the parsonage at Tshipise and the plot at Harper.

2. To bring back the subsidies which were cut and the interest that accrued from it. In this case we claim about R250 000 00 that will help us in healing our wounds.

Extract from the testimony of Bishop Mvume Dandala, TRC faith community hearings, 17 November 1997

A number of our ministers suffered public humiliation at the hands of the government and its agents of evil. A large number of Methodist families suffered at the hands of the tyrannical system as they responded to the prophetic call to resist apartheid. These, for us, are not a cause for boasting, for the pain that accompanied such witness is still [felt]. In 1978 the

Methodist Church of Southern Africa suffered a major blow when it was banned and declared an undesirable organisation from Transkei, one of the areas where Methodism is strongest in Southern Africa. All our properties in Transkei were confiscated without compensation. The most valuable of them were then sold and they are now lost to us. Apartheid effectively wanted to alienate the Methodist Church from part of its roots in the Eastern Cape. The reason being simply the refusal of our conference in 1977 to accommodate the fracturing of the people of Southern Africa according to their ethnic backgrounds and their balkanisation into independent Bantu states. For ten years we were forbidden from ministering to our mothers and fathers. We were forbidden from [burying] our own without the permit of the oppressor. To minister to our own people, turned either into a criminal offence or an act for which one could be labelled . . . [inaudible] from the Church Catholic. Today we wish to offer an unreserved apology to those who felt that our refusal to minister in Transkei under these stringent conditions imposed by that government was to abandon them.

We also wish to offer an apology on behalf of those who felt compelled by the needs of our members there to serve within the Methodist churches formed according to the law of the government of Transkei. The wounds of that blow are still fresh for us, because some of our people were permanently alienated from us as a result. We deeply long for a reconciled Methodist Community, restored to its full fellowship and connection. We thank God for the changes that have come to our land. We wish to state without ambiguity that we are committed to our responsibility to help bring healing and reconciliation to South Africa. We will continue to build racially mixed congregations where individuals are honoured and their heritage welcomed for the growth of all together. We have committed ourselves to joining hands with other Christian communities to fight hunger and poverty, which is often, if not always, a direct consequence of our unjust history. We are prepared to be in dialogue with people who may have a claim on some of our property, as a result of having been unjustly removed from their land. We have called on our congregations to use our facilities for projects that will assist those who were denied opportunities to gain valuable skills for their future. We have opened our facilities for healing and counselling sessions such as Kulumani, and we have set as one of the three goals of our connection that the church at every level will encourage the creation of speaking forums where people can speak about their pain and help one another to heal. We are deeply conscious of the breakdown of morality in our land as a result of apartheid and we seek to place emphasis again on values such as family life, that were broken down by apartheid acts such as the migratory labour laws. We have, and we will continue to write, liturgies that allow people to look back at their history and see that their heroes were not victims, but people, who like Jesus, laid their lives down for the freedom of the nation. We will endeavour not to flinch or hesitate when required to say a prophetic word that will help our country and all its organs so that we will never allow ourselves to repeat the mistakes of the past as a nation. We believe that it is all the people of South Africa who must have the will to move their country to a destiny of freedom, wealth, charity and respect for creation and human dignity. We believe that it is our task that we should appeal to the gospel of Jesus Christ for such a will to be nurtured and strengthened among our people. I thank you, Sir.

Submission to the Truth and Reconciliation Commission: Johannesburg Central post-hearing, public follow-up workshop, by Lesley Morgan

I am 47 years old. I am a middle-aged, middle-class, South African housewife, an elder in my congregation, a wife, a mother, a nursing sister. However, I do not come before you as a representative of any of these groups. I cannot speak for middle-aged white housewives, nor for the medical community, nor for my denomination, nor for my congregation, nor even for my family. I am here in my personal capacity, as Lesley, stripped of my titles and my relationships.

I grew up with all the advantages and opportunities afforded me because I was white. I was oblivious of the fact that their [*sic*] were so many people around me who were not as privileged as I was, not because I was unfeeling, but because I was unaware. I became more aware by the time I reached high school and can remember heated discussions in classrooms because of the inequalities I was beginning to notice. In hindsight I realise the gross distortions I was taught but it is only in looking back that I can see that our education system prepared me for accepting the totally unacceptable. In learning things without questioning, in obeying authority without challenge, I came to accept as normal the totally and grossly abnormal.

When I was in my twenties, I had many friends at university, including young people who were arrested and harassed by security policemen. It filled me with anger, but also with a sense of helplessness. We tried so hard with no result. The feeling of uselessness was quite overpowering. The state just carried on and things got more and more difficult.

By the late '70s and early '80s I was married with a young family. Although I was fully aware of the dreadful things that were happening all around me, fear paralysed me. I was no activist. I was afraid of being arrested, afraid of being detained without trial, afraid of being tortured or killed. I do not even have the excuse of not knowing. I was well aware of what was happening. I read the Black Sash publications and knew the terrible consequences of the Group Areas Act, the Mixed Marriages Act, the Land Appropriation Act, the Separate Development Act, the Bantu Education Act. God forgive me, I did nothing to speak out against these obscene laws.

In April this year, I attended the first of several meetings on the churches' response to the TRC hearings. One of the things discussed was the fact that so few white people attend the hearings and/or make submissions. I have been thinking of nothing else since then. I started talking about it in my community and discussing it with my friends. I started asking myself why I have not attended. I know it is causing great pain amongst the black community. I cannot imagine what it must be to bear your pain and suffering so openly and publicly. I can imagine what it must feel like to stretch out your hand in an attempt to forgive and reconcile and have no one there to grasp it. The hurt must be enormous and there must be anger and frustration too.

[. . .]

I have been thinking about what I would submit today. I thought about saying how apartheid had violated us all, as it has, but in the face of the submissions that have preceeded mine, and the millions that have not been heard, what could I say to them? I thought I could say 'I'm sorry' and that would somehow make it all right. But God kept nudging me, pulling at my arm. I was at a loss to explain how I feel, and how our past has somehow diminished me. We are so separated, you and I, our experiences so vastly different. How do we bridge that gap? I am a Christian. How do I reconcile what I believe with what I practised?

[. . .]

I am of the Reformed tradition. We are not given to Pentecostal or charismatic experiences. On Wednesday, I was driving to a conference of the eradication of poverty. I drove 8 km past my turnoff on the highway. For the first time in my life, I truly heard the voice of Christ. In all the years I ignored the oppressed, I ignored him. In my fear and concern for my own safety, like Peter before me, I denied my Lord. Like Peter, the realisation of that denial has filled me with unbearable sorrow. The realisation that my faith is so small, so selfish, so empty, has broken me. It has made me understand why I feel such shame. I profess to be a follower of Christ, but have been unwilling to go where He has led me. I have realised my sins of omission are still alive.

I cannot change the past and it would be so much easier to blame apartheid for all of it. The truth is, I made my own choices. I know of so many people who chose differently. I have read the letter submitted to the TRC by Beyers Naudé. So many people have said, 'Of all people, why would he need to make a submission?' I have been greatly humbled by it . . . He helped me find my way here.

The choices I made in the past to avoid what I perceived, in my fear and cowardice, as having consequences too dangerous to deal with have resulted in consequences far worse than I ever feared. Poverty has moved into my street, crime has moved in next door, unemployment is knocking at my gate. The results of systemic human rights violations have left us all with a legacy of mistrust, suspicion and anger. I will not run away from what is happening. I acknowledge my part in the creation of our present. I pray that together we will secure our future.

[. . .]

Finally I need to say one last thing . . . the hardest part is at the end. It is so hopelessly inadequate to make right what has happened, so puny in the face of so much suffering . . . but it is all I have to give – I'm sorry.

'An open letter to all pastors in South Africa,' written by Nico Smith
By the time of its presentation at the hearings this letter had been signed by some 400 pastors.

To us as preachers of the Word of God, the responsibility is entrusted to proclaim at all times the gospel of reconciliation with God and our fellow human beings in Christ.

This responsibility entails the prophetic denouncement of all forms of injustice, oppression and violence committed against any human being. As we read and hear what happened in South Africa during the years of Nationalist Party rule, we, as preachers of God's Word, are confronted with the question how could it possibly have happened while we as preachers of reconciliation, justice and peace were preaching this message from our pulpit every Sunday.

But the question which disturbs us even more is this, how was it possible that those who intentionally committed murders and sabotage against fellow citizens could have been, as is now becoming evident, members of churches and even regular churchgoers?

Was there nothing in our preaching, liturgies and sacraments that disturbed the conscience of those who were directly involved in all the evil deeds committed?

Therefore we have indeed more than enough reason to feel deeply guilty for having spiritualised and even gagged the gospel to such an extent that those in government and those responsible to execute government policy didn't feel confronted by our preaching.

We are guilty of having allowed the rulers to execute the ideology of forced separation for the sake of so-called law and order without offering united resistance as preachers of justice and peace.

We admit and confess that we too were blinded by an ideology which presented itself as justifiable from the Bible.

We lacked the gift of discerning the spirits because we had not real desire to receive this gift. In the light of the above, we want to confess publicly that we as preachers were co-responsible for what happened in South Africa. In fact our guilt should be considered as more serious than that of any other person or institution.

We who were supposed to be the conscience of the nation didn't succeed in preventing the most serious forms of abuse of the human conscience. As a result of this, the criminal violation of people's human dignity and even the destruction of human life continued for too long.

But this confession of guilt is not intended to be vague and general. We confess our guilt by mentioning specific examples of our failure to be faithful to the gospel. We first of all acknowledge and confess that for many of us, especially those in the white community, life was very convenient and comfortable under Nationalist Party rule.

Many of us therefore couldn't and wouldn't see the oppression and violation of millions of people in our country, hear their cries for justice and failed to take action.

We furthermore acknowledge and confess that when we sometimes did feel uncomfortable about the way the government and other institutions persisted in its abuse of power, we did nothing because of fear.

We thereby allowed evil, with the co-operation of Christians, to continue its devastating work against the people of God.

In the same breath we commit ourselves to call upon Christians to be careful in their support of political leaders and their policies. We furthermore commit ourselves to challenge Christians concerning their political and socio-economic responsibilities.

We also want to make amends for neglecting the needs of the poor and the oppressed, therefore we commit ourselves to the task of guiding God's people towards involvement in actions to eliminate the socio-economic inequalities of our country.

We have evaded this responsibility for too long. We furthermore commit ourselves to the task of encouraging people with the gospel of hope. Especially in these days when many have lost hope and are despairing of the future of our country.

This we will do by replacing the longing for the previous so-called better days, by dreams of an even better future. The same gospel, therefore, also urges us to commit ourselves to engage in the reconstruction of our society.

Although we recognise that some ministers have stood bravely in the struggle for justice, it is our hope that every church minister who reads this document will recognise the challenge facing us all, which we dare not push aside.

We are compelled to make a choice. Either we confess our guilt in order to be set free for greater and more faithful service to the gospel of Jesus Christ, or we ignore this challenge to confess our guilt and thus declare ourselves not guilty of what happened in our country.

'The Salvation Army and the Truth and Reconciliation Process in South Africa – A Policy Statement', approved by the Territorial Executive Council, 21 January 1997

. . . The Salvation Army internationally has, by policy, generally refrained from political involvement but has, where deemed appropriate, been willing to condemn practices which are morally and socially unacceptable. Still, for many years, the Salvation Army in South Africa remained silent about the growing evils of apartheid. It was only in November 1986 that General E. Burrows, international leader of the Salvation Army, issued a statement clearly condemning apartheid.

The Salvation Army in 1995 initiated a territory-wide process of reconciliation including a pledge card with signatures publicly presented to the General and a memorial plaque erected in Soweto. We recognise that the process must continue and the Salvation Army is willing to participate constructively in the continuing process at national level. The following general principles will guide us in participation, being offered in response to SACC recommendations to the churches.

1. The territorial executive council will continue to monitor the reconciliation process and advise on policies and programmes which will further the process.

[. . .]

Two significant aspects of Salvation Army meetings include personal testimony and confession at the mercy seat. We recognise the immense value of being able to share one's story in public, with emphasis on God's way with us. We also understand the benefit of private confession shared in confidence with a counsellor. Both these aspects of Salvation Army meetings can be utilised in exploring the truth of the past and building the reconciliation process. Especially important is the acceptance by a congregation of a member witnessing in this way.

2. The following theological emphases will be upheld in the reconciliation process. [A brief statement of Salvation Army doctrinal essentials follows, including substitutionary atonement, regeneration, conversion and reconciliation, and a statement on social responsibility.] . . .

3. We uphold our position of political neutrality in our relationship with the state.

The Salvation Army recognises the authority of the state and of the governing authority (Romans 13: 1–5). It nevertheless retains the freedom to obey God rather than man (Acts 5: 29). The Army's position of neutrality in matters of party politics has proved to be of longterm benefit. At times it may have been misunderstood as abdication of moral duty. Our neutrality is not a passive withdrawal from difficult issues, but active engagement with all. It frees us to minister to all people at all times.

[. . .]

4. The Salvation Army is committed to the just redistribution of resources in South Africa. This includes a willingness to participate in land reform and to reassign land under Salvation Army ownership where this qualifies for reallocation. The allocation of central funds of the Salvation Army takes account of traditionally disadvantaged communities.

5. The Salvation Army will offer pastoral care to both the victims and perpetrators of crimes during the apartheid era.

The ministry of preaching balanced with sensitive listening will challenge and guide people, congregations and communities with whom we are in contact. The aim will be spiritual conversion which should include attitude change and whole person transformation (Romans 12: 2). We will promote the concepts of Health, Healing and Wholeness as outlined in the General's vision and direction statement.

[. . .]

6. We recognise the importance of good relations with neighbouring states.

South Africa is one of the countries of the Salvation Army's Southern Africa territory including Mozambique, Lesotho and Swaziland, countries which have been affected by events in South Africa and to whom South Africans therefore have a responsibility for good-neighbourliness. We will cultivate good relations with neighbouring countries and discourage anti-foreigner sentiments.

7. We acknowledge that the Salvation Army together with many other churches in South Africa should have been more active in opposition to the evils of apartheid.

[. . .]

8. We will cultivate a balanced attitude to our history and nurture hope for the future but concentrate positively on the realities of the present.

Whilst there are many painful and unpleasant elements to our history we will cultivate a balanced view of our history, recognising especially the giftedness of the people of all backgrounds in the Salvation Army in South Africa. We will view the reconciliation process as a very positive aspect of our history. We will cultivate forward planning, through a visioning process with the setting of goals and strategic plans. We will nevertheless concentrate on the present realities, and work on the present strengths and abilities of the people of the organisation, at the same time committing ourselves to human resource development and building up capacity.

[. . .]

10. We will continue to develop programmes and policies which combat racism and strengthen reconciliation.

• We will encourage people to recognise themselves and each other primarily as South Africans rather than as members of a particular ethnic group.

• We will work for the empowerment of the historically disadvantaged communities. Human and community development in the spirit of partnership rather than charity, welfare and paternalism will be our emphasis.

• In united gatherings we will attempt to cultivate respect for and participation in the differing traditions of worship prevalent in the Salvation Army in South Africa.

• We will continue to cultivate a unity of purpose for Salvationists of all ethnic backgrounds and language groups.

Extracts from the testimony of Rabbi Cyril Harris, TRC faith community hearings, 18 November 1997

I want to explain in a few moments the range of practical projects the South African Jewish community is undertaking under the broad umbrella of a programme called Tekun, which Bertie Lubner and I have the honour of being co-chairmen. *Tekun* is a Hebrew word meaning repairing, trying to put things right. It is a wonderful exercise, we are trying to apply Jewish resources, skills, expertise and know-how, to be of maximum benefit to the upliftment programme. One instance in food: the Jewish housewife, when she shops, is asked to buy an extra tin or extra packet. She is buying half a dozen tins, buy a seventh tin; a dozen packets of something, buy a thirteenth packet. That goes in a separate part of the trolley, goes to the nearest Synagogue . . . and we take that to the hungry.

We have many projects. I give you one instance on welfare. Nokatula, which is a home for the physically and mentally handicapped in Alexandra Township, is consistently visited by the Selwyn Segal Centre, which is a similar home for physically and mentally handicapped people in Johannesburg. We share expertise and facilities and we all go together to Camp David at Magaliesberg. May I point out that here we are not being patronising. I know it sounds terribly patronising, we are trying to empower people to help themselves, and that's why we are handing over the skills. We have a major agricultural project at Rietfontein. It is an educational experience in farming, based on the success in Israel. Many of our projects, I mention this not, God forbid, to make a political point! I mention it because the state of Israel has expertise in things like water conservation, solar energy and all forms . . . helping at the moment seventeen African countries, and we feel very proud that the Israelis want to help us with some of our projects. And they are helping us with this Agricultural Education Centre at Rietfontein. Two weeks ago 100,000 spinach seedlings . . . were planted and we are all helping with this exercise. We have very many educational projects. We have enrichment programmes in which SADTU[1] and COSAS[2] have co-operated with us. Sometimes they have requested, sometimes we have gone to them. Our King David Schools in Johannesburg and the schools in Cape Town are helping in the townships with computer literacy programmes. It's where I'm computer illiterate but the youngsters, bless them, have to be computer literate, and we're helping in East Bank High School for example, in Alex, with many adult education programmes, basic literacy courses. My wife . . . is the Chairperson of Ossac. Ossac is a black adult education school in Killarney, run in the Oxford Synagogue. We get over 100 every evening. The ages range from 20 to 60. There are domestic workers, security personnel, shop assistants, unemployed people. They do the IEB tests in English and Maths, and we have a 95% success rate, and there is nothing more joyous in the world than seeing somebody over 50 who has been denied an education actually coming every night and studying and the glow on that person's face when they hold their certificate. It is wondrous to behold. We are encouraging education in many ways. Our Union of Jewish Women has programmes in Soweto in HIPPI (home instruction for pre-primary youngsters which is geared to the mothers) and MATAL (upgrading the qualifications of pre-school teachers).

. . . Some of the things I am mentioning to you have been going on for donkey's years. The Rabbi Wyler's School in Alexandra was founded by the Reformed Jewish Movement over 50 years ago. Rabbi Wyler put in a primary school then and thank God it's still going. We have arranged to take groups of young professionals to Israel to train them in entrepreneurial skills, business development skills, banking skills. We are already on our fourth group there. Every single person who has been in one of these groups and come back, they have actually been given promotion. If they were a bank clerk, they are now assistant manager in the bank. And it's a wonderful thing.

We are using the expertise of ORT, which is an international Jewish organisation, and we have at Midrand a college of Science and Technology, which is again wonderfully successful. We are doing things for employment and there is a very wonderful lady called Helen Leverman, in the Cape, who [is involved in a programme] making toys and bead decorations and they are sold all over the world: in Paris, London and New York. And it's a way of getting, including blind people, who can be taught how to string the beads and by the touch on a colour system, and it's a marvellous thing. We have sporting activities . . . we have soccer in Soweto and they love it. And we have cultural activities. We have joint choral concerts. We have the black choir of Soweto, the Johannesburg Jewish Choir and something called the Welsh Male Choir. We are trying to build bridges, we are going across the board.

I have only given you, Mr Chairperson, . . . a few examples. I know it's a drop in the ocean, but we are trying to galvanise our Jewish community in order that we can actually help. It is our responsibility to be of help.

Extracts from the women's submission to the TRC by Ms Cathy P. Makhenya

. . . All religions are patriarchal, based on the 'rule of the fathers'. This was reinforced by the missionaries. The legacy of this tradition is that women remain largely powerless and voiceless. In the Christian tradition, spirituality has largely been the preserve of men. The language of prayer and worship is generally male, the symbols and images of God are male, the Scriptures have been used [to support] male dominance, the ruling structures of the Church are predominantly male and there is a prevailing male consciousness. This is somewhat of an anomaly, as the congregations are predominantly female.

Women are excluded from Christian religious language. In hymns, liturgy and the Scriptures people are referred to as men, the sons of God or brothers, not to mention the militaristic language commonly used, too. The language for God is predominantly male (Lord, King, Master, Father). Not only do these terms entrench patriarchy, but they are also the terms of the ruling classes. God is presented as a ruling, controlling male. Thus, the male is seen as more fully representative of God than the female. I believe that this male language and imagery has contributed to the Churches' sanctioning of men dominating women.

[. . .]

The patriarchal nature of Church structures, regrettably, has condoned, encouraged and, in some cases, actively enforced the subjugation of women to men, denying them the realisation of their full potential, not only within the Church, but politically, socially and economically. It is a matter of debate that our new political Constitution grants women more status than any religious one. Our clergy need to be trained in the understanding of the rights now legally granted to us constitutionally, but withheld from us spiritually.

[. . .]

There exists a classism and racism within the Church that has resulted in a differentiation of the facilities provided for pastors, usually with an urban bias. Though aimed at the clergy, it also has resulted in the suffering of indignities by the spouses (overwhelmingly women) and their children. Lack of adequate sewerage, water and other basic needs are common, especially in the rural areas. Urban areas differentiate between township and suburban facilities, thus reinforcing classism and, inevitably, racism.

The wives of clergy are often exposed to conscious and unconscious patriarchy that would make a weaker person buckle at the knees. While studying, their husbands are accommodated in seminaries, spouses and their children are not, often living in conditions that are simply disgraceful because of poor or nonexistent stipends. Little or no training is offered to wives to equip them for the contribution they make to their husbands' ministry. There is little choice in the matter of wives' ministry; the expectation of the congregation, the denomination and the ministers themselves is that wives will participate actively and fully in the life and work of the congregation or parish. Ministers are called, they have a vocation, wives are not recognised for the contribution they make, called or not.

Ministers' wives, often professional people, have little choice in the decision to work or not. Their financial contribution to the family economy often exceeds that of their spouses and is often what keeps the family clothed, fed and educated. Should their husbands predecease them, they lose their homes if provision has not been made to purchase a home prior to his death. Given the stipends most clergy are paid, the chances of that having taken place are usually remote. Newly widowed, and usually with a family to provide for, what support can this woman expect from the Church? Often marginalised and isolated by their position as the wife, and neglected by their husbands because of Church commitments, many of them are lonely and depressed.

[. . .]

Although women have had no authority within the Church, they have had a profound influence. Women and women's organisations have made a significant and valuable contribution to the life and work of their denominations, especially in areas concerning family and social issues. Their service has brought no positions of responsibility outside of the domestic. For example, women raise much of the Church funds, but are not in a position to decide how these funds should be allocated. That important decision is made by the male church council . . .

There are Faith Communities represented at these hearings whose female believers are not allowed to worship in the same area as their husbands, fathers, brothers and sons. They are separated from the fullness and richness of their spiritual and family life, not because of any sin of omission or commission, but merely because of their gender. They are absolutely voiceless and powerless and suffer denigration and humiliation because they are women. God hears the cries of the oppressed – when will we?

A Creed

We believe in God,
Who created women and men in God's image,
Who created the world and gave both sexes the care of the earth;
We believe in Jesus, Child of God, chosen by God, born of the woman Mary,
Who listened to women and stayed in their homes,
Who looked for the Kingdom with them,
Who was followed and supported by women disciples;
We believe in Jesus,
Who discussed theology with a woman at a well,
Who received anointing from a woman at Simon's house
And rebuked the men guests who scorned her;
We believe in Jesus,
Who healed a woman on the Sabbath,
Who spoke of God as a woman seeking a lost coin,
As a woman who wept, seeking the lost;
We believe in Jesus,
Who thought of pregnancy and birth with reverence;
We believe in Jesus,
Who appeared first to Mary Magdalen
And sent her with the message 'Go and tell';
We believe in the wholeness of God, in whom there is neither Jew nor Greek, slave nor free,
Female nor male, for we are one in God;
We believe in the Holy Spirit,
As she moves over the waters of creation and over the earth,
The woman spirit of God, who created us and gave us birth
And covers us with her wings. Amen.

Dutch Reformed Church in South Africa: Synod of the Western and Southern Cape, submission to the Truth and Reconciliation Commission, 7–9 October 1997, pp. 10–12.

4. *Testimony, confession of guilt, forgiveness, reconciliation & obedience*

4.1 The Synod bears testimony with this submission that over the years the Lord mercifully made use of the Dutch Reformed Church, specifically the Dutch Reformed Church in South Africa (Western and Southern Cape), in the service of His cause, and for this we wish to thank and praise Him. However, we did not always hear His Word correctly for the times in which we lived, and we often failed to do that which He required of us. This we wish to confess to Him. Where we offended our neighbours, we wish also to sincerely confess our sins to them.

4.2 The Synod accepts that the confession of that which had been done wrongly in the past, and forgiveness for that which had happened, indeed give rise to absolution, as well as a commitment to repair broken ties, and even more importantly, it demands a life of obedience to God. We confess our guilt and, in the forgiveness that we receive in Christ, we wish to take each other's hands and go into the future together.

4.3 The Synod accepts that the purpose of confessing your guilt to your fellow human beings is not merely to remove the burden from your shoulders but also to eliminate the stumbling blocks between yourself and others. Therefore our confessions of guilt and deeds of forgiveness in South Africa may not come to an end.

4.4 The Synod calls on church members to live a life of ongoing confession, continued willingness to forgive, and obedience to God.

4.5 The Synod collectively undertakes to accompany the Dutch Reformed Church in the Western and Southern Cape on a new journey – a journey of reconciliation. The Dutch Reformed Church wishes in the years ahead to strive actively to promote the expansion of the Kingdom of God, the elimination of injustice in every direction and at all levels of our society, and Christian reconciliation. In this regard the Synod would like to co-operate with the other members of the family of Dutch Reformed Churches, the Afrikaans Reformed churches and the other churches in South Africa, and it will strive wherever possible to ensure that a unified, collective Christian testimony may be heard.

4.6 The Synod requests that the Moderature take the lead in this reconciliation process in the synodal area of the Western Cape as a matter of great urgency. The Synod resolves to make this declaration/submission available to church members, ecclesiastical assemblies, the press and the Truth and Reconciliation Commission.

Appendix 2: A List of Written Materials Received by the TRC from Faith Communities[3]

Traditional Religion

• Submission from Nokuzola Mndende, Lecturer in African Religion, UCT. February 1997.

Protestant Christianity

Baptist Convention of South Africa

• Submission, 19 November 1997, presented to the hearings by Des Hoffmeister, General Secretary.

• Press statement regarding the Assembly of the Baptist Convention of South Africa, meeting at Durban, 10 to 14 December 1997.

• Sample programmes of 'Discovering Truth Workshops'.

• 'Kempton Park Thembisa Resolution II', dated 6-8 November 1997, from a joint BCSA and BUSA retreat.

Baptist Union of South Africa

• Submission, forwarded on behalf of the Executive Committee of the Baptist Union of South Africa by Terry Rae, General Secretary, 26 June 1997.

Belydende Kring

• Submission dated 11 Nov. 1997, signed by Rev. Dr Z. E. Mokgoebo.

Church of England in South Africa

• Submission by Joe Bell, Presiding Bishop, dated 18 July 1997.

• †Submission dated 17 November 1997, presented to the hearings by Bishop Frank Retief.[4]

Church of the Province of South Africa

• Submission, dated 30 June 1997, signed by Archbishop Njongonkulu Ndungane.

• †Submission, presented to the hearings, 17 November 1997, by Bishop Michael Nuttall.

Dutch Reformed Church

• English extract from the Afrikaans document *The Story of the Dutch Reformed Church's Journey with Apartheid*, General Synodal Commission of the Dutch Reformed Church.

• 'Dutch Reformed Church in South Africa: Synod of the Western and Southern Cape, submission to the Truth and Reconciliation Commission' (with covering letter signed by Fritz Gaum, Synod Moderator), undated (the document comes out of a decision taken at Synod on 7, 8 and 9 October 1997).

• 'What does Reconciliation Mean, and What Role Should the Church Play to Promote National Unity and Reconciliation?' Appended to the above document.

• 'Skuldbelydenis en Vergifnis – 'n Getuienis uit Zimbabwe', *Die Kerkbode,* 6 September 1996.

• 'Speech Given on Behalf of the Dutch Reformed Church in South Africa on Occasion of the Official Centenary Celebrations of the Reformed Church in Zimbabwe, 14 Sept. 1991', by C. M. Pauw.

• 'Witness of Dutch Reformed Church Delegates', undated document reflecting on the International Global Consultation on World Evangelism, 1997, signed by Drs Louis Louw and Danie Nel and Revs. Sampie Niemand and Leon Westhof.

• 'Voorlegging aan die Kommissie vir Waarheid en Versoening by sy sitting op 14 tot 16 Oktober in die Paarl', NGK Ring van Stellenbosch.

Evangelical Lutheran Church in Southern Africa (Natal–Transvaal)

• Letter to Commission from Bishop D. R. Lilje, dated 30 June 1997, notifying them that no submission would be forthcoming from the church.

• Letter written to congregations, dated 18 March 1996, signed by Lilje, supporting the Commission and asking members to pray for the reconciliation process.

• Submission dated 19 March 1998, signed on behalf of the Church Council of the Evangelical Lutheran Church in Southern Africa (Natal–Transvaal) by Bishop D.R. Liljie.

Institute for Contextual Theology

• Submission, undated, and signed by Rev. Wesley Mabuza.

• †Further submission, presented at hearings 17 November 1997, signed by Rev. Wesley Mabuza and McGlory Speckman.

Methodist Church of South Africa

• Submission dated August 1997, signed by H. Mvume Dandala, Presiding Bishop.

Moravian Church in South Africa

• Submission, dated 20 November 1996, signed by W. M. Majikijela, President.

Presbyterian Church of Southern Africa

• Submission, dated 18 August 1997, signed by the Moderator, the General Secretary and the Director of the Justice and Social Responsibility Division.

Reformed Presbyterian Church of South Africa

• Submission, presented at hearings on 18 November 1997 and presented by Dr Gideon Khabela, Rev. D.M. Soga and Rev. J.V. Mdlalose.

Religious Society of Friends (Quakers)

• Submission, dated June 1997, coming from the central and southern district yearly meeting. Covering letter, dated 9 July, states that a further submission may be forthcoming from the full body.

Rosebank Union Church

• Statement of Repentance, date obscured, signed by Rev. Ellis André.

Salvation Army

• Submission, dated 17 March 1997, signed by Paul A. du Plessis (Territorial Commander), with the executive officers of the Salvation Army in Southern Africa.

• 'The Salvation Army and the Truth and Reconciliation Process in South Africa – A Policy Statement', approved by the Territorial Executive Council, 21 January 1997.

• 'Army makes submission to the Truth Commission', supplement to *The War Cry*, 7 June 1997.

Scripture Union

• Submission, dated 15 August 1997, signed by Dr Christian S. Abels, National Chairperson.

Seventh Day Adventist Church

• 'Statement of Confession', undated and unsigned. Note that a signed version was submitted to the Commission which was not made available to the writers of the RICSA Report.

South African Council of Churches

• Submission, August 1997, submitted by B. H. Bam, General Secretary.

United Congregational Church of Southern Africa.

• Submission, dated 8 August 1997, signed by B. T. Maluleka, administrative secretary.

• †Submission, dated October 1997, submitted by Des van der Water and Steve de Gruchy.

Uniting Reformed Church in Southern Africa

• Submission, signed by J. D. Buys, Moderator of General Synod, 16 Sept. 1997.

• Submission by URCCSA Messina Congregation, no date, signed by the Church Council.

Historically African Churches

United Methodist Church of South Africa

• Statement, dated 17 November 1997, signed by Mr Nkosinathi Madikezela, Ecumenical Affairs Officer.

Zion Christian Church

• Statement, dated 18 November 1997, signed by Bishop B. E. Lekganyane.

Ibandla lamaNazaretha

• Submission, dated 18 November 1997, presented to the hearings by Mthembeni P. Mpanza. (The written submission was in English, the presentation in Zulu.)

Roman Catholicism

• Submission, 15 August 1997, unsigned.

• Submission by South African Catholic Bishops' Conference, presented to the hearings by Bishops Kevin Dowling and Buti Thlagale, 17 November 1997.

Pentecostal and charismatic Christianity

Apostolic Faith Mission

• Submission, dated 4 August 1997, signed by I. S. Burger, President.

Rhema Church / IFCC

• Submission, presented by Rev. Ray McCauley at hearings, 19 November (plus addendum).

Hatfield Christian Church

• Submission, with covering letter signed by Dr Graham Catto on behalf of the steering committee and dated 16 September 1997.

The Evangelical Alliance of South Africa (TEASA)

• Submission, with covering letter dated 15 September 1997, signed by Moss Nthla, General Secretary.

• Written remarks presented at hearings by Dr Derek Morphew of Vineyard Ministries.

Islam

Jamiatul Ulama Transvaal

• Submission, dated 18 November 1997, signed by E. I. Bham, Assistant Secretary.

Muslim Judicial Council

• Submission, presented by Imam Hassan Solomon at the hearings, 18 November 1997.

Muslim Youth Movement

• Submission, dated 18 November 1997, signed by Nissar Dawood, General Secretary.

Judaism

Chief Rabbi of South Africa

• Submission, dated 1 July 1997, signed by Rabbi Cyril K. Harris.

• Gesher Movement.

• 'Reconciliation: a Jewish View', dated January 1997, with covering letter signed by Geoff Sifrin, Chairperson.

Hinduism

South African Hindu Maha Sabha

• Submission, dated 18 November 1997, signed by Ashwin Trikamjee, President. Also presented at hearings.

Ramakrishna Institute of Spirituality and Hinduism

• Submission, dated 25 June 1997, signed by Prof. P. Joshi, President.

Buddhism

• Dharma Centre

• Submission by Ron Schiff, Rodney Downey and Heila Downey, dated 25 June 1997.

The Baha'i Faith

• Submission from National Spiritual Assembly of the Baha'is in South Africa together with a covering letter signed by Brett Hone, Secretary, and dated 15 September 1997.

Other submissions

World Conference on Religion and Peace

• Submission presented by Franz Auerbach, 18 November 1997.

• 'Justice, Retribution and the Truth and Reconciliation Commission' by Imam Rashid Omar, Vice President, 7 November 1997.

• 'Proposal for Action by People of Faith on December 16.'

Nico Smith

• Open letter to South African Christian Pastors, undated.

Gereformeerde Kerk (unofficial representation)

• ''n Openbare Belydenis (Uit Potchefstroom) / An Open Confession from Potchefstroom', dated 6 August 1997 and signed by Alwyn du Plessis, Bennie van der Walt, Amie van Wyk and Ponti Venter.

Women in religion

• 'Submission to the Truth and Reconciliation Commission, Faith Communities Hearings', Ms Cathy P. Makhenya.

Rev. Douglas Torr, dated 8 July 1997.

Lesley Morgan, dated 27 June 1997.

Daryl D. Bredenkamp, 'Comment on the Present Hearings within Church Groups', dated 19 November 1997.

Statement (with covering letter) from Karoo Mobile Law Clinic on behalf of the Old Apostolic Church, 17 November 1997, signed by Mxolisi Tshaliti.

Appendix 3: Testimony at the Faith Hearings

Monday 17 November

- South African Council of Churches (Ms Hlope Bam, Revs. Bernard Spong, Eddie MacKew and Inlama Ntshingwa)
- Institute for Contextual Theology (Revs. Wesley Mabuza and McGlory Speckman)
- Church of the Province of Southern Africa (Bishops Michael Nuttall and Zambule Dlamini)
- Church of England in South Africa (Bishops Frank Retief and Martin Morrison, Rev. Elias Majozi and Mr Noel Wright)
- Methodist Church of Southern Africa (Bishop Mvume Dandala and Rev. Vivian Harris, Bishops Simon Gubule, Alec Diko and Dabula)
- Catholic Church (Bishops Kevin Dowling and Buti Thlagale)
- Presbyterian Church of Southern Africa (Revs. Douglas Bax, Pakiso Tondi and Allistair Roger)
- United Congregational Church of Southern Africa (Rev. David Wanless and Prof. John de Gruchy)
- Reformed Presbyterian Church of South Africa (Dr Gideon Kabela and Revs. D. M. Soga and J. V. Mdlalose)

Tuesday 18 November

- World Conference on Religion and Peace (Dr Franz Auerbach)
- Dr Faried Esack
- Hindu Maha Sabha (Mr Ashwin Trikamjee and Mr R. Kallideen)
- National Spiritual Assembly of the Baha'i Faith (Mr Z. Zitandele and Mrs Vera Rezavi)
- African Religious Community (Mr K. Koka)
- Council of African Instituted Churches (Archbishop T. W. Ntongana and Rev. S. Moliswa)
- Women in religion (Ms Cathy Makhenya and Ms Hlope Bam)

- lamaNazaretha (Mr M. P. Mpanza)
- Belydende Kring (Drs Z. E. Mokgoebo, Henry Thyes and Kwaho, and Mrs Julia Tladi)

Wednesday 19 November

- Muslim Judicial Council (Iman Hassan Solomon)
- Zion Christian Church (Bishop Barnabas Lekganyane, Rev. Immanuel Lothola and Thomas Mahope)
- Evangelical Alliance of South Africa (Mr Moss Nthla, Dr Derek Morphew and Rev. Colin LaVoy)
- Rhema Church / International Fellowship of Christian Churches (Rev. Ray McCauley and Pastors Ron Steele, Mosa and Chris Lodewyk)
- Apostolic Faith Mission (Pastors Izak Burger, Frank Chikane, George Mahlobo, Peter de Witt)
- Uniting Reformed Church in Southern Africa (Revs. James Buys and Marcus Maphoto)
- Dutch Reformed Church (Ds Freek Swanepoel and Dr Willie Botha)
- The Rev. Nico Smith and Mr Moss Nthla
- Profs. Bennie van der Walt and Ponti Venter

Notes

Introduction

1. The Report itself was essentially written by Stephen Martin, working with Cochrane and De Gruchy.

2. Recent attempts by the National Church Leaders' Forum and the Archbishop of Cape Town to deal with issues related to poverty may reflect the beginning of a deeper concern with economic rights.

The Report on Faith Communities and Apartheid

1. Richard Elphick, 'Introduction: Christianity in South African History', in *Christianity in South Africa: A Political, Social and Cultural History*, Richard Elphick & Rodney Davenport, eds. (Cape Town; Oxford: David Philip; James Currey, 1997), 1.

2. All these points will be elaborated below.

3. Both President Mandela and Deputy President Mbeki have stressed the important role faith communities can play in the construction and legitimation of democratic values. In underlining this, we of course recognise that faith communities must not be ruled by the state. This would be to repeat the practices of the apartheid government which imposed its norms upon faith communities, to the point of not recognising marriages conducted according to Muslim and Hindu law. Most of the faith communities, however, saw themselves as committed to the promotion of good citizenship. For this reason we say that they can be (and even go as far as to say that they must become) places where democratic values are learned.

4. Interview with Piet Meiring, 17 December 1997. A document presented at a TRC meeting in Cape Town on 15 May 1997, and supplied to RICSA by the Commission, stated:

A Church hearing may prove to be of significant value to the TRC process, interpreting the different denominations' understanding of the context within which they operated, as well as their own possible contributions to creating a climate within which gross human rights violations could take place, either by their commissions or their omissions (p. 1).

These 'churches' hearings, the document went on to state, were to include also 'other faith communities' – naming specifically the WCRP, the Hindu community, the Union of Orthodox Synagogues and, strangely enough, the ANC religious desk (p. 2).

5. In some ways this accounts for the sloppiness with which other faith communities (particularly the Muslim) were approached. The intention seems to have been to include Christian churches and the inclusion of the others was an afterthought.

6. Many examples of analyses of African Initiated Churches that uncover their many sources, dimensions and functions could be provided. See Linda E. Thomas, 'African Indigenous Churches as a Source of Socio-Political Transformation in South Africa', *Africa Today*, first quarter 1994, 39–56; Luke L. Pato, 'The African Independent Churches: A Socio-Cultural Approach', *Journal of Theology for Southern Africa*, no. 72 (September 1990), 24–35; and Glenda Kruss, 'Religion, Class and Culture: Indigenous Churches in South Africa, with Special Reference to Zionist-Apostolics', Masters dissertation (University of Cape Town, 1985).

7. See section 2.3.8 on Islam. The different class origins and profiles of the Cape and Transvaal Muslim communities (Malay and Indian, respectively) played out in theological and ideological differences, particularly exemplified in the conservative, Indian Ulamas.

8. For purposes of simplicity, written submissions that the Commission received either before, during or after the hearings will simply be referred to as 'submissions' and presentations at the hearings as 'presentation'. Further details (including dates of presentations and signatories of submissions) may be found in the appendices.

9. See Nokuzola O. Mndende, 'The Voice of the Red People' (University of Cape Town, Department of Religious Studies, 1994), as well as her submission to the Commission. Nevertheless, within contemporary South Africa, African Traditional Religion is, for better or for worse, coming to conform to the shape of the other faiths. Those who call for a return to it as the 'authentic' religion of Africans (usually versus Christianity) indeed treat it as one option among many (albeit a more 'authentic' option), as a faith community self-conscious and distinct from the body politic. A helpful understanding of the transformation of communal religion within more differentiated societies may be found in William Everett, *Religion, Federalism and the Struggle for Public Life* (New York: Oxford University Press, 1997).

10. This was noted by Prof. Piet Meiring, coordinator of the faith community hearings (interview December 1997). He was not able to be more precise on the particular definition of 'player' with which the Commission worked.

11. A complete listing is included in the appendix to this volume.

12. Undoubtedly the sexism latent in faith communities was exacerbated by the conditions of apartheid South Africa. We shall refer to this important submission again below, but recommend that it also be dealt with in the gender section of the final report. See also section 5.2.4.

13. Note how these categories parallel those identified by the *Kairos Document*. See the Kairos Theologians, *Challenge to the Church: The Kairos Document* (Johannesburg: Skotaville, 1986).

14. A number of introductions to faith communities in South Africa are available. Especially helpful are David Chidester, *Religions of South Africa* (London: Routledge, 1992); Martin Prozesky & John de Gruchy, *Living Faiths in South Africa* (Cape Town: David Philip, 1995); and Elphick & Davenport, *Christianity in South Africa.*

15. African Indigenous Churches grew from 4.67 to 5.37 million members between 1980 and 1991, according to the respective censuses. The Zion Christian Church grew dramatically from 0.53 to 1.5 million during the same period. At the same time, membership in Methodist churches dropped from 2.2 to 1.8 million; Anglican churches from 1.6 to 1.17; and DRC family churches from 3.49 to 3.2 million – in spite of a population size increase from 29.36 to 37.7 million during the same period. Unless otherwise specified, all statistics quoted in the present report are from J. J. Kritzinger, 'The Religious Scene in Present-day South Africa', in *Religious Freedom in South Africa*, J. Kilian, ed. (Pretoria: UNISA, 1994), 2-4.

16. On the Dutch Reformed Church and Afrikaner nationalism, see Johan Kinghorn, 'On the Theology of Church and Society in the DRC', *Journal of Theology for Southern Africa*, no. 70 (March 1990), 21–36, and 'Modernization and Apartheid: The Afrikaner Churches', in *Christianity in South Africa*, Elphick & Davenport, eds., 135–54.

17. The Apostolic Faith Mission also had a number of state officials and politicians as members. See section 3.2.1.1.

18. On primal religion see David Chidester, 'Primal Religions' in *A Southern African Guide to World Religions*, John de Gruchy and Martin Prozesky, eds. (Cape Town: David Philip, 1991). On African religion as primal see Chidester, *Religions of South Africa*, chapter 1.

19. Nokuzola Mndende submission. For a helpful account of the resurgence of African Religion in contemporary South Africa, and the contentiousness of its relations with Christianity, see 'African Religion Comes in from the Cold', *Cape Times,* 24 December 1997.

20. Chidester, *Religions of South Africa*, 1.

21. John W. de Gruchy, *Christianity and the Modernisation of South Africa* (Cape Town: David Philip, in press), chapter 1.

22. See Cochrane, *Servants of Power: The Role of English-Speaking Churches 1902–1930* (Johannesburg: Ravan, 1987).

23. The CI was more broadly 'ecumenical' than the SACC, welcoming Jews, Muslims and agnostics/atheists into its ranks. It was a victim of state repression, a strong opponent of human rights abuses and proponent of social transformation. Several references were made to the CI in the submissions and at the hearings. The failure to invite a representation from it is therefore a serious oversight. As we cannot tell the story of Christian (and other) faith communities during the years 1960–1994 apart from considering the CI, this report will take the liberty of referring to its work when appropriate. For a more detailed history of the Christian Institute, see Peter Walshe, *Church Versus State in South Africa* (Maryknoll: Orbis Books, 1983) and John W. de Gruchy, 'A Brief History of the

Christian Institute', in *Resistance and Hope*, John W. de Gruchy & Charles Villa-Vicencio, eds. (Cape Town; Grand Rapids: David Philip; Wm. B. Eerdmans, 1985).

24. Known for its involvement in the writing of the *Kairos Document*, the ICT supplied a number of important leaders to the SACC, including Frank Chikane, ICT director in the 1980s, who would later become general secretary of the Council. The ICT, as Wesley Mabuza said in his presentation, 'operates outside church and government structures in order that it could provide an ongoing independent critique'.

25. See the next section. The Apostolic Faith Mission is now also a member of the SACC.

26. Hence the way the term is used here is closer to the American than the European sense.

27. While this was not mentioned in their submissions, there can be little doubt that such churches benefited from the charged political situation of the 1980s; as mainline churches became more radical, many members joined conservative evangelical churches.

28. For a debate about the legacy of apartheid amongst evangelicals, especially concerning the Baptist Union, see the articles by David Walker, 'Evangelicals and Apartheid: An Enquiry into Some Dispositions', *Journal of Theology for Southern Africa*, no. 67 (June 1989); 'Evangelicals and Apartheid Revisited', *Journal of Theology for Southern Africa*, no. 89 (December 1994); and Frederick Hale, 'Coming to Terms with Evangelicals and Apartheid', *Journal of Theology for Southern Africa*, no. 84 (September 1993). It is notable that some prominent progressive evangelicals such as Walker, Peter Moll and Richard Steele (the latter two both conscientious objectors) have migrated to more ecumenical churches.

29. Hale, 'Coming to Terms', provides a helpful summary of Baptist Union history. More details on the split between Union and Convention can be found in Louise Kretzschmar, 'The Privatisation of the Christian Faith amongst South African Baptists', Ph.D. (University of Cape Town, 1992).

30. Here we refer to the Nederduitse Gereformeerde Kerk.

31. This church was mentioned by Clive Derby-Lewis at the first amnesty hearings into the assassination of Chris Hani. Though English-speaking, Derby-Lewis counted himself a loyal member. At its 1997 synod the church termed apologising for the principles of apartheid 'cultural suicide' for Afrikaners. 'The Church is Sorry, but Not Too Sorry', *Mail & Guardian,* 17 September 1997.

32. The other Afrikaans churches have also historically identified themselves with Afrikaner nationalism and National Party (and later Conservative Party) policies. The Hervormde Kerk prohibited non-whites from joining it. Some members of the Gereformeerde Kerk – particularly some teaching at Potchefstroom University – began to dissent from National Party policies in the mid-seventies, signing a document called *The Koinonia Declaration*. It was from members of this group that the TRC received an 'Openbare Skuldbelydenis', apologising for the sin of apartheid and failing to act decisively against human rights violations.

33. David Bosch, 'Introduction', in I. Daneel, *Quest for Belonging* (Gwero: Mambo Press, 1987), 9. We shall simply refer to them as AICs.

34. This was according to the 1991 census. The 1980 census placed them at just over a quarter of South Africa's Christians.

35. The term 'contextual innovation' is from Darrel Wratten's work on South African Buddhism. 'Buddhism in South Africa: From Textual Imagination to Contextual Innovation', Ph.D. dissertation (University of Cape Town, 1995).

36. This is true except insofar as the Order of Ethiopia, which resulted from an agreement between the CPSA and James Dwane, an early Ethiopian leader, is represented in the submission of the CPSA. Having failed to get recognition from the African Methodist Episcopal Church in the United States, Dwane had his church constituted as an Order in the CPSA in 1900. For historical background on Ethiopianism, see Hennie Pretorius and Lizo Jafta, "A Branch Springs Out: African Initiated Churches', in *Christianity in South Africa*, Elphick & Davenport, 211–26 and Chidester, *Religions of South Africa*, ch. 4.

37. James P. Kiernan, 'The African Independent Churches', in *Living Faiths in South Africa*, 118. A more extensive analysis of the class base of the Zionist and Zionist-Apostolic churches is Kruss, 'Religion, Class and Culture'.

38. Precisely why the ZCC grew at such a significant rate during the turbulent eighties is an important question.

39. See the ZCC submission. Most notable among these leaders was P. W. Botha in 1985. During this time, no liberation movement leaders were invited to Moria.

40. Pretorius and Jafta, 'A Branch Springs Out', 218.

41. Although as separate institutions they constitute an early form of resistance to colonialism. See section 3.2.3. An important analysis of African Christianity and its resistance to colonialism is John and Jean Comaroff's *Of Revelation and Revolution* (Chicago: University of Chicago Press, 1991).

42. The invitation to Moria of leaders such as Botha was seen by many as an act of blatant legitimisation. Allegations have also been made about connections between the ZCC, Inkatha and the South African Defence Force in the late 1980s, chiefly arising out of documents released during the trial of Gen. Magnus Malan in 1996. See 'Pulling the Strings on the Buthelezi Marionette', *Mail & Guardian*, 8 March 1996.

43. The Christian Institute assisted in establishing the African Independent Churches Association in the 1960s. In the 1980s, the Spiritual Churches Institute and the Khanya Theological College were involved in ecumenical activity. See CAIC presentation.

44. Seventeen per cent of the mission schools affected by the 1953 Bantu Education Act were Catholic. Eventually the church was forced, in 1972, to close or hand over its primary schools. Joy Brain, 'Moving from the Margins to the Mainstream: The Roman Catholic Church', in *Christianity in South Africa*, Elphick & Davenport, eds., 204.

45. This marginality led David Chidester to deal with it in his chapter on 'religious pluralism', along with Islam, Hinduism and Judaism. Chidester, *Religions of South Africa*.

46. Allan H. Anderson & Gerald J. Pillay, 'The Segregated Spirit: The Pentecostals', in *Christianity in South Africa*, Elphick & Davenport, eds., 227.

47. Anderson and Pillay, 'The Segregated Spirit', 234. See also Anderson's 'The Struggle for Unity in Pentecostal Mission Churches', *Journal of Theology for Southern Africa* no. 82 (March 1993), 67ff.

48. See Anderson & Pillay, 'The Segregated Spirit', 238–39. The Pinkster Protestante Kerk was formed by former members of the AFM who thought it too

politically involved.

49. It is notable that Rhema churches often flew the South African flag during the turbulent eighties, a blatantly political act.

50. The assistance of Imam Rashid Omar of the Claremont Mosque in Cape Town in the drafting of this section is gratefully acknowledged.

51. See Ebrahim Moosa, 'Islam in South Africa', in *Living Faiths in South Africa*, 129–30.

52. On the Maetsuycker edict, which tolerated Islam 'at a private' but not a public level, see A. Rashid Omar, 'An Islamic Experience of Religious Freedom in the South African Context', in Killiam, ed., *Religious Freedom*, 74–5.

53. It is notable, however, that the MJC claims itself to be the first faith community in South Africa to declare apartheid a heresy (in 1961). MJC submission, 3.

54. Moosa, 'Islam in South Africa', 149. See also A. Rashid Omar, 'The Impact of the Death in Detention of Imam Abdullah Haron on Cape Muslim Attitudes', Honours dissertation (University of Cape Town, 1987).

55. We highlight the COI, although recognising that Faried Esack's being a 'representative' of them at the Commission is not 'official'.

56. See Moosa, 'Islam in South Africa', 149–50.

57. This, it should be noted, it denies in its submission.

58. Moosa, 'Islam in South Africa', 151. This solidarity, notes Moosa, was exhibited especially at funerals, protest marches and rallies.

59. The assistance of Prof. Milton Shain of the University of Cape Town in drafting this section is gratefully acknowledged.

60. A. A. Dubb, *Jewish Population of South Africa: The 1991 Sociodemographic Survey* (Cape Town: Kaplan Centre, 1994).

61. Hellig mentions also disputes over orthodoxy which divided along ethnic (English and East European) lines. Hellig, 'The Jewish Community', in *Living Faiths in South Africa*, 162. See Milton Shain, *Jewry and Cape Society* (Cape Town: Historical Publication Society, 1983) and *The Roots of Anti-Semitism in South Africa* (University Press of Virginia, 1994).

62. Hellig, 'The Jewish Community', 156.

63. Dubb, *Jewish Population.*

64. Hellig, 'The Jewish Community', 169.

65. Milton Shain, 'South Africa', in *American Jewish Year Book, 1997*, David Singer and Ruth R. Seldin, eds. (New York: American Jewish Committee, 1997), 422.

66. The assistance of Mr R. Kallideen of the Hindu Maha Sabha, Durban, in the drafting of this section is gratefully acknowledged.

67. Louis H. van Loon, 'Buddhism in South Africa', in *Living Faiths in South Africa*, Prozesky and De Gruchy, eds., 209–16.

68. Baha'i Statement, 2.

69. The DRC did not supply an official submission like the other communities. What functions in this report as their 'submission' is actually a document written for the World Alliance of Reformed Churches entitled *Our Journey with Apartheid*, which they provided the Commission. They did, however, make a presentation at the hearings.

70. Perhaps all this resembles a broader dilemma of the Commission – that

those who confess crimes appear more guilty than those who may have committed even more heinous acts, but who refuse to come forth.

71. This is also evident in the correspondence the Commission received around the representation of Islam at the hearings. See section 5.2.1.

72. Hence present struggles for church and denominational identity (both within and between groups) are a factor in 'remembering' and 'reconstructing' the past. What Rev. Beyers Naudé said of the DRC could also be applied to other churches, that it fears schism and especially losing members to conservative rivals (in the DRC's case, the Afrikaanse Protestantse Kerk) and this will govern how far it is prepared to own responsibility. See 'The Church is Sorry, but Not Too Sorry', *Mail & Guardian,* 17 September 1997.

73. The original reads 'denomination'.

74. See previous note.

75. The original reads 'church'.

76. From a sample letter provided by the Commission, dated 29 May 1997 and signed by Commissioner Wynand Malan.

77. Those who did not apologise or confess complicity included the Moravian Church, United Methodist Church, Zion Christian Church, the amaNazaretha and the Baha'i faith. In its initial letter to the TRC, the Evangelical Lutheran Church (Natal and Transvaal) claimed it saw no reason to apologise: however, it admitted that members might have committed violations. In its submission to the Commission, which came late in the process, ELCSA confessed its complicity in the sins of apartheid. Although it freely admitted its support for the liberation movements, the Institute for Contextual Theology offered no apology nor admitted complicity in human rights abuses, nor did the Belydende Kring. Koka, who spoke on behalf of the ATR community, claimed to have tried to find something to apologise for but saw Africans as victims rather than perpetrators. In her submission on behalf of African Traditional Religion, Nokuzola Mndende did not offer any apology or confession.

78. We must bear in mind that the DRC, while admitting its support of apartheid, has never equated it with a gross violation of human rights.

79. The use of prayer – whether to invoke divine support for the government or for its removal – was an important symbolic activity as well, though not in itself necessarily supporting human rights violations. It is arguable that mobilising religious symbols in the envisioning of the conflict in terms of 'forces of darkness' against 'forces of light' helped create a climate for human rights violations.

80. The DRC in its *Journey* document, however, confessed to supporting apartheid when applied 'with Christian love' (no doubt seeing the essence of apartheid as 'good neighbourliness'), yet insisted that when this norm was not applied, they confronted the state behind closed doors.

81. SACC submission, 10.

82. As already noted with regard to the Baptist submissions.

83. See Anthony. O. Balcomb, *Third Way Theology* (Pietermaritzburg: Cluster Publications, 1993) for a critique of theologies which tried to find ways between the dominant political options in the 1980s.

84. See Robin M. Petersen, 'Time, Resistance and Reconstruction: Rethinking Kairos Theology', Ph.D. dissertation (University of Chicago, 1995) for an analy-

sis of AICs which criticises the narrowly ethical understanding of 'political engagement' of the Kairos theologians.

85. The most obvious example of this would be of course the DRC. However, in their *Journey* document they made no reference to the way the Dutch Reformed 'family' mirrored apartheid. Perhaps this was because the establishment of their structures along racial lines had predated the government policy.

86. For example the CPSA apologised for its English pride and attitude of moral superiority towards Afrikaners.

87. MCSA submission, 2.

88. Nico Smith presentation. The phrase 'willing executioners' is carefully chosen and refers to a controversial book entitled *Hitler's Willing Executioners: Ordinary Germans and the Holocaust* (New York: Alfred A. Knopf, 1996), which argues that Nazi Germany's extermination of Jews could only succeed because of the tacit co-operation of ordinary German people.

89. RC submission, 3.

90. Commissioner Bongani Finca at the hearings on day three.

91. DRC presentation.

92. DRC *Journey*, 15.

93. DRC *Journey*, 21f.

94. DRC *Journey*, 35.

95. UCCSA submission, 1. For an analysis of the original document submitted by the DRC to the TRC (which was a translation of a longer document and was prepared for the World Alliance of Reformed Churches to make a case for the DRC's readmission), see H. Russel Botman, 'The DRC Continues Its Journey with Apartheid', *Challenge*, October–November 1997, 26–7.

96. DRC *Journey*, 36.

97. CPSA submission, 2.

98. PCSA submission 8. The policy was defended against a British Council of Churches report entitled *The Future of South Africa.*

99. The symbolic power inherent in 'praying for' state operatives and agents as well as the sway this kind of practice held within churches is underlined by the controversy around the campaign in 1986 to promote prayer to end unjust rule. See Allan A. Boesak & Charles Villa-Vicencio, *When Prayer Makes News* (Philadelphia: Westminster Press, 1986).

100. SAPA press report 23 July 1997. From http://www.truth.org.za/sapa9707/s970723a.htm. For a response, claiming that the situation was one of war and that the church was justified in lending support to the military, see the editorial in *Die Kerkbode*, August 1997.

101. Nico Smith presentation.

102. URCSA submission, 9.

103. Mention should be made in this connection of the other Afrikaans Reformed Churches: the NHK and the GK.

104. AFM submission, 4. Colin LaVoy confessed at the hearings that many 'evangelical Pentecostals' participated in government commissions, including the commission that led to the banning of Beyers Naudé.

105. BCSA submission, 6. For this and other reasons, the BCSA appealed to the Commission to investigate the relationship between state security structures and the Baptist Union. The Brigadier was a high-ranking chaplain in the SADF. The

Kimberley meetings sparked much controversy within the Union, and protests from black and coloured members forced them to be moved.

106. Hindu presentation. This is questionable, however. The Muslim (Indian) Ulamas co-operated with the state and, according to Yasmin Sooka (in a personal communication, April 1997), the Hindu Maha Sabha did also. Indeed, Sooka strongly underlined the fact that resistance within Indian Hindu communities was on the part of a minority.

107. Ronald Sider, 'Interview with Frank Chikane', in *Conflict and the Quest for Justice: National Initiative of Reconciliation Reader No.* 2, Klaus Nürnberger, John Tooke and William Domeris, eds. (Pietermarizburg: Encounter Publications, 1989), 352–58.

108. BCSA submission, 6. The ministers mentioned were Pastor Lukwe and Rev. Gideon Makhanya.

109. Venter presentation. Venter and Van der Walt also alluded to the monitoring of the communications of members of the GK and staff at Potchefstroom University who voiced criticism of the government (and the restrictive racial policies of the University itself).

110. It is worth noting that all the examples given here were well established long before 1948, the 'official' advent of apartheid. Indeed, it is arguable that apartheid was ethically and theologically more palatable to its proponents precisely because it was anticipated in the way churches were organised.

111. Quoted in Anderson, 'The Segregated Spirit', 240.

112. Burger also said that, 'by the grace of God, all four divisions [of the AFM] prospered.' AFM submission 1.

113. Scripture Union submission, 2.

114. RC submission, 3

115. PCSA submission, 9. See also Sipho Mtetwa, 'Ministering to a Bleeding South Africa', in *The Making of an Indigenous Clergy in Southern Africa,* P. Denis ed. (Pietermaritzburg: Cluster Publications, 1995), 181–6.

116. PCSA submission, 9. Archbishop Tutu also made this admission of the CPSA at the hearings, noting that 'it was only very recently that we had an equalisation of stipends'.

117. We could also add in the case of the PCSA a rejection of union with other confessionally similar churches for fear of being 'swamped' by new black members.

118. MCSA presentation.

119. BCSA submission, 7.

120. These included two racially divided Union conferences, as well as secondary and tertiary educational institutions. SDA submission, 6.

121. The Kairos Theologians, *Challenge to the Church: The Kairos Document* (Grand Rapids: Eerdmans, 1985), 17. We have changed the tenses of the verbs in this sentence. It is important to recognise, whether implicitly or explicitly, the confessions of even the conservative churches that identified the liberation theology of the *Kairos Document* as anti-Christ, in this definition. See especially the submission of CESA.

122. This term refers to a number of groups which espoused extreme conservative politics and justified them with Christian symbols. Strongly anti-communist and often using relief as a front, they had no qualms about involvement in poli-

tics (unlike more conservative churches which would have eschewed politics). It must be recognised that the term may or may not represent the self-understanding of the many different groups this Report summarises under it.

123. Paul Gifford's work investigated the links between right-wing groups and the Rhema Bible Church in the 1980s. See Gifford, *The Religious Right in Southern Africa* (Harare: Baobab Books, 1988). Also useful is Michael Worsnip, *The Gospel of National Security*, unpublished typescript (Pietermaritzburg: Fedsem, 1989).

124. In what became known as 'Muldergate', some 64 million rands of government funds were spent on buying newspapers and other media, both domestically and overseas, as well as infiltrating civil organisations including churches. 'The conspiracy also involved attempts to undermine opposition groups and especially the churches within South Africa and abroad by denigrating their leadership, their policies and their integrity.' Derrick Knight in Roger A. Arendse, 'The Gospel Defence League: A Critical Analysis of a Right Wing Christian Group in South Africa', *Journal of Theology for Southern Africa*, no. 69 (December 1989), 97. Over one million rands of public money went to the Christian League – the purpose of which was to drive a wedge between the SACC and its member churches. Arendse, 'Gospel Defence League', 97. *The Aida Parker Newsletter*, United Christian Action and Victims Against Terrorism are further examples of organisations that were covert SADF projects. All three were involved in disseminating information about Allan Boesak's extra-marital relations with Di Scott in 1985 – information which had been fed them through security agents. See 'How Media did the State's Dirty Work', *Mail & Guardian,* 19 September 1997.

125. TEASA presentation. The example they gave was the youth camps.

126. AFM submission, 5, 3. Interestingly, Izak Burger, the President of the now united AFM church, had himself previously argued that the segregation of Pentecostalism was not so much a result of political influences as a spontaneous spiritual movement, suggesting divine origins (cited in Anderson and Pillay, 'The Segregated Spirit', 240). See above, section 2.2.5.

127. TEASA presentation at the hearing by Colin LaVoy.

128. Cochrane, *Servants of Power* and Charles Villa-Vicencio, *Trapped in Apartheid: A Socio-Theological History of the English-Speaking Churches* (Maryknoll; Cape Town: Orbis Press; David Philip Publishers, 1988) provide important exposés.

129. See Jonathan Draper, '"In Humble Submission to Almighty God" and its Biblical Foundation: Contextual Exegesis of Romans 13:1–7', *Journal of Theology for Southern Africa* no. 63 (June 1988), 30–8.

130. Nico Smith's Open Letter alluded thus to the calling of Christian ministers.

131. Specifically they note a general lack of condemnation of apartheid before 1971, and a general silence about the migrant labour system. URCSA submission, 6.

132. Faried Esack's presentation.

133. Maha Sabha submission, 4; Ramakrishna submission, 2.

134. CESA, RC and PCSA submissions. CAIC presentation.

135. Salvation Army submission.

136. ELCSA submission.

137. MCSA, UCCSA, Nico Smith submissions.

138. And here we should note that it is not only specific members that were privileged – faith communities themselves (for instance the English-speaking churches) had a prominent, secure place within the society and we can also speak of some of them as 'privileged'.

139. RC submission, 2.

140. Nico Smith presentation.

141. See for instance the URCSA submission.

142. URCSA submission, 6.

143. CPSA submission, 2.

144. BCSA submission, 5.

145. Faried Esack presentation.

146. URCSA submission, 9–10.

147. Salvation Army policy statement, 2.

148. SDA submission, 2.

149. See for example the SDA submission.

150. One example of this was the declaration of the Cato Manor site in Durban (where many Indians had settled) a 'white area'. Maha Sabha submission, 5.

151. The SDA spoke of members who, having decided to marry across the colour line, were forced to leave the country.

152. Despite Faried Esack's claim at the hearings that Muslims suffered not as Muslims, but as coloured or Indian people, it is clear from other submissions that the state did target faith communities, trying to win their loyalties and marginalise their members opposed to the state.

153. BK submission, 2.

154. See James R. Cochrane, 'Christian Resistance to Apartheid: Periodisation, Prognosis', in *Christianity in South Africa*, Martin Prozesky, ed. (Bergvlei: Southern Books, 1990), 94ff.

155. Low-intensity conflict describes a war in which the traditional armed forces take a back seat to psychological, political and economic operations of the state or counter-insurgent forces. Theology is also used. 'Everything is welded into a comprehensive military unit in the service of the prevailing state ideology.' Michael Worsnip, 'Low Intensity Conflict and the South African Church', *Journal of Theology for Southern Africa*, no. 69 (December 1989), 84.

156. SACC submission, 7–8. The BK mentioned a Rev. Conradie, who died under mysterious circumstances after being branded a traitor to the *volk* by the DRC for his membership in the movement. BK presentation.

157. James Buys, now moderator of the Uniting Reformed Church, had a chemical substance injected into his car while in Oudtshoorn. URCSA submission, 21.

158. RC submission, 4. The loss of life was narrowly averted when the fire was put out before it reached explosives placed by the perpetrators.

159. UCCSA submission, Moravian submission, 16. Archbishop T.W. Ntongana was barred from attending funerals of activists. CAIC presentation.

160. The loss of a mosque is, the MJC explained at the hearings, especially significant within the Muslim community. More than a building, it is a sacred site and must never be abandoned. Group Areas legislation was a direct attack on this principle, assuming that the sacrality of such spaces is transferable to wherever the state decided to resettle the community.

161. UCCSA submission, 5.

162. Moravian submission, 5–7. In addition to losing land and space, the churches were sometimes forced to relocate a distance away from where their members lived.

163. SDA submission, 4; Moravian submission, 7.

164. UCCSA submission, 2; MCSA submission, 2; RPC submission, 5.

165. RPC submission, 5. The United Methodist Church claimed to have lost properties under the Holomisa regime in the late eighties. UMCSA submission.

166. SDA submission, 4.

167. UCCSA submission, 7. The land was originally donated by the Church of Scotland.

168. UCCSA submission, 7. An account of Fedsem against the backdrop of contextualised theological education issues may be found in John W. de Gruchy, 'From the Particular to the Global: Locating Our Task as Theological Educators in Africa Within the Viability Study Process', *Bulletin for Contextual Theology in Southern Africa and Africa* 3, no. 3 (October 1996), 20–4.

169. URCSA Messina congregation submission.

170. Maha Sabha submission, 6; JUT submission, 3.

171. AmaNazaretha submission, 10.

172. JUT submission, 3. Marriages within the Shembe Church were recognised neither by state nor traditional customary law, forcing members to have three separate ceremonies. AmaNazaretha submission, 10.

173. MYC submission, 2. Pressure from other Muslim organisations forced the Ulamas to withdraw.

174. Baha'i statement, 3.

175. CESA submission, 8. The impossibility of remaining politically neutral in apartheid South Africa was underlined for CESA when its Kenilworth congregation was attacked in July 1993 by APLA (Azanian People's Liberation Army) cadres, who later told the TRC amnesty committee that they were motivated by the fact that the churches were responsible for taking land away from the African people.

176. See Alan Brews, 'Vulnerable to the Right: The English-Speaking Churches', *Journal of Theology for Southern Africa*, no. 69 (December 1989), 41–51.

177. Faried Esack presentation at hearings.

178. See the submission of the NG Kerk in Afrika, Messina.

179. See De Gruchy and Villa-Vicencio, *Apartheid is a Heresy*. This is not new. The line between political and theological heresy has often been blurred by 'Christian' politicians as well as by theologians and church leaders. The heresy trials of Johannes du Plessis in the 1920s and 1930s provide good examples. See De Gruchy's discussion of the trials in *Christianity and the Modernisation of South Africa* (in press).

180. The UCCSA, for example, testified at the hearings to the loss of its mother church in Cape Town over its support for the PCR.

181. The Evangelical Fellowship of Congregational Churches, a breakaway from the UCCSA, was set up in the wake of the debate over the UCCSA's membership in the WCC. It was linked to churches funded by the state and exposed in the 1979 Information Scandal (UCCSA submission, 12). The state also set up the

Western Cape Council of Churches, linked closely with JMC (Joint Management Committee) structures, in counterposition to the SACC and the Western Province Council of Churches. Worsnip, 'Low Intensity Conflict', 94. Bishop Dowling pointed out that the Catholic Church was not exempt either, with the Catholic Defence League and Tradition, Family and Property – two groups which counterpoised themselves to the SACBC.

182. Martin Prozesky, 'The Challenge of Other Religions for Christianity in South Africa', *Journal of Theology for Southern Africa*, no. 74 (March 1991), 39.

183. Nokuzola Mndende submission.

184. MCSA, UCCSA, RC and PCSA submissions. This was also detailed by the SACC.

185. In his presentation at the hearings, Bishop Michael Nuttall recalls 'a synod resolution in which it was decided that any Anglican who was in the security police could not be elected to serve on a parish council. The opposition to this decision in some quarters of our church was immediate.'

186. SACC submission, 8. At the hearings, SACC director of communications Bernard Spong said that 'the Council of Churches was a Council at one level in that the leaders and representatives of the churches made the decisions, but in fact the action was by individuals from those churches who were actually committed to the cause and the struggle against apartheid and were prepared to make that stand.'

187. The Jewish community, which did not collectively speak up against oppression, had many members who nevertheless were active in opposing apartheid. In his submission, Rabbi Cyril Harris indicated that this is how Jews opposed apartheid: through individuals. And Kader Asmal's comment, that 'the Jewish community of South Africa has produced proportionately more heroes in the struggle against apartheid than any other so-called white group', must be noted. Submission of the Chief Rabbi, 2.

188. See Petersen, 'Time, Resistance and Reconstruction'.

189. Cochrane, 'Christian Resistance to Apartheid', 92.

190. What follows comes from Cochrane, 'Christian Resistance to Apartheid'. Cochrane concludes from this that 'the churches as human institutions tend to reflect rather than challenge their social milieu, and, that they do so with prevailing symbols of social and political legitimacy.' Cochrane, 'Christian Resistance to Apartheid', 95.

191. Interestingly it seems that the more evangelical communities (especially the BUSA, Rosebank Union Church and Hatfield Christian Church), while claiming to have 'made many submissions' to the government opposing apartheid, were vague and did not mention particular instances. Hence parts of this section are lacking in concreteness in their documentation.

192. See Richard Elphick, 'The Benevolent Empire and the Social Gospel: Missionaries and South African Christians in the Age of Segregation', in *Christianity in South Africa*, Elphick and Davenport, eds., 347–69 and Cochrane, *Servants of Power* for historical background.

193. For an analysis of Cottesloe, see John W. de Gruchy, *The Church Struggle in South Africa* (Grand Rapids and Cape Town: Eerdmans and David Philip, 1986), 62–9.

194. PCSA submission, 1. This statement, while a watershed, was relatively

mild and even paternalistic compared to later ecumenical statements.

195. The English-speaking churches had united four years previously to oppose the church clause which segregated worship, but had failed to respond adequately to the education crisis caused by the Bantu Education Act in 1953, and had almost all lost their schools to the state.

196. DRC submission, 9–12.

197. DRC submission, 12. Naudé would go on to establish the Christian Institute, originally to agitate for change in the DRC. It is worth mentioning that dissent within DRC ranks, while controlled, was not completely lacking. In 1982 the so-called 'Ope Brief' was issued by 123 ministers and theologians and caused a major controversy in the church. See David J. Bosch, Adrio König and Willem Nicol, eds., *Perspektief op die Ope Brief* (Cape Town: Human & Rousseau, 1982).

198. SACC submission, 3.

199. It must be added, however, that support for the Call for Prayer from the member churches of the SACC was mixed, with vocal opposition coming from Anglican Archbishop Philip Russell and Methodist President Peter Storey. For documentation, see Boesak and Villa-Vicencio, *When Prayer Makes News*.

200. UCCSA submission, 14. For the debate in the 1980s, see the articles in the series 'Southern Africa Today: The Kairos Debate', *Journal of Theology for Southern Africa*, no. 55 (March 1986), also *Perspektiewe Op / Perspectives on Kairos*, J. W. Hofmeyr, J. H. H. du Toit and C. J. J. Froneman, eds. (Cape Town: Lux Verbi, 1987). The latter contains a fairly extensive bibliography of commentaries and articles on the *Document* during its first two years. A recent account of the writing of the *Document* may be found in Albert Nolan, 'Kairos Theology', in *Doing Theology in Context: South African Perspectives*, John W. de Gruchy & Charles Villa-Vicencio, eds. (Cape Town; Maryknoll: David Philip; Orbis, 1994). The Document remains contentious today, with John Kane-Berman of the Institute for Race Relations calling for a confession of guilt from its signatories, accusing them of complicity in violence. 'Let the Priests Confess', *Frontiers of Freedom,* 14:4 (1997), 1 and 'The *Kairos* Controversy', *Frontiers of Freedom,* 15:1 (1998), 11–12.

201. See also A. Rashid Omar, 'Muslim–Christian Relations in the Midst of the Anti-Apartheid Struggle', unpublished paper, 11–14, on assessments of the *Document* (and a critique of its Christian particularism) within Muslim and WCRP circles.

202. See *Die Koinonia Verklaring*, pamphlet (Potchefstroom & Germiston, 1977) and Bennie van der Walt, *'n Skuldbelydenis oor Apartheid*, pamphlet (Potchefstroom: Institute for Reformational Studies, 1997). The struggle within the Gereformeerde Kerk provides a good example of the mobilisation of the same set of religious resources in two contrary directions.

203. *A Different Gospel* (Johannesburg: Presbyterian Church of Southern Africa, n.d.). This work anticipated the declaration of the theology behind apartheid being declared a heresy by the Belhar Confession in 1982 and was used as the basis for Allan Boesak's appeal to the World Alliance of Reformed Churches to suspend the DRC's membership.

204. RC submission, 2; UCCSA submission, 2. According to the MJC submission, the declaration of apartheid as a heresy in terms of Islamic theology dates to

the Call of Islam Declaration in 1961. MJC submission, 3.

205. UCCSA submission, 2; PCSA submission, 2.

206. Belhar, of course, predated the formation of the Uniting Reformed Church and was an initiative mainly of the Sendingkerk. For a location of the Confession in relation to the German Barmen Declaration (its most important historical parallel) and the *Kairos Document*, see Nico Horn, 'From Barmen to Belhar and Kairos', in *On Reading Karl Barth in South Africa*, Charles Villa-Vicencio, ed. (Grand Rapids: Eerdmans 1988), 105–19.

207. Salvation Army submission, 2.

208. SDA submission, 3.

209. MJC submission, 2–3.

210. Gerrie Lubbe cited in MJC submission, 3.

211. CESA submission (Bell), 2; UCCSA submission, 15.

212. UCCSA submission, 15. It goes on, however, to say that 'Whilst the UCCSA was concerned about the loss of innocent civilian life in guerrilla attacks, it never allied itself with the hysterical reaction against "terrorism" that the apartheid government orchestrated.'

213. The URCSA stated that 'the ambiguous nature of decision with regard to justified actions against apartheid was often left to the conscience of members'.

214. RPC submission, 3.

215. In 1985, the CESA's national synod expressed its 'abhorrence of all violence and all oppression'. CESA submission (Bell, 2). Interestingly, while CESA put forth that the 'only solution' to the problem of violence was dealing with sin through 'reconciliation to God', the UCCSA said in its submission that the only answer to the problem of violence (and here it specifically referred to the struggle on the borders between the SADF and the liberation movements) was justice for the people of South Africa. UCCSA submission, 15.

216. The RPC's submission (3) notes this as well. For the debate on violence and revolution, see Charles Villa-Vicencio, ed., *Theology and Violence: The South African Debate* (Johannesburg: Skotaville Publishers, 1987).

217. See Villa-Vicencio, *Trapped in Apartheid*.

218. In both their submissions, CESA spoke of how their leaders discreetly approached P. W. Botha and F. W. de Klerk to express 'concern about wrongs'. CESA submissions by Bell (2) and Retief (5). They did not, however, indicate what the response of the state was, nor did they spell out precisely the nature of their 'concern'.

219. Baha'i presentation.

220. MJC submission, 5.

221. SACC submission, 4. See 'The Church–State Confrontation: Correspondence, February–April 1988', *Journal of Theology for Southern Africa*, no. 63 (June 1988), 68–87. Notable in this regard is Archbishop Tutu's letter to Prime Minister Vorster in May 1976, warning of the situation at Soweto. This is reprinted in Desmond Tutu, *Hope and Suffering* (Grand Rapids: Eerdmans, 1984), 28–36.

222. DRC *Journey*, 20.

223. Not insignificantly the tricameral constitution in its preamble declared South Africa a Christian state, even though the structures it put forth were aimed at co-opting groups with many Muslim and Hindu members.

224. MJC submission, 6.

225. UCCSA submission, 9.

226. Quaker submission, 1; SDA submission, 5. Seventh Day Adventists faced a dilemma here, as their conservative doctrine of church–state relations also held loyalty to the state in high esteem. Some resolved the dilemma by serving in the medical corps. Others became objectors and suffered for it. Whether they were doing this to oppose apartheid, or to oppose war on principle, is an important question which the church, according to its submission, only started to address after the evil of apartheid became apparent.

227. The PCSA mentioned especially Peter Moll and Richard Steele. PCSA submission, 4. See also the submission of Rev. Douglas Torr.

228. Mentioned as 'religious objectors' in the URCSA submission were Revs. D. Potgeiter, B. Nel, N. Theron, C. Krause and Brother B. de Lange.

229. UCCSA submission, 12–13.

230. PCSA submission, 4.

231. Something which illustrates the gap between resolutions and actions in churches.

232. PCSA submission, 7.

233. UCCSA submission, 15.

234. CPSA submission, 2. The CPSA was in the unusual position of its SADF chaplains supplying support to what its Namibian members could only see as an army of occupation. In the late eighties, the CPSA took a decision not to appoint any more military chaplains.

235. PCSA submission, 3.

236. PCSA submission, 3, citing Dawid Venter. Robertson's work is chronicled in R. J. D. Robertson, *The Small Beginning* (Cape Town: Salty Print 1997).

237. JUT submission, 4.

238. And indeed in their submission, the Baha'is spelt out clearly that they had no intention to challenge the state.

239. RC submission, 5.

240. RPC submission, 5.

241. MJC submission, 5. Indeed the idea of a 'common struggle' meant inter-faith co-operation at a number of levels – something condemned by more conservative Muslim groups. It is notable that the Western Province Council of Churches and the Witwatersrand Council of Churches also affiliated with the UDF – the only two regional partners of the SACC to do so – for the same reasons as the MJC: as being part of a 'common' struggle. In fact the inter-faith co-operation was probably the strongest in the Western Cape amongst Muslims and Christians, and later with Jews for Justice, precisely because of this factor.

242. UCCSA submission, 15.

243. See J. Kinghorn, B. C. Lategan and C. F. van der Merwe, *Into Africa: Afrikaners in Africa Reflect on 'Coming Home'* (Stellenbosch: The Centre for Contextual Hermeneutics, 1988).

244. WCRP presentation.

245. RC submission, 6.

246. Peter Walshe points out that as by 1988 the political activities of the UDF and COSATU were severely curtailed, faith community leaders filled in important gaps. Indeed he goes as far as to say that the activities of 'prophetic Christian'

leaders and liberation movements were 'enmeshed'. Peter Walshe, *Prophetic Christianity and the Liberation Movement in South Africa* (Pietermaritzburg: Cluster Publications, 1995), 123f.

247. The MYM noted that most Muslim countries cut their ties to South Africa during the apartheid years. Ironically, this created difficulties for South African Muslims, those on pilgrimage, who 'suffered tremendous hardship, financial and personal loss and humiliation when undertaking their trip to Mecca'.

248. The ZCC opposed disinvestment. ZCC submission, 4–5.

249. CPSA submission, 2. Ironically it was the CPSA Archbishop of Cape Town who was one of the most vocal proponents of sanctions.

250. RC submission, 5. 'History', it said, 'will be the judge.' On the debate within the Catholic Church over sanctions, see Villa-Vicencio, *Trapped in Apartheid*, 120–1.

251. The UCCSA Assembly adopted a resolution supporting 'immediate and comprehensive sanctions' in 1986. UCCSA submission, 13.

252. For a defence of sanctions, see Cecil Mzingisi Ngcokovane, 'Economic Sanctions: The Only Remaining Non-Violent Means to Dismantle Apartheid', *Journal of Theology for Southern Africa,* no. 62 (March 1988), 53–61.

253. See Villa-Vicencio, *Trapped in Apartheid,* 13-24.

254. Spong presentation, 17 November 1997.

255. Mention could be made of *Pro Veritate, The Voice* and *Crisis News* – all of which were eventually banned.

256. RC submission, 3; Muslim Youth Movement submission, 2.

257. UCCSA submission, 14.

258. Ramakrishna submission, 2.

259. Written by James Wyllie, Vido Nyobole and Sue Brittion.

260. WCRP presentation.

261. See *The Road to Rustenburg: The Church Looking Forward to a New South Africa,* Louw Alberts and Frank Chikane, eds. (Cape Town: Struik Christian Books, 1991).

262. Details on the above and further examples may be found in Peter Walshe, *Prophetic Christianity and the Liberation Movement in South Africa* (Pietermaritzburg: Cluster Publications, 1995), 145–53, and John W. de Gruchy, 'Midwives of Democracy', *Journal of Theology for Southern Africa*, no. 86 (March 1994), 14–25.

263. In his presentation at the hearings on behalf of the WCRP, Franz Auerbach observed that 'we don't actually know a great deal as communities of the experiences of other communities in South Africa in the past and therefore we often talk to each other without knowing enough of the background'.

264. WCRP presentation at the hearings.

265. It reflects an ethical, rather than a symbolic, understanding of religion.

266. PCSA submission, 10. In its policy statement, the Salvation Army spoke of initiating an internal process of reconciliation. Others who made this recommendation included the ICT and Imam Rashid Omar, the latter in a document appended to the WCRP submission.

267. Although as we stated in section 2.3.1 the relation between the PCSA and the RPC is not the same as that between the DRC and the URCSA, nor between the BUSA and the BCSA, nevertheless similar economic dynamics keep them apart.

268. See the PCSA submission.

269. BCSA submission, 8. 'Our people are drowning in a sea of unanswered questions.'

270. Although the PCSA noted in its submission that union with the UCCSA was rejected in 1983–4, largely it seems because of fear of a black majority church. PCSA submission, 8.

271. Under the initiative of Archbishop Ndungane, the CPSA is currently engaged in a programme to encourage its wealthier (and whiter) parishes to contribute to paying off the debt of poorer (and blacker) parishes. We shall make a recommendation concerning this kind of process in section 5.3.

272. According to Matlhodi Malope of the National Land Committee, churches had been making these kinds of resolutions since 1984 but there had yet to be action. 'Besides confessing', he said at a joint SACC and NLC conference in 1997, 'there has been no major action to show remorse or repentance from the church.' 'Pressure on the Churches to Hand over Land', *Mail & Guardian,* 19 November 1997.

273. Salvation Army policy statement, 2.

274. BCSA submission, 8.

275. See Gesher, 6.

276. CPSA submission (Ndungane), 1–2.

277. PCSA submission, 10. One such confession was included in the submissions by Lesley Morgan.

278. PCSA submission, 5.

279. Salvation Army policy statement, 2.

280. SU submission, 4.

281. URCSA submission, 21.

282. RC submission, 7.

283. Salvation Army policy statement, 2.

284. ELCSA submission, 3.

285. Gesher document, 4.

286. TEASA submission, 3.

287. Chief Rabbi submission, 3.

288. SDA submission, 8.

289. IFCC submission addendum.

290. SACC submission, 11.

291. URCSA submission, 21–2. The Catholic presentation at the hearings did as well, adding the idea of a symbolic burial for all who had disappeared in exile and whose bodies have not been found.

292. RC presentation.

293. The Maha Sabha, CESA, AFM, MJC, IFCC and ZCC all expressed concern at the hearings over crime.

294. AmaNazaretha submission, 13.

295. BUSA submission, 2.

296. CESA submission, 7. Significantly, the CESA placed 'the ongoing struggle to uplift the poor and needy and to think through the issue of the redistribution of wealth from a Christian perspective' alongside its traditional agenda concerning abortion, pornography, gambling and so forth.

297. IFCC submission, 6.

298. IFCC submission, 5.

299. ICT presentation at hearings.

300. The PCSA was concerned about the perception that the process was being hijacked to settle older political scores.

301. ICT submission, 4ff; RC presentation.

302. CAIC presentation, Koka presentation, COI presentation and others.

303. RC submission, 8.

304. For a study of Frontline Fellowship and Gospel Defence League, see Lesley Fordred, 'Sacred Nation, Holy War', Honours dissertation (University of Cape Town, 1990). *The Journal of Theology for Southern Africa* also published a theme issue in December 1989 on right-wing religious movements, including Muslim groups.

305. For a fascinating account of right-wing 'missionaries' in Mozambique, see Steve Askin, 'Mission to RENAMO: The Militarisation of the Religious Right', *Journal of Theology for Southern Africa*, no. 69 (December 1989), 106–16. Overseas evangelical groups such as the Church of the Christian Crusade helped disseminate the idea that the South African government was opposing communism and supporting Christian civilisation in maintaining its national security policies. For a particularly striking example, see Billy James Hargis, *The Communist Threat to Southern Africa* (Pretoria: Southern African Christian Crusades, n.d.).

306. Abdulkader Tayob, 'Fitnah: The Ideology of Conservative Islam', *Journal of Theology for Southern Africa*, no. 69 (December 1989), 65–71, and Ebrahim Moosa, 'Muslim Conservatism in South Africa', *Journal of Theology for Southern Africa*, no. 69 (December 1989), 73–81.

307. ELCSA's submission was literally at the last minute, and was received by the Commission the night before the faith communities section of the final report was due.

308. Commissioner Yasmin Sooka was to have served on the panel but was unable to attend the hearings.

309. Originally Moulana Ebrahim Bham of the conservative JUT was scheduled to speak on behalf of the Muslim community. When Moulana Faried Esack (with whom Bham is engaged in the dispute over Radio Islam) heard of this, he requested space to appear. As the controversy over representation grew, the MJC contacted the Commission and offered to make a special appearance. In a fax to Meiring, dated 17 November 1997, Nisaar Dawood of the Muslim Youth Movement denied his organisation had been approached by the Commission to make a submission or to testify, and called the fact that the JUT was to speak 'a slap in the face of many who gave their lives for the struggle'. The MYM later made a submission. While it ended up with a variety of submissions from the Islamic community, the way they came about was an embarrassment for the TRC.

310. Letter of the Mujlisul Ulama to TRC, 21 November 1997.

311. See especially the CESA and IFCC submissions. At the hearings, Rev. Colin LaVoy of the Assemblies of God identified Beyers Naudé as a truly prophetic figure during the 1970s.

312. ZCC and amaNazaretha submissions.

313. Bishop Lekganyane is a revered figure amongst ZCC members, and is rarely seen outside of the annual gathering at Moria. His appearance (on the third

rather than the second day) was a kind of epiphany. He refused to take the oath and had an assistant speak for him. In fact, he did not speak a word during the entire event.

314. Or alternatively it could be argued that faith communities are simply doing what they have historically done in South Africa: reflect the discourse of those in power.

315. Though with the growing numbers amongst AICs, this is becoming less and less so.

316. Villa-Vicencio, *Trapped in Apartheid*, 93.

317. Again we emphasise that we speak of institutions. There were important, strong voices within each church who made their influence known in what would have otherwise been more moderate organisations.

318. In some ways this meant that as institutions they occupied the same space as the liberal parliamentary opposition in the 1980s.

319. It is notable that the DRC did not shy away from using the term 'prophetic' of its identity – even during the apartheid years. DRC *Journey*, 37. Interestingly it pledges that same prophetic voice to government in the future. See our comments on language in the previous section.

320. At the hearings, CESA described its feelings at facing its past as 'embarrassment, heartache and pain' – as if it were surprised by the testimonies of victims.

321. See the presentation and discussion of women in religion.

322. Sixty-six different persons sat as representatives of their faith communities at the hearings. Only four were women. At the hearings, while the question of gender was raised by commissioners during the question times, only the SACC, BK and Faried Esack made explicit reference to the oppression of women in their communities within their presentations.

323. When at the CPSA's Cape Town synod meeting, which took place shortly after the TRC faith communities hearings, a motion was introduced to declare support for the Commission, confessions spontaneously began to happen, including confessions of sexism as well as racism on the part of clergy and lay representatives.

324. We (the writers of this report) are utilising the term 'process of healing' rather than 'a TRC for the faith communities', both to get away from the problems with the term 'reconciliation' noted above and also to capture what we consider the normative role for faith communities – namely facilitators of healing – in a post-apartheid South Africa. The term 'healing' has a resonance within many if not most faith traditions. It is therefore a more inclusive term than 'reconciliation'. It also gets beyond the quasi-juridical nature of the TRC, trying to promote confession on the part of individuals, to addressing the pathologies of the past. It also speaks more strongly to the apartheid past, envisioning it as a wound that continues to be a source of pain for the majority of South Africans, as well as for the land which has also been deeply gouged. It also speaks of the need for cleansing, for the removal of harmful influences, and warns of the dangers of merely covering over the past. Healing is multidimensional, and we can use the term to refer to wounded and broken relationships (including economic and political relationships), families, institutions, and even faith. Finally, 'healing' speaks of a positive future, of a wholeness in which all (people and land) share equally.

325. The year 1999 will also see South Africa's first 'normal' government elected – something that also signals a fresh start.

326. See Denise Ackermann, 'On Hearing and Lamenting: Faith and Truth Telling', in *To Remember and to Heal: Theological and Psychological Reflections on the Truth and Reconciliation Commission*, H. Russel Botman & Robin Petersen, eds. (Cape Town: Human & Rousseau, 1996), 47–56.

Chapter 2

1. Knight (1982) states that the CLSA project received at least R340,000 of taxpayers' money to carry out its campaigns against the SACC.

2. See *Journal of Theology for Southern Africa*, no. 69 (December 1989). This issue is a useful resource for reflection on RWCGs in the churches. A good deal more was exposed about RWCGs in the late 1980s. For example, in 1988 the Institute for Contextual Theology (ICT) and the Ecumenical Documentary and Information Centre for East and Southern Africa (EDICESA) held separate conferences on the theme of right-wing religion in Johannesburg and Harare (Zimbabwe) respectively. Participants at each conference highlighted the unmistakable reality of RWCGs in South Africa and produced documented evidence of their active role in the propagation of 'state theology'. Around this time, the phenomenon of RWCGs was the subject of research at various places in South Africa such as the ICT offices in Johannesburg and the Department of Religious Studies at the University of Cape Town. Critical analyses of RWCGs in South Africa appeared in various books and articles (e.g. Knight 1982; Knight 1989; Gifford 1988) and progressive news bulletins and magazines (e.g. *Crisis News*, November 1988; *People's Church,* July/August 1988). In 1989, the story of right-wing Christianity was outlined in *The Road to Damascus*, an international version of the South African *Kairos Document*. Even influential church bodies in Cape Town, including the Church of the Province, the Roman Catholic Church and the Methodist Church, adopted a statement in 1988, accusing RWCGs of their political abuse of the Christian faith in South Africa (see 'The Political Abuse of Religion', in *Crisis News,* 1988).

3. See note 2 above.

4. E.g. the Gospel Defence League (GDL), Tradition, Family and Property (TFP), Frontline Fellowship (FF), Jimmy Swaggart Ministries (JSM), *Signposts Magazine* (Signposts), the Catholic Defence League (CDL), United Christian Action (UCA), and the Conference for Christian Action (CCA).

5. E.g. the Western Cape Council of Churches (WCCC), the United Christian Conciliation Party (UCCP), the Bophuthatswana Ministers' Fraternal (BMF), the Reformed Independent Churches Association (RICA), Jesus for Peace in South Africa (JPSA), and the Christian Alliance of South Africa (CASA).

6. E.g. *The Aida Parker Newsletter* (APN), FF, the GDL, *Signposts*, and UCA (which acted as an umbrella and co-ordinating body for many different RWCGs, including those mentioned here).

7. E.g. Anglicans Concerned for Truth and Spirituality (ACTS), the CDL, and TFP. Not mentioned by *Crisis News*, but referred to in the RICSA Report (sec. 5.1.1) and directly implicated in the Information Scandal (Muldergate), is the Evangelical Fellowship of Congregational Churches (EFCC).

8. E.g. the Church of England (CESA) and the ultra-right Afrikaanse

Protestante Kerk.

9. E.g. Bet-El Group of Ministries, the JSM and Christian Mission International (CMI).

10. E.g. UCCP, WCCC, RICA, JCP and CASA.

11. By this I mean the analysis of the description and classification of the content of the primary material put out by RWCGs. No explicit sociological analysis of the material is attempted in this study (Arendse 1989a, 28).

12. This analysis was undergirded by what I believed to be the strong dualistic worldview that pervaded the theology of RWCGs. 'In Platonic fashion, sharp contrasts are drawn in each case between two opposing spheres: God and Satan; good and evil; the kingdom of light and the kingdom of darkness; spiritual and material; supernatural and natural; Christian and secular humanism; Christ and antichrist; church and politics. RWCGs decide what fits into a particular sphere. This makes it easier to identify the enemy and call for strong counter-action. For example 'Christian values which are good are made synonymous with capitalism, whereas communism and socialism are evil and satanic' (Arendse 1989a, 42–3). My treatment of the worldview of RWCGs here must be read alongside the treatment of their worldview in Fordred's study (1990) described in this essay.

13. This case study is therefore useful not only for understanding the essential character of RWCGs but also to illustrate the traceable connections between 'older' RWCGs of the 1970s and 'newer' RWCGs in the 1980s and 1990s.

14. Scarborough edited the English-language version of the journal *Vox Africana* that was identified earlier as one of the apartheid state's secret funding projects to promote its cause among former West German Christians. Its first English edition was published in January 1988, and was designed to discredit liberation theology among the English-speaking churches (Arendse 1989b, 98). She also worked closely with young American missionaries, such as Mark Kreitzer, who shared the ideological agenda of the GDL. Kreitzer wrote a series of pamphlets entitled *What does the Bible say about ...?* They covered a variety of themes such as reconciliation, justice, peace, the oppressed poor, capitalism and socialism. All themes claimed an absolute connection between identified 'biblical blueprints' and the fundamentalist US-based movement for 'Christian reconstruction' (Arendse 1989b, 99). See my comments on biblical fundamentalism below.

15. E.g. Arendse 1989a & 1989b; Gifford 1988 & 1989; Walker 1989. Gifford's earlier work connects RWCGs in South Africa with the New Christian Right (NCR), while his second provides an account of their major theological features such as nationalism, dispensationalism, reconstruction, the gospel of prosperity and otherworldliness. Walker analyses the foundational doctrines of evangelicalism and illustrates how these predisposed evangelicals to grant support to the apartheid system.

16. Fordred's analysis draws heavily on the insights of post-structuralism (e.g. Foucault 1980; 1986), which aims, among other things, to understand first, rather than judge, the production of meaning and the construction of reality that gives rise to any discourse. While an important corrective to earlier work (including my own), I believe she has largely underrated and underplayed the dominant social function of right-wing Christian discourse and practice which I and others have sought to emphasise.

17. What Fordred's (1990, 20) conception of RWCGs in terms of 'conservative

Christian' does help us to see, however, is the very close relationship that exists between the phenomenon of RWCGs and a new Christian fundamentalism once thought to be unique to the United States but now gaining influence across the globe (see e.g. Diamond 1989; Brouwer et al. 1996).

18. This kind of analysis is a more detailed and extended focus on the 'militarist' character of RWCGs, one of several 'dominant ideological trends' of these groups (cf. Arendse 1989, 34–8; Arendse 1989b, 102–3).

19. Askin (1989, 113 n.40) draws this directly from one of Peter Hammond's own prayer and praise newsletters entitled *A New Field: South West Africa*, July/August 1985. Other comments by Askin are carefully grounded in several actual FF documents and related sources that can be easily examined and corroborated.

20. Fordred (1990, 21–3) provides a revealing interview with Hammond in which he describes the events that prompted the launch of FF and, according to him, its evangelistic missionary goals. This is just one example of how Hammond uses Christian discourse to mask an ideological militancy that served the South African state's agenda of oppression. See also my own study (Arendse 1989a, 34–8) for a revealing exposé of the undeniable links between the SADF, the military chaplaincy, and RWCGs such as FF, the GDL, Signposts Publications and Research Centre, *The Aida Parker Newsletter* and Women for South Africa (WOSA) during the 1980s. Veterans for Victory – a RWCG specifically dedicated to the elimination of the End Conscription Campaign during the 1980s – has this to say about FF: 'This is a Christian Mission group, but don't be fooled by the name, Christian or Mission. These fellows go into Angola and Mozambique doing research and exposing communist murder and slaughter of innocents ... They can supply information and photos of SWAPO and other terror groups' (undated letter, early 1987). In 1989, local newspapers reported the capture of FF members in Mozambique, and described them among other things as 'Renamo-supporting' missionaries (*Sunday Times*, 29 Oct.) and 'mercenary priests' (*Cape Argus*, 31 Oct.).

21. See the RICSA Report (sec 5.2.2 n.155). Worsnip's analysis is grounded in his fuller unpublished study, *The Gospel of National Security* (1989b, esp. ch. 5).

22. Here Worsnip (1989b, 91) mentions the Rhema Bible Church, founded by Ray McCauley in 1978, together with other related charismatic and Pentecostal churches, such as the Hatfield Christian Church. These church groups are also identified as RWCGs in other sources (e.g. *Crisis News* 1989, 6; Arendse 1989a, 24; Gifford 1989, 38–40). Both these church groups made submissions at the TRC hearings, yet they never defined themselves as RWCGs during the 1980s. Instead, they included themselves among the many other faith communities that apologised in more general terms for their involvement in apartheid. The suggestion made in the RICSA Report (sec. 5.1.1) that no RWCG made any submission at the TRC hearings, therefore, may need to be somewhat amended in light of the specific submissions of Rhema, Hatfield and even the Church of England (CESA). The positive and encouraging theological and political 'shift' that these submissions suggest cannot be underestimated (see below). This does not mean, however, that the content of their submissions should not be included among those of other church groups that are carefully evaluated and ultimately tested against the practical actions of reconciliation and healing that they undertake in the future.

23. Des Hoffmeister, representing the Baptist Convention of South Africa, noted how RWCGs had used churches as fronts to propagate their theology and politics.

24. But see note 23 above.

25. At the time, Finca noted that he had made the response, from which this quote is taken, in his personal capacity and not as commissioner.

26. Having raised the question about the apparent omission of RWCGs from the TRC hearings, I am aware that most of these groups remain militantly opposed to the entire TRC process itself. One example of this opposition is the vitriolic rhetoric of *The Aida Parker Newsletter*: 'After 12 months of an avalanche of TV histrionics, backed by hysterical media headlines, this R130 million extravaganza has degenerated into little more than a series of one-sided show trials aimed, it would appear, at the moral annihilation of the Afrikaners. Academics prefer the term, "cultural genocide."'

27. See the next section where I provide additional recommendations in this regard.

28. This is not to suggest that RWCGs should not enjoy with all South African citizens the 'freedom of religion, belief, and opinion', 'freedom of expression', and 'freedom of association' enshrined in the Bill of Rights of our new Constitution (Sections 15, 16 & 18). But it does mean that RWCGs should be held seriously accountable for their activities, especially those activities that in the past may have promoted gross human rights violations in any form either within South Africa or beyond her borders.

29. Many Christian leaders and lay people often lack an adequate awareness of how societies function, how power relations work, or how various ideas are used to promote or maintain certain political, economic and cultural practices. 'Religious' ideas are particularly vulnerable at this point because they appear to their adherents, at least, to be absolute, divinely inspired and unquestionable. Yet religion and religious ideas are social realities and have definite social functions in relation to prevailing ideologies and authority structures in society.

30. Worth further investigation is how many RWCGs of the 1980s, which may seem to have 'disappeared', still continue to operate in local churches or communities in the 1990s, albeit under new names.

31. These topics include pornography, gambling, abortion, the death penalty, and drugs. More recently, RWCGs such as UCA have been vehemently opposed to the Gun-Free Campaign in South Africa (see *UCANEWS*, edition 2/97). These concerns should not be ignored, but should be more constructively engaged than RWCGs seem to suggest.

32. See the helpful article of Wanamaker (1989).

33. See *Cape Times*, 15 June 1998, p. 17 for the full account of this story.

Chapter 3

1. While I recognise the wisdom of a deliberate reflection on the significance of the faith community hearings for people of faith, this contribution will look more broadly at the TRC as a whole. Though not commenting directly on the faith community hearings, I hope it will nevertheless contribute to the deepening of reflection on the issues of reconciliation and truth-telling that confront all religious people in this country.

2. Participants in this discussion, entitled 'Transforming society through reconciliation: myth or reality?', also included Charles Villa-Vicencio, Heidi Grunebaum-Ralph, Wynand Malan and others. Citations of Mamdani, Villa-Vicencio, Grunebaum-Ralph and Malan below are taken from the transcripts of that discussion, available at http://www.truth.org.za/debate/recon2.doc. A further account of these issues with special reference to memorialising may be found in the contribution by Grunebaum-Ralph & Stier to this volume.

Chapter 4

1. The referent for the term AIC has been variously described as 'African Independent Churches', 'African Indigenous Churches', 'African Instituted Churches' and 'African Initiated Churches'.

2. *Speaking for Ourselves* (ICT, 1985) is one of the few theological books published by AIC theologians.

3. As happened on numerous occasions during the 1980s and early 1990s. The chapter by Arendse in this volume gives an account of the apartheid government's (ab)use of such groups.

4. I use the notion of 'prophetic theology' to describe that theology usually known as Black theology, liberation theology or 'contextual theology'. For a fuller description, see Petersen (in press).

5. For an account of the visit, and an analysis of some of the issues at stake, see Petersen (in press).

Chapter 5

1. Mbali (1987) was one of the first scholars to point to the relationship between apartheid, its racism and institutions, on the one hand, and the theory of value formation on the other.

2. Further discussion of the 1857 synod may be found in Loff (1983).

3. *Our Journey with Apartheid* was originally written for the World Alliance of Reformed Churches conference in August 1997, to appeal for the re-inclusion of the DRC after a fifteen-year suspension of its membership.

4. As this book was going to press, the DRC had just voted to accept in principle a merger with the Uniting Reformed Church, although the acceptance of the Belhar Confession remains a point of contention. The synod also voted in favour of a motion denouncing apartheid as sinful. We have decided to leave the present text as it stands, first because the acceptance of unity in principle is still not an acceptance in practice and, second, because its main point remains: conversion, manifest in structural and confessional reunification with its former 'daughter' churches, remains the imperative for the DRC.

Chapter 7

1. The authors would like to acknowledge the important and relevant work of Claudia Braude, Pumla Gobodo-Madikizela, and Steven Robins, and we thank them for their contributions to a dialogue on many of the issues raised in this essay.

2. Claudia Braude (1996, 62–3) illustrates this point in a close reading of how Giliomee manipulates a neo-conservative ideology in the form of amnesiac historiography, clearly demonstrating how Giliomee evokes the uniqueness of the

Holocaust in order to support his revisionist claims.

3. For another example of the juxtaposition of apartheid and Holocaust-related issues, see Robins (1998).

4. Promotion of National Unity and Reconciliation Act (No. 34, 1995). See also Mahamod (1996).

5. In recent years, with survivors ageing and passing away, many have found both their voices and their audiences in the context of video testimony archiving projects such as the Fortunoff Video Archive for Holocaust Testimonies at Yale University and the Survivors of the Shoah Visual History Foundation started by Steven Spielberg. We note as well that, in many cases, it is only the children of those Shoah survivors who, having inherited the legacy of silent suffering from their parents, engage the process of healing and articulating a relationship to that past.

6. Such activity has parallels in the South African case. For example, in April 1997, the families of the Pebco Three (Sipho Hashe, Qwaqwahuli Godolozi, and Champion Galela) and of the Cradock Four (Fort Calata, Sparrow Mkhonto, Sicelo Mhlawuli, and Matthew Goniwe) held a memorial service on the banks of the Fish River in the Eastern Cape, consecrating a memorial space at the site of the disposal of the activists' ashes. All seven activists had been abducted, tortured and murdered by security forces in 1985.

7. This is not unlike the call of the RICSA's Report (sec. 5.3) for the TRC to allow space for the expression of lamentation, a mode the authors suggest requires small, safe spaces rather than public, political forums for its unfolding. RICSA suggests that faith communities can provide the space for such lamentation for sites of mourning and loss, while we would argue that the sites themselves could be made into lamentational spaces in which the discourse of faith communities could organise ritualised remembrance.

Chapter 8

1. The following sketches of issues in Germany, India and America are worked out in much greater detail in Everett (1997).

2. For some helpful sources in a very complex history, see Boraine, Levy & Scheffer (1994), chapters 3–4; Harper (1996).

3. The essays in Nuttall & Coetzee (1998) exhibit many facets of this difficulty.

4. Notice the contrasting emphases and ways of relating these two approaches in the essays by Smit, Petersen and Tsele in Botman & Petersen (1996).

5. For a much fuller historical and theological development of these ideas, see Everett (1988).

6. For the most extensive historical and systematic development of this theme, see Elazar (1994 & 1996).

Chapter 11

1. South African Democratic Teachers Union.

2. Congress of South African Students.

3. We have organised these according to the categorisation used in the RICSA Report. Note that a list of oral testimony follows.

4. † indicates the primary submission in cases where two or more were sent to the Commission. The RICSA Report makes reference to this one unless otherwise indicated.

Bibliography

The Aida Parker Newsletter. Number 204 (1997). Available at <http://www.cycad.com/cgi-bin/Aida/204/>.

Ackermann, Denise M. 1996. 'On Hearing and Lamenting: Faith and Truth Telling.' In *To Remember and to Heal: Theological and Psychological Reflections on Truth and Reconciliation*, edited by H. Russel Botman and Robin M. Petersen, 47–56. Cape Town: Human & Rousseau.

Adonis, J. C. 1982. *Die afgebreekte Skeidsmuur weer opgebou* [*The broken dividing wall rebuilt*]. Amsterdam: Rodopi.

Arendse, Roger. 1989a. 'Right Wing Christian Groups in South Africa: An Analysis and an Evangelical Critique.' Honours Dissertation. Cape Town: University of Cape Town.

Arendse, Roger. 1989b. 'The Gospel Defence League: A Critical Analysis of a Right Wing Christian Group in South Africa', *Journal of Theology for Southern Africa* no. 69 (December), 95–105.

Askin, Steve. 1989. 'Mission to Renamo: The Militarisation of the Religious Right.' *Journal of Theology for Southern Africa*, no. 69 (December), 106–16.

Asmal, Kader, Louise Asmal, and Ronald Suresh Roberts. 1997. *Reconciliation Through Truth: A Reckoning of Apartheid's Criminal Governance*. Second edition. Cape Town; Oxford; New York: David Philip; James Currey; St. Martin's Press.

Balcomb, Anthony O. 1993. *Third Way Theology: Reconciliation, Revolution and Reform in the South African Church During the 1980s*. Pietermaritzburg: Cluster.

Baum, Gregory and Harold Wells. Eds. 1997. *The Reconciliation of Peoples: Challenge to the Churches*. Maryknoll: Orbis.

Baum, Gregory. 1975. *Religion and Alienation: A Theological Reading of Sociology*. New York: Paulist Press.

Berlant, Lauren, 1991. *The Anatomy of National Fantasy: Hawthorne, Utopia, and Everyday Life*. Chicago: University of Chicago Press.

Bernstein, Michael André. 1994. *Foregone Conclusions: Against Apocalyptic History*. Berkeley: University of California Press.

Biko, Steve. 1978. *I Write What I Like*. San Francisco: Harper & Row.

Boesak, Allan A. 1977. *Farewell to Innocence*. Johannesburg: Ravan Press.

Bonhoeffer, Dietrich. 1966. *Christology*. London: Collins.

Bonhoeffer, Dietrich. 1972. *Letters and Papers from Prison*. New York: Macmillan.

Bophuthatswana, Republic of. 1987. *A Nation on the March*. Melville: Hans Strydom Publishers.

Boraine, Alex and Janet Levy. Eds. 1995. *The Healing of a Nation*. Cape Town: Justice in Transition.

Boraine, Alex, Janet Levy and Ronel Scheffer. Eds. 1994. *Dealing with the Past: Truth and Reconciliation in South Africa*. Cape Town: Institute for Democracy in South Africa.

Bosch, David. 1985. 'The Fragmentation of Afrikanerdom and the Afrikaner Churches.' In *Resistance and Hope: South African Essays in Honour of Beyers Naudé*, edited by Charles Villa-Vicencio and John W. de Gruchy, 61–73. Cape Town: David Philip.

Botha, D. P. 1980. 'Church and Kingdom in South Africa.' Unpublished address. Johannesburg: South African Council of Churches.

Botman, H. Russel. 1994. 'A Critical Testimony on the Document "Church and Society."' In *Studies from the World Alliance of Reformed Churches no. 25*. Geneva: World Alliance of Reformed Churches.

Botman, H. Russel. 1996a. '"Dutch" and Reformed and "Black" and Reformed in South Africa: A Tale of Two Traditions on the Move to Unity and Responsibility.' In *Keeping Faith: Embracing the Tensions in Christian Higher Education*, edited by R. A. Wells. Grand Rapids: Eerdmans.

Botman, H. Russel. 1996b. 'Narrative Challenges in a Situation of Transition.' In *To Remember and to Heal: Theological and Psychological Reflections on Truth and Reconciliation*, edited by H. Russel Botman and Robin M. Petersen, 37–44. Cape Town: Human & Rousseau.

Botman, H. Russel and Robin M. Petersen. Eds. 1996. *To Remember and to Heal: Theological and Psychological Reflections on Truth and Reconciliation*. Cape Town: Human & Rousseau.

Botman, H. Russel. 1997. 'The DRC Continues Its Journey with Apartheid.' *Challenge*, October–November, 26–27.

Braude, Claudia. 1996. 'The Archbishop, the Private Detective and the Angel of History: The Production of South African Public Memory and the Truth and Reconciliation Commission.' *Current Writing* 8, no. 2.

Brews, Alan. 1989. 'Vulnerable to the Right: The English-Speaking Churches.' *Journal of Theology for Southern Africa*, no. 69 (December), 41–51.

Bronkhorst, Daan. 1995. *Truth and Reconciliation: Obstacles and Opportunities for Human Rights*. Amsterdam: Amnesty International.

Brouwer, S., P. Gifford and S. D. Rose. 1996. *Exporting the American Gospel: Global Christian Fundamentalism*. London: Routledge.

Brown, Roger, and James Kulik. 1982. 'Flashbulb Memories.' In *Memory*

Observed: Remembering in Natural Contexts, edited by Ulric Neisser, 23–40. San Francisco: W. H. Freeman.

Caputo, John D., and Jacques Derrida. 1997. *Deconstruction in a Nutshell: A Conversation with Jacques Derrida*. New York: Fordham University Press.

Chidester, David. 1992. *Shots in the Streets: Violence and Religion in South Africa*. Cape Town: Oxford University Press.

Cloete, G. Daan and Dirkie J. Smit. 1987. *A Moment of Truth*. Grand Rapids: Eerdmans.

Cochrane, James R. 1990. 'Christian Resistance to Apartheid: Periodisation, Prognosis.' In *Christianity in South Africa*, edited by M. Prozesky, 81–100. Bergvlei: Southern Books.

Comaroff, John L. and Jean Comaroff. 1997. *Of Revelation and Revolution, Volume Two: The Dialectics of Modernity on a South African Frontier*. Chicago: University of Chicago Press.

Crisis News. 1988. November. Special Issue on Right-Wing Christian Groups.

De Certeau, Michel. 1984. *The Practice of Everyday Life*. Berkeley: University of California Press.

De Gruchy, John W. 1989. 'Confessing Guilt in South Africa Today in Dialogue with Dietrich Bonhoeffer.' *Journal of Theology for Southern Africa* no. 67 (June), 37–45.

De Gruchy, John W. 1994b. 'Midwives of Democracy.' *Journal of Theology for Southern Africa*, 86 (March), 14–25, 86.

De Gruchy, John W. and Charles Villa-Vicencio. Eds. 1983. *Apartheid is a Heresy*. Grand Rapids: Eerdmans.

De Gruchy, John. 1994a. 'Waving the Flag.' *The Christian Century*, 15–22 June, 596–8.

De Kok, Ingrid. 1998. 'Cracked Heirlooms: Memory on Exhibition.' In *Negotiating the Past: The Making of Memory in South Africa*, edited by Sarah Nuttall and Carli Coetzee, 57–71. Cape Town: Oxford University Press.

Diamond, S. 1989. *Spiritual Warfare: The Politics of the Christian Right*. London: Pluto Press.

Die Koinonia Verklaring. 1977. Pamphlet. Potchefstroom and Germiston.

Draper, Jonathan. 1988. '"Humble Submission to Almighty God" and its Biblical Foundation: Contextual Exegesis of Romans 13:1–7.' *Journal of Theology for Southern Africa*, 63 (June), 30–38.

du Toit, André. 1983. 'No Chosen People: The Myth of the Calvinist Origins of Afrikaner Nationalism and Racial Ideology.' *American Historical Review*, 88 (October), 920–52.

Dunn, James. D. G. 1987. *The Living Word*. London: SCM.

Dutch Reformed Church. 1990. *Church and Society*. Cape Town: N.G. Kerk Uitgewers.

Elazar, Daniel J. 1994. *Covenant and Polity in Biblical Israel*. New Brunswick, NJ: Transaction Publishers.

Elazar, Daniel J. 1996. *Covenant and Commonwealth: From Christian Separation through the Protestant Reformation*. New Brunswick, NJ: Transaction Publishers.

Elphick, Richard and Rodney Davenport. Eds. 1997. *Christianity in South Africa: A Political, Social and Cultural History*. Cape Town; Oxford: David Philip;

James Currey.

Elphick, Richard. 1997. 'Introduction.' In *Christianity in South Africa: A Political, Social and Cultural History*, edited by R. Elphick and R. Davenport, 1–15. Cape Town; Oxford: David Philip; James Currey.

Everett, William Johnson. 1988. *God's Federal Republic: Reconstructing Our Governing Symbol.* New York: Paulist Press.

Everett, William Johnson. 1997. *Religion, Federalism, and the Struggle for Public Life: Cases from Germany, India, and America.* New York: Oxford University Press.

Finca, Bongani. 1997. 'Challenging a Divided Church, Summary of Response at the Presbyterian Church Annual Challenge Lecture.' *Challenge*, June–July, 17–18.

Fordred, Lesley. 1990. 'Sacred Nation, Holy War: Cosmology and Ideology in the South African Mission of Frontline Fellowship and the Gospel Defence League.' Honours diss. Cape Town: University of Cape Town.

Foucault, Michel. 1986. 'Disciplinary Power and Subjection.' In *Power*, edited by Steven Lukes. Oxford: Basil Blackwell.

Foucault. Michel. 1980. *Power/Knowledge.* New York: Pantheon.

Franz, Collette. 1996. 'South Africa's Truth and Reconciliation Commission: An Enquiry into the Nature of the "Truth" Produced at Hearings of the Committee of Human Rights Violations.' Honours dissertation. Cape Town: University of Cape Town.

Friedländer, Saul. 1994. 'Memory of the Shoah in Israel: Symbols, Rituals, and Ideological Polarization.' In *The Art of Memory: Holocaust Memorials in History*, edited by James E. Young, 149–57. Munich; New York: Prestel; The Jewish Museum.

Gerhart, Gail M. 1978. *Black Power in South Africa: The Evolution of an Ideology*. Berkeley: University of California Press.

Gerlof, Roswith. 1998. 'Truth, a New Society and Reconciliation: The Truth and Reconciliation Commission in South Africa from a German Perspective. *Missionalia,* 26, no. 1 (April), 17–53.

Gerstner, Jonathan N. 1997. 'A Christian Monopoly: The Reformed Church and Colonial Society under Dutch Rule.' In *Christianity in South Africa: A Political, Social and Cultural History*, edited by R. Elphick and R. Davenport, 16–30. Cape Town; Oxford: David Philip; James Currey.

Gevisser, Mark. 1996. 'The Ultimate Test of Faith.' *Mail & Guardian*, 18 April, 12.

Gifford, Paul. 'Theology and Right Wing Christianity.' *Journal of Theology for Southern Africa*, no. 69 (December), 28–39.

Gifford, Paul. 1988. *The Religious Right in Southern Africa*. Harare: University of Zimbabwe Press.

Giliomee, Hermann. 1996. 'Liberal and Populist Democracy in South Africa: Challenges, New Threats to Liberalism.' Presidential Address. South African Institute of Race Relations. Braamfontein: SAIRR.

Goba, Bonganjalo. 1988. *Agenda for Black Theology: Hermeneutics for Social Change*. Johannesburg: Skotaville Press.

Grunebaum-Ralph, Heidi et al. 1998. 'Public Discussion: 'Transforming Society Through Reconciliation: Myth or Reality?' Participants included Pumla

Gobodo-Madikizela, Heidi Grunebaum-Ralph, Wynand Malan, Mahmood Mamdani, Mxolisi Mpambani, and Rowan Smith.' Available at <http://www.truth.org.za/debate/recon2.doc>.

Grunebaum-Ralph, Heidi. 1997. '(Re)Membering Bodies, Producing Histories: Silence, Collective Memory and Historical Narration in Holocaust Survivor Narrative and Truth and Reconciliation Commission Testimony in South Africa.' Paper, American Comparative Literature Conference, Puerto Vallarta, Mexico, 10–13 April.

Harper, Charles. 1996. *Impunity: An Ethical Perspective. Six Case Studies from Latin America*. Geneva: WCC.

Hay, Mark. 1998. *Ukubuyisana: Reconciliation in South Africa*. Pietermaritzburg: Cluster Publications.

Hodgson, Janet. 1987. 'Ntaba KaNdoda: Orchestrating Symbols for National Unity in Ciskei.' *Journal of Theology for Southern Africa,* no. 58 (March), 18–31.

Hopkins, Dwight N. 1989. *Black Theology USA and South Africa: Politics, Culture and Liberation.* Maryknoll: Orbis Books.

Huber, Wolfgang. 1996. 'Violence: The Unrelenting Assault on Human Dignity'. Trans. Ruth C. L. Gritsch. Minneapolis: Fortress.

Institute for Contextual Theology (ICT). 1985. *Speaking for Ourselves*. Braamfontein: Institute for Contextual Theology.

Jabès, Edmond. *The Book of Questions, Vols. I & II.* Trans. Rosmarie Waldrop. Hanover; London: Wesleyan University Press; University Press of New England, 1991.

Kairos Theologians. 1986. *Challenge to the Church: The Kairos Document.* Second Edition. Johannesburg: Skotaville.

Kistner, Wolfram. 1994. 'The Legacy of the Past in the New South Africa.' Unpublished Paper.

Knight, Derrick. 1982. *Beyond the Pale: The Christian Political Fringe.* Lancashire: Caraf Publications.

Knight, Derrick. 1989. 'Wolves in Sheep's Clothing, Part One: Within South Africa.' Briefing paper, Feb.

Krog, Antjie. 1998a. *Country of My Skull.* Cape Town: Random House.

Krog, Antjie. 1998b. 'The Truth and Reconciliation Commission: A National Ritual?' *Missionalia,* 26, no. 1 (April), 5–16.

Lamola, John. 1988. 'Does the Church Lead the Struggle? A Caution.' *Sechaba,* July, 7–11.

Langer, Lawrence. 1993. 'Memory's Time: Chronology and Duration in Holocaust Testimonies.' *Yale Journal of Criticism,* 6, no. 2 (Fall), 263–73, 2.

Laub, Dori. 1992a. 'An Event Without a Witness: Truth, Testimony and Survival.' In *Testimony: Crises of Witnessing in Literature, Psychoanalysis and History*, edited by Shoshana Felman and Dori Laub. London: Routledge.

Laub, Dori. 1992b. 'Bearing Witness, or the Vicissitudes of Listening.' In *Testimony: Crises of Witnessing in Literature, Psychoanalysis and History*, edited by Shoshana Felman and Dori Laub. London: Routledge.

Levi, Primo. 1986. 'The Memory of Offense.' In *Bitburg in Moral and Political Perspective,* edited by Geoffrey Hartman, 130–7. Bloomington: Indiana University Press.

Loff, Chris. 1983. 'The History of a Heresy.' In *Apartheid is a Heresy*, edited by J. W. de Gruchy and C. Villa-Vicencio. Cape Town; Grand Rapids: David Philip; Eerdmans.

Lyotard, Jean-François. 1988. *The Differend.* Trans. Georges van den Abbeele. Minneapolis: University of Minnesota Press.

Mahamod, D. P. 1996. 'Azanian People's Organisation (AZAPO) and Others *v* President of the Republic of South Africa and Others.' *Constitutional Law Reports,* 8, no. BCLR 1015 (CC), BCLR 1015 (CC).

Maluleke, Tinyiko S. 1997a. '"Dealing Lightly with the Wound of My People"? The TRC Process in Theological Perspective.' *Missionalia,* 25, no. 3 (November), 324–43.

Maluleke, Tinyiko S. 1997b. 'Truth, National Unity and Reconciliation in South Africa: Aspects of the Emerging Theological Agenda.' *Missionalia*, 25, no. 1 (April), 59–86.

Maluleke, Tinyiko S. 1997c. 'The "Smoke-Screens" Called Black and African Theologies: The Challenge of African Women's Theology.' *Journal of Constructive Theology,* 3, no. 2 (December), 39–63.

Mamdani, Mahmood. 1996. 'Reconciliation Without Justice.' *Southern African Review of Books*, no. 46 (December).

Marty, Martin E. 1981. *The Public Church: Mainline–Evangelical–Catholic*. New York: Crossroad.

Mbali, Z. 1987. *The Churches and Racism: A Black South African Perspective.* London: SCM.

Minkley, Gary, Ciraj Rassool, and Leslie Witz. 1996. 'Thresholds, Gateways, and Spectacles: Journeying Through South African Hidden Pasts and Histories in the Last Decade of the Twentieth Century.' Paper: The Future of the Past: The Production of History in a Changing South Africa. University of the Western Cape, 10–12 July.

Mndende, Nokuzola O. 1994. 'The Voice of the Red People.' University of Cape Town, Department of Religious Studies.

Mofokeng, Takatso. 1986. 'Reconciliation and Liberation.' In *Cry Justice*, edited by John de Gruchy. London: Collins Liturgical Publications.

Moltmann, Jürgen. 1994. *Jesus Christ for Today's World.* Minneapolis: Fortress Press.

Moosa, Ebrahim. 1989. 'Muslim Conservatism in South Africa.' *Journal of Theology for Southern Africa*, 69 (December), 73–81.

Mosala, Itumeleng J. 1985. 'African Independent Churches: A Study in Socio-Theological Protest.' In *Resistance and Hope: South African Essays in Honour of Beyers Naudé*, edited by Charles Villa-Vicencio and John de Gruchy. Cape Town; Grand Rapids: David Philip; Eerdmans.

Mosala, Itumeleng J. 1987. 'The Meaning of Reconciliation: Black Perspective.' *Journal of Theology for Southern Africa*, no. 59 (June), 19–25.

Mosala, Itumeleng J. 1989a. *Biblical Hermeneutics and Black Theology in South Africa*. Grand Rapids: Eerdmans.

Mosala, Itumeleng J. 1989b. *Race, Class and Gender as Hermeneutical Factors in the African Independent Churches' Appropriation of the Bible: A Final Report to the Human Sciences Research Council.* Pretoria: Human Sciences Research Council.

Mosala, Itumeleng J. 1994. 'Jesus in the Parables: Class and Gender Readings.' *Journal of Black Theology in South Africa* 8, no. 2 (November), 142–47.

Mosala, Itumeleng J. 1995. 'Spirituality and Struggle: African and Black Theologies.' In *Many Cultures, One Nation: Festschrift for Beyers Naudé*, edited by Charles Villa-Vicencio and Carl Niehaus, 79–89. Cape Town: Human & Rousseau.

Müller-Fahrenholz, Geiko. 1996. *The Art of Forgiveness: Theological Reflections on Healing and Reconciliation*. Geneva: WCC.

Mutua, Makau wa. 1995. 'The Banjul Charter and the African Cultural Fingerprint: An Evaluation of the Language of Duties.' *Virginia Journal of International Law*, 35, no. 333, 340–80.

Niebuhr, H. Richard. 1951. *Christ and Culture*. New York: Harper & Row.

Niehaus, Carl. 1993. *Om te veg vir Hoop*. Cape Town: Human & Rousseau.

Nolan, Albert. 1994. 'Kairos Theology.' In *Doing Theology in Context: South African Perspectives*, edited by John W. de Gruchy and Charles Villa-Vicencio. Cape Town; Maryknoll: David Philip; Orbis.

Ntoane, L. R. L. 1983. *A Cry for Life: An Interpretation of 'Calvinism' and Calvin*. Kampen: Kok.

Nuttall, Sarah and Carli Coetzee. Eds. 1998. *Negotiating the Past: The Making of Memory in South Africa*. Cape Town: Oxford University Press.

Pauw, Jacques. 1997. *Into the Heart of Darkness: Confessions of Apartheid's Assassins*. Johannesburg: Jonathan Ball.

Petersen, Robin M. In press. *Time, Resistance and Reconstruction: A Theology of the Popular and Political*. Maryknoll; Pietermaritzburg: Orbis Books; Cluster Publications.

Prozesky, Martin and John W. de Gruchy. Eds. 1995. *Living Faiths in South Africa*. Cape Town: David Philip.

Reamonn, P. 1994. 'Farewell to Apartheid? Church Relations in South Africa.' In *Studies from the World Alliance of Reformed Churches no. 25*. Geneva: World Alliance of Reformed Churches.

Robins, Steven. 1998. 'Silence in My Father's House: Memory, Nationalism, and Narratives of the Body.' In *Negotiating the Past: The Making of Memory in South Africa*, edited by Sarah Nuttall and Carli Coetzee, 120–40. Cape Town: Oxford University Press.

Ross, Fiona. 1996. 'Existing in Secret Places: Women's Testimony in the First Five Weeks of Public Hearings of the Truth and Reconciliation Commission.' Unpublished paper: Faultlines Conference, University of Cape Town, July.

Rubenstein, Richard L. 1992. *After Auschwitz: History, Theology, and Contemporary Judaism*. Second edition. Baltimore; London: Johns Hopkins University Press.

Sacks, P. M. 1985. *The English Elegy: Studies in the Genre from Spenser to Yeats*. Baltimore; London: Johns Hopkins University Press.

Schreiter, Robert. 1992. *Reconciliation: Mission and Ministry in a Changing Social Order.* Maryknoll: Orbis.

Scott, James C. 1985. *Weapons of the Weak: Everyday Forms of Peasant Resistance*. New Haven: Yale University Press.

Scott, James C. 1990. *Domination and the Arts of Resistance: Hidden Transcripts*. New Haven: Yale University Press.

Shriver, Donald. 1995. *An Ethic for Enemies: Forgiveness in Politics*. London: Oxford University Press.

Smit, Dirkie J. 1992. 'Reformed Theology in South Africa: A Story of Many Stories.' *Acta Theologica*, 1.

Smit, Dirkie J. 1996. 'Covenant and Ethics? Comments from a South African Perspective.' In *The Annual Society of Christian Ethics*, 265–82. Washington: Society of Christian Ethics.

Sobrino, Jon. 1994. *The Principle of Mercy: Taking the Crucified People from the Cross*. Maryknoll: Orbis Books.

South African Council of Churches. 1989. 'Confessing Guilt in South Africa: The Responsibility of Churches and Individual Christians.' Johannesburg: SACC.

South African Council of Churches. 1995. 'The Truth Will Set You Free.' Johannesburg: SACC.

Sparks, Allister. 1994. *Tomorrow is Another Country: The Inside Story of South Africa's Negotiated Revolution*. Cape Town: Tafelberg.

Stier, Oren Baruch. 1995. 'Lunch at Majdanek: The March of the Living as a Contemporary Pilgrimage of Memory.' *Jewish Folklore and Ethnology Review* 17, no. 1–2: 57–66.

Strauss, P. J. 1995. 'Abraham Kuyper, Apartheid and Reformed Churches in South Africa in their Support of Apartheid.' *Theological Forum*, 23, no. 1, 4–27.

Sturken, Marita. 1997. *Tangled Memories: The Vietnam War, the AIDS Epidemic, and the Politics of Remembering*. Berkeley: University of California Press.

The Church–State Confrontation: Correspondence, February–April 1988. 1988. *Journal of Theology for Southern Africa*, 63 (June), 68–87.

The Kairos Theologians. 1986. *The Kairos Document: Challenge to the Churches*. Second Edition. Johannesburg: Skotaville.

Tutu, Desmond M. 1976. 'Church and Nation in the Perspective of Black Theology.' *Journal of Theology for Southern Africa*, no. 15 (June).

Tutu, Desmond M. 1997. 'Speech to the South African Press Club,' 21 October. Available at <http://www.truth.org.za/reading/press.htm>

Van der Walt, Bennie. 1997. *'n Skuldbelydenis oor Apartheid*. Pamphlet. Potchefstroom: Institute for Reformational Studies.

Villa-Vicencio, Charles. 1989. 'Right Wing Religion: Have the Chickens Come Home to Roost?' *Journal of Theology for Southern Africa*, no. 69 (December), 7–16.

Villa-Vicencio, Charles. 1987. *Theology and Violence: The South African Debate*. Johannesburg: Skotaville Publishers.

Walker, D. 1989. 'Evangelicals and Apartheid: An Enquiry into Some Dispositions.' *Journal of Theology for Southern Africa*, no. 67 (June), 46–61.

Walshe, Peter. 1983. *Church versus State in South Africa*. Maryknoll: Orbis Books.

Walshe, Peter. 1995. *Prophetic Christianity and the Liberation Movement in South Africa*. Pietermaritzburg: Cluster Publications.

Wanamaker, Charles A. 1989. 'Right Wing Christianity and the Bible in South Africa.' *Journal of Theology for Southern Africa*, no. 69 (December): 17–27.

Wieviorka, Annette. 1992. *Deportation et Génocide*. Paris: Plon.

World Conference on Religion and Peace, South African Chapter. 1993.

'Declaration on Religious Rights and Responsib+ilities (1992).' *Journal of Theology for Southern Africa,* no. 82 (March): 107–110.

Worsnip, Michael. 1989a. 'Low Intensity Conflict and the South African Church.' *Journal of Theology for Southern Africa*, no. 69 (December): 82-94.

Worsnip, Michael. 1989b. 'The Gospel of National Security.' Unpublished typescript. Pietermaritzburg: Federal Theological Seminary.

Young, James E. 1988. *Writing and Rewriting the Holocaust: Narrative and the Consequences of Interpretation.* Bloomington; Indianapolis: Indiana University Press.

Index